ANCIENT SLAVS

by
Frank A. Kmietowicz

WORZALLA PUBLISHING CO.
3535 Jefferson Street, Stevens Point, Wis. 54481
U. S. A.

CONTENTS

ILLUSTRATIONS

MAPS

INTRODUCTION

When the Slavs appeared on the international arena as a political factor the Old World had been closing its antiquity. The newcomers acquiring new territories for colonization, by peaceful penetration or by force, met resistance and disdain. It found its reflection in literature. Ancient chroniclers and historians left scanty and somewhat contradictory descriptions of the Slavs.

Next to it came another negative factor, the centuries old struggle for extermination of the Slavs. The German propaganda which was put in operation many years before World War I had tended to convince that the world needs to consider only the history of "western civilization" — meaning, of course, Germany as the center of this civilization — and that the states east of Germany, that is, mostly the Slav states, did not need to be considered at all, since they were made upon only of "barbarians", and "uncivilized" people who, by the grace of the Lords, the Hohenzollerns, the geopoliticians and the Nazis, were destined to be "civilized" by the "master race".

Fortunately, this ridiculous attitude met its fate with the end of World War II. Although the Slav countries suffered immense losses, they emerged victorious with the Soviet Union as the second superpower in the world next to the United States. This configuration on the international arena has forced researchers to dig harder into the past to find out the true meaning of many Slavic manifestations. After all, according to The World Almanac in 1970 were in millions: Russians — 132.6; Ukrainians — 35.5; Poles — 32.5; Yugoslavians — 20.5; Czechs and Slovaks — 14.5; Byelorussians — 8.6; and Bulgarians — 8.5. To these nations should be numbered about 15 millions Slavs scattered all around the world with 100,000 Serbo-Lusatians who live in autonomous district in East Germany.

1

The second good aspect in archaeology. It is a most fascinating study, and never in the world's history was there a greater desire to preserve antiquities than at the present day. The archaeological digging on a spectacular scale is being done in Russia, Poland, Czechoslovakia, Yugoslavia and Bulgaria. But not only in these Slavic countries. The research is going on in Austria, East and West Germany, where the Slavs were Germanized, as well as in Romania, where they were Romanized, and in Hungary, where they were Magyarized. Findings are so impressive that they force us to rewrite the history of the Ancient Slavs.

Next to the archaeological findings, the researchers have turned to the auxiliary sciences, like ethnography, anthropology, linguistics, paleozoology and paleobotany for explanation of the most complex Slavic phenomena, with the most startling results.

This book represents an attempt of the history of the Ancient Slavs, based on the latest scientific achievements. Starting with the remote past, this book should end with the Slavic Great Migrations which closed antiquity. Since the process of making Slavic nations was not ended with this epoch, it was necessary to include the history of the early Slavic states until the 13th century A.D.

Thus, this book is composed of three parts:

A. Proto-Slav epoch from the earliest times to 2000 B.C.;

B. Ancient Slav epoch from 2000 B.C. to the end of the 6th century A.D.

C. Early Slavic States epoch from the 6th to 13t century.

Owing to its complexity the mythology of the Ancient Slavs is not included in this book.

Author

A. PROTO-SLAV EPOCH

from the earliest times to 2000 B.C.

CHAPTER I
ETHNOGENESIS

At the end of the 6th century A.D. the Balkan possessions of the Byzantine Empire saw the new invasion. Masses of people, more ore less organized, flooded down the peninsula, seeking booty and land for colonization. Some of them were the warriors led by their own or foreign war leaders, some belonged to the groups of men, women and children carrying their meagre possessions.(1)

Invaders crushed many resistances of imperial units, pushed down and down and the Balkan peninsula and even stormed the walls of Constantinople.

The Byzantinians already survived attacks of many invaders. Their European domains devastated the Teutonic nations like Bastarns, Vandals, Marcomans, Ostrogoths, Visigoths and others, then came Asiatic marauders: Huns and Avars.

The new invaders looked different to the Byzantinian observers in many aspects. They had been admired for their courage and detested for their language which sounded to some Byzantinian ears as "the most barbaric".

Who were they?

Where they came from?

Where were their cradlelands?

Answers to the two questions met no difficulity: the new invaders were Slavs flooding the Balkan peninsula from northern Europe. But the answer to the third question was controversial from the beginning down the centuries. Historians even today are not unanimous in this subject.

There was no nation in European antiquity which some scholars had not connected with the Slavs, and some other scholars vigorously denied that the Slavs had had as forebearers any European nation.

Since there is no historical document regarding the original homeland of the Slavs, many theories try to solve the mystery. Some of them attempt to localize it in Asia, some in Asia Minor, and some in Europe, especially in the region at the Danube, Vistula and Dnieper.

The oldest theory was formulated by the Russian monk, Nestor, who lived in Kiev (1056-1114). According to his calculations, the Slavic cradlelands were at the rivers Danube and Tissa, but being persecuted, they migrated to the region of the Vistula and the Baltic.(2) This idea, called the "Balkan theory" won many famous researchers, among them Paul Safarik (1796-1861).

There was, however, strong argument against it, which forced the Slavists to abandon the Balkan theory. Surprisingly enough, it has been raised again by the Yugoslavian scholar, V. Trbuhovic.

The second European conception of the Slavic home country appeared as a result of the rejection of the Balkan theory. Some historians have placed the cradlelands of the Slavs somewhere to the north and north-east of the Carpathians. This conception, called the "Sub-Carpathian theory" was introduced by the famous Czech archaeologist, Lubor Niederle (1865-1944). It won many scholars, like the German paleo-ethnographer Max Vasmer (1886-1962), Polish ethnographer-anthropologist, Jan Czekanowski (1882-1964), the Polish archaeologist, Józef Kostrzewski (1885-), the Russian archaeologist, P. N. Tretiakov (1897-), the Spanish archaeologist, P. Bosch-Gimpera (1911-), and many others.

According to their deliberations, the homeland of the Slavs was north of the Carpathians, with the borders as far as the river Elbe in the west, the Volga in the east, and the Baltic Sea in the north.

The third European conception of the Slavic cradlelands is called the "Kiev theory". According to it, Max Vasmer placed the original home of the Slavs in the region around the city of Kiev in Ukraine.

Some of the researchers have tried to localize the Slavic cradlelands somewhere in Asia. Among them, it is worth to mention the Polish ethnographer, Karol Moszyński (1887-1964), and the Polish historian, Henry Łowmiański (1898-). The first, in his book published in 1925, localized the original Slav home in the center of Asia. Under the strong criticism of the Orientalists he changed his mind, explaining that the forebearers of the Proto-Slavs dwelt somewhere deep in Asia.(3)

There were two scholars who tried to localize the Slavic cradlelands in Asia Minor: the Polish historian, Władysław Surowiecki (1769-1827), and the Russian researcher, T. Florinski.

Although in many of these theories is a grain of truth, two scientific disciplines argue strongly for the European home country of the Slavs: anthropology and linguistics.

The excavation of ancient European tombs and places of burial has confirmed that the doichocephalic type had not before the fifth century moved southward over the Carpathians, and as has been scientifically proved, the dolicephalic type was predominant among the Slavs.

The linguistics also shows that the Proto-Slavs belonged to the Indo-European nations as their western branch.

NOTES TO CHAPTER I

1. **Bibliography:** Bruckner A., 'Słownik etymologiczny języka polskiego', Warszawa 1970; Czekanowski J., 'Wstęp do historii Słowian', Poznań 1957; Georgiev W.; Balgarski etnologiczen recznik', Sofija 1962; Kostrzewski J., 'Prasłowiańszczyzna', Poznań 1946; Łowmiański H., 'Początki Polski', Warszawa 1970; Moszyński K., 'Kultura ludowa Słowian', Warszawa 1969; Nestor, 'Powieść minionych lat', Wrocław 1968; Niederle L., 'Slovanske starożitnosti', Praha 1924; Portal R., 'The Slavs', New York 1969; Surowiecki W., 'Śledzenie początku narodów słowiańskich', Warszawa 1965; Tretiakov P.N., 'Wostoczno slawianskije plemiena'., Moskva 1953; Vasmer M., 'Russisches etymologische Wörterbuch,' Heidelberg 1950.

2. Nierderle proves that the Nestor chronicle regarding the migration of the Slavs is based, not on historic documents, but on scripture, which narrates the exodus of the human race from the land of "Sinear". On this belief he probably built his theory about the Slavs being led by St. Paul or St. Jerome (340-420) to the Balkan, from whence they later migrated north.

3. About the Asian theory R. Portal writes: "They (Slavs) came from central Europe in the first place and did not become any less European when they extended their civilization eastward to the Pacific. Even during the period when they were largely subjected to Mongol overlordship and out of touch with the west, their essentially European civilization, the heir to the traditions of both Kiev and Byzantium, remained essentially intact". (R. Portal, The Slavs, p. 3).

7

CHAPTER II

EXODUS

It was quite a thrill when the liguists discovered a community in all European and most south-west Asian nations.(1) Some researchers started feverishly digging in dictionaries, grammars and the oldest written records to find out when and where this community existed and what caused its disappearance. In this way the comparative linguistics developed.

The new branch of science based on the sacred books of the east came to startling results. Here is an example:

English	Veda	Polish	German
brother	bhrater	brat	Bruder
beaver	babhra	bóbr	Bieber
day	dina	dzień	deinam (Old G.)
knowledge (Wit)	veda	wiedza	Wissen

The comparative linguistics led the German linguist, Franz Bopp (1791-1867), to reconstruct the language of the community,(2) and others to determine the time of its duration and disintegration into national languages.

The liguists came to the conclusion that the community of language existed some six thousand years ago. Since it gave birth to all European languages and some in south-west Asia, especially in India, they called it the "Indo-European Community".(3)

Some linguists do not believe that the joint language called "Pre-Indo-European" ever existed, but some are clearly convinced it was in use, but between the 6th and 4th millennium (4) disintegrated into four linguistis groups: the northern, the Balto-Slavic-German; the western, the Celtic-Ithalic-Venedig; the

8

central, the Greek-Armenian-Thracian-Indoiranian; and the southern, with the Hettic and others.(5)

It is not known what people used the Indo-European language and to what material culture they could be assigned. Some archaeologists believe they produced the cord ceramic.

Judging by the oldest writings (6) the Indo-European nations started to depart from the community and to individualize around the 3rd millennium B.C.(7)

When researchers discovered the possibility of existence of the Indo-European linguistic community the second question was: where this community might have been? There are two theories trying to localize this community. The first, the "forest theory" accepts possibility that the cradlelands of the Indo-Europeans were the forest regions somewhere in Europe. This theory is favored by anthropologists and archaeologists.(8)

More fortunate is the second theory, called the "steppe theory". It accepts the possibility of the huge Eurasiatic steppe as being the cradlelands of the Indo-Europeans.(9) This theory appears to be more logical than the first one. If the Indo-Europeans had to occupy the vast regions of whole Europe and a large chunk of the Asian continent in a relatively short time, they would have to have been numerous and in constant contact with themselves, since they had one language. They would have to have lived on the steppe, because forests as well as mountains made obstacles in traveling; besides, grassy plains present good habitation for hunters and nomads. Many rivers made traveling and communication easier.

If the steppe offered such good conditions, why did the Indo-European community disintegrate and their nations part?

There could have been many reasons for exodus from the Eurasiatic steppe. Perhaps, from time to time, the grassy plains were overpopulated, and some tribes left voluntarily or had been pushed out by the stronger tribes, and had to look for a new homeland. Some atmospheric calamities, like drought or flood, as well as infectious sicknesses of the game, could have contributed to the escape, too.

Why they did not farm? Farming economy was well established in Europe in times of exodus from the Euraistic steppe. After all, the Ukrainian steppes and American and Canadian prairies became the world famous grannaries. But it had not happened until man learned how to fertilize and irrigate the soil, a trick the primitive farmers in Europe in those times didn't know.

It appears that exodus from the Eurasiatic steppe in all directions started about four thousand years B.C. and ended after two millennia. The Indo-Europeans migrated as far to the east as the Tien-Shaw province in western China.(10)

The Indo-European language community disintegrated in Neolithic times, somewhere about 2000 B.C., before the introduction of metallurgy into economy.(11)

Migrating east, west and south, the Indo-Europeans met on their way different ethnic groups which they absorbed. Assimilation of foreign linguistic communities helped to develop the new languages. Only Lithuanian made an exemption. Its archaic structure is close to Indo-European, which means that marching north-west the forebearers of the Lithuanians of today met no ethnic groups, or those groups were so small and insignificant that they were of no influence on Lithuanian language.

Today, one-third of man-kind uses languages which root in Indo-European community.

The last nations to leave the Eurasiatic steppe were the forebearers of the Slavs, Balts and Germans. They are usually called the Proto-Slavs, Proto-Balts and Proto-Germans.

It appears those three groups were of one group in their homeland before they split, especially Slavs and Balts.(12) The question arises as to where their homeland might have been. The answer is also difficult, as in determining the Indo-European homeland. There are many speculations in this field, based on linguistics.

Some basis for these speculations was brought about by archaelogical findings at Volossovo at the lower Oka River.(13) In light of it and linguistics it could be assumed that the Proto-Slav-Balt-German homeland was somewhere at the lower Oka and the upper Volga, with the Proto-Germans occupying the northern part, the Proto-Balts in the middle, and the Proto-Slavs in the southern region.

Sometime about 2000 B.C. this community started to migrate. The reason is not known. It could be assumed the community was pushed out by the warfaring Fatyanovo people.

North of the Black Sea, as far as the Dnieper, were settlements of the primitive farmers belonging to the Tripolye culture. Their northern neighbors were the people of Fatyanovo culture, who first brought grain-growing and stock-raising economy into the forest zone of central Russia.(14) They are best known in the basin of the Oka, upper Volga and the surrounding uplands. It has been supposed that the creators of Fatyanovo culture were warlike folk given to the cattle-raiding as much as to cattle-raising. These belligerent people were in struggle with Tripolye settlers, although

10

there is an open question as to who was the aggressor. Anyway, they fought each other.

It could have happened that the Fatyanovo folk pushed the Proto-Slav-Balt-German people out of their homeland so they could occupy it.

The Proto-Slavs-Balts could not have migrated south, because the fertile southern plains were occupied by the Tripolye people, who were on a higher cultural level and better equipped to fight off marauding nations. They could not have marched north because the Proto-Germans were there. The only way left was to go west. So, they gathered their meagre possessions and followed the sun.(15)

The Proto-Germans left their homelands, too. They took the northern way up the Volga, about 2000 B.C., crossed the Finland Bay and marched down the Scandinavian peninsula, to be in Jutland around 500 B.C.(16)

Map I. Possible routes from Eurasiatic steppes

11

The exodus did not take a form of massive migration with a hundred thousand participants. The migrants were not on the level to organize themselves into spectacular hordes, as Mongols showed to Europeans in the early times of our era. Their clannish organization allowed them to move west in small independent groups.

Archaeologically, it seems possible to trace the route of their migration through finds of painted pottery decorated with spirals and meanders belonging to a culture that flourished between Neolithic and Bronze ages.(17)

What was the economy of the migrants? Many researchers believe that the inhabitants of the Eurasiatic steppe were hunters, fishermen and food-gatherers. No matter how vast their homeland was, it is impossible to think that they made their living by the most primitive economy. Since they occupied the big territories of Europe and Asia, they must have known animal herding in some way,(18) especially cattle-raising, as linguistics indicate.(19)

NOTES TO CHAPTER II

1. **Bibliography**: Brandstein W., 'Studien zur indogermanischen Grundsprache', Wien 1952; Hawkes J., 'Prehistory', New York 1964; Hencken H., 'Indo-European Languages and Archaeology', American Anthropologist 1955; Krahe H., 'Sprache und Vorzeit', Heidelberg 1954; Meiler A. 'Wstęp do językoznawstwa indoeuropejskiego', Warszawa 1958; Milewski T., 'Zarys językoznawstwa ogólnego', Lublin 1948; Miller F. M., 'Lectures in Science and Language', Oxford 1864; Pokorny J., 'Indogermanisches etymologische Wortenbuch', Bern 1948; Safarewicz J. 'Problematyka językoznawstwa indoeuropejskiego', Warszawa 1959; Schrader H., 'Sprachvergleichung and Urgeschichte', Jena 1906.

2. F. Bopp, 'Vergleichende Grammatic des Sanskrit, Zend, Griechischen, Lateinischen, Littauischen, Gotischen and Deutschen', Berlin 1833.

3. There are two other names of this linguistic community. One is the Aryans, popularized by Max Muller. It was intended to embrace all those whose languages in Europe, Persia and India spring from a single original speech, distinct from other Asiatic families, Turanian or Semitic. But on one hand it is often loosely used to describe many long-headed races of Europe and Asia, even those of early geological ages, while, on the other, it has been restricted to that branch of the Iranian race which spoke the language of the Vedas or other dialects of Sanskrit. The word "Aryans" appeared in the most ancient Sanskrit writings, the Veda, and was signifying "excellent", "honorable" or "lord of the soil", as 'Encyclopedia of

Religions', New York 1964, Vo. III, p. 151 states. The other name is the Indo-Germanic. It seems the German researchers who contributed much to reconstruct the Indo-European language gave their name to it to satisfy German national ambitions. In this way the German scholars usually operate with the term "Indo-Germanic".

4. V. J. Georgiev, 'Issledwanija po sravnitel'no-istoriceskomu jazykoznaniju', Moskva 1958, p. 277-282, as well as J. W. Hauer, 'Die vergleichende Religionsgeschichte und Indogermanenproblem', Heidelberg 1936, p. 200

5. Max Müller subdivided Aryan languages into southern and northern groups. The southern is subdivided into two classes: a) Indic, b) Iranic. The northern has six classes: a) Celtic, b) Ithalic, c) Illyric, d) Hellenic, e) Windic, f) Teutonic.

6. The oldest writings of the Indo-European are in Hettic, dated on the 17th century B.C. According to 'Encyclopedia of Religions', Vol. III, p. 472, the formation of the Rig-Veda, the early hymns of the Aryan shepherds of Baktria, is dated 1400 B.C. The Iranian Zend-Avesta comes a little later than the Vedas.

7. If the Rig-Veda is dated 1400 B.C., then the forebearers of the authors of the sacred books must have left the Indo-European community a thousand years before they settled in India.

8. Th. Peschke, 'Die Arier', Jena 1878, p. 67, suggests that the marshlands of Pinsk at the Pripet were cradlelands of his Aryans (Indo-Europeans) which were a blonde race. K. Penka, 'Die Herkunft der Arier', Wien 1886, thinks that following the melting away of the last glacier, people settled in Sweden, and then they disintegrated as the Indo-Europeans. G. Kosinna, 'Übergang und Verbreitung der Germanen in vor — und frühgeschichtlicher Zeit', Leipzig 1934, p. 112, sees the cradlelands of the Indo-Europeans in eastern Jutland and southern Sweden, with the center in Ellerbeck near Koln in northern Germany.

9. The steppe theory is most recognized. O. Schräder, 'Reallexikon der indogermanischen Altertumskunde', Berlin 1929, Vol. II, p. 585, thinks the cradlelands of the Indo-Europeans were somewhere near the Aral and Caspian Seas. H. Guntert, 'Der Ursprung der Germanen', Heidelberg 1934, p. 116, sees the homeland of the Indo-Europeans in a region stretching from the northern shores of the Aral and Caspian Seas to the Volga. J. Kuryłowicz, 'Stosunki etniczne w przedhistorycznej Europie', Lwów 1934, p. 543-550, denotes the Eurasiatic steppe from middle Asia to the east of the Dnieper as the territory of the Indo-European community.

10. T. Milewski, 'Zarys językoznawstwa', Lublin 1948, Vol. II, p. 228, states that the Tochars settled in this region used the Indo-European language when the Buddhist missionaries met them in the 7th century A.D.

11. H. Krahe, 'Sprache und Vorzeit', Heidelberg 1954, p. 33, concludes that since there is no common word for copper or bronze in Indo-European languages, the linguistic community must have been disintegrated before the metallurgy was introduced.

12. The theory of the Baltic-Slavic community is especially favored by the linguists: T. Lehr-Spławiński, 'Podstawy indoeuropejskiej wspólnoty językowej bałto-słowiańskiej', Warszawa 1958, p. 125-136; J. Otrębski, 'Rozwój wzajemnych stosunków między grupą językową bałtycką a słowiańską', Warszawa 1958, p. 146-148; J. Kuryłowicz, 'O balto-slavjanskom jazykovom odinstve', Warszawa 1958, p. 15-49.

13. C. Engel, 'Die ostgermanische Stamme in Ostdeutschland, die gotische Ostseeherschaft und das Gotenreich in Osteurope', Leipzig 1942, p.136; A. M. Tallgren, 'Volossovo, Reallexikon der Vorgeschichte', Berlin 1939, Vol. XIV, p. 179; C. F. Meinander, 'Die Bronzenzeit in Finland, Helsinki 1954, p. 26.

14. J. Hawkes, 'Prehistory', New York 1964, p. 342-344.

15. H. Łowmiański, 'Początki Polski', Warszawa 1963, Vol. I. p. 62.

16. G. Klingberg, 'Den germanska bebyggelsens alder i Norden', Fornvannem 1950, p. 148-158.

17. 'Encyclopedia Britannica', New York 1972, Vol. XX, p. 648.

18. E. I. Krupnov, I. V. Sinicyn, 'Drevnee naselenie Niżnego Povolż'ja', Moskva 1956, p. 73, 75; O. S. Labodovska, 'Serednij i pozdnij neolit', Kyiv, 1957, p. 42.

19. Since the word daughter has the same sound in Indo-European languages (in Swedish — dotter; Danish — datter; Dutch — dochter; German — Tochter; Gothic — dauhtar; Lithuanian — duktere; Greek — thygater; Armenia — dustr; in Sanskrit — duhitri, and according to 'Encyclopedia Americana', New York 1944, Vol. II, p. 372, daughter meaning "milkmaid" that being the function in the early Brahman and Aryan household which the daughter discharged) it could be assumed that migrating west and north the Proto-Slavs, Proto-Balts and Proto-Germans were not only hunters, fishermen, food-gathers, but cattle-raisers as well.

CHAPTER III
VENETI

Estonian chronicler Heinrici of the beginning of the 13th century mentions the nation called the Wendi.(1) They lived at the river Winda (Vente, today in Latvia), but chased from this region, they moved and settled where is now the city of Riga. They had been chased from this area by the Kurs, and sought refuge with the Letgals occupying the left bank of the river Dvina. Here they built the fortified town, Cesis. Under pressure of the Teutonic Knights they embraced Christianity. The Knights were not sure how far the Wendi accepted the new religion, so they built their own fortress, called Wenden, to keep their eyes on the converts.(2)

The nation, chased from place to place because they were faithful to their pagan gods, was the last remnant of the big nation which for some millennia occupied almost all of Europe. It was of the same Indo-European stock as the Proto-Slavs, only it left its Eurasiatic homeland probably two thousand years earlier.

Some historians call it the Old European people, some the Venedi, Veneti or Wenden.(3) The nation disappeared, but before they left the historic scene their successors picked up the geographical names which they used with the root "ven".

A closer look at the map of Europe allows us to notice Venetic names in the north-west Gaul, known now as Morbihan in France. It led a lively trade with England with a good profit. The region was conquered by Romans in 57 B.C. There are Venetic traces on British Isles, and the names of Vendsyssel and Vendilskagi appeared in Jutland and Vendel in Uppland. Then, the Wenden had been mentioned by Heinrici in Estonia and some historians (4) think the name Veneti survived in the Vyatitchi, the name of one of the eastern Slavic nations. There had been the Eneti settled in Asia Minor, which L. Niederle classifies as the Veneti. They might have

15

left their original homeland in the Balkan and migrated to Asia Minor. One more Venetic center located in north-east Italy with the city of Ateste (Este, today) and Patavium (Padua, today) was recorded by history. Its name perpetuates the city of Venice. The Veneti in this region were known as skillfull horse-raisers and horse-traders. They fought wars with Etruria siding Romans against Gaul. At the end of the 3rd century B.C. they had been defeated by the Romans and Romanized.

If all those regions including the highly controversial territory of the Vyatitchi and Eneti are connected with a line it gives a circle and proves the "waves theory" is right. It says that if there are no obstacles in terrain, like mountains, marshlands, deserts, lakes and sea, or some hindrance caused by dense population and pests, like the tse-tse fly, the migration goes in all directions in the way the waves rise when a stone is thrown into a quiet pond. The farthest wave gives the name of a migrating force because the natives, when seeing the newcomers, always met them with the same questions: Who are you? What it your name? Where do you come from?(5)

These questions should give answers why the migrants to central Europe 4000 B.C. called themselves Veneti, but the problem is controversial. The literature trying to explain the origin of the word Veneti is quite numerous.

There are three conceptions to explain this term. One represented by Hilferding assumed that the name Veneti derives from the Indo-European 'vanita' — honorable, revered. J. Perwolf accepted this idea with some correction. He thought that the word Veneti derives from the Slavic term 'vęt' — more.(6)

The second conception accepts the possibility that the Germans or Celts created the word Veneti to describe the Slavs. It could derive from the Lithuanian word 'vandu' or Latin 'unda' — wave. After all, Slavs preferred to settle at the rivers and in marshlands. One of their nations, the Dregovitchi, were even called "the people of the marshlands".

R. Much (7) thinks the word 'Veneti' derives either from the Old German words with the root 'ven' — friendly, or Celtic 'venia' — (wine in Old English) friend. Another German scholar, K. Mullenhoff (8) accepts a possibility that the word 'Veneti' comes from the Gothic 'vinja' — people having good and numerous pastures.

The third conception maintains that the Veneti were an Illyrian nation who lived in the neighborhood of the Germans, whose name was transferred to the Slavs.(9)

16

Not one of these three conceptions gives a convincing explanation, but in some might be a grain of truth. After all, the Veneti must had been a big nation if they colonized almost all of Europe. They must have been a peaceful people as the historical records and archaeologial findings indicate, and perhaps because of that they had been venerated by other nations. Their settlements were at the rivers and lakes, as settlements of primitive farmers usually were.

As the question of the Veneti name is open, so is their language.

Max Muller, classifying the Indo-European languages, distinctly mentions the Venetic (Windic) language as one of six European proto-languages. The other scholars do likewise, but there is no proof that such a language ever existed. The Estonian chronicler, Heinrici, describing persecution of the Wenden in the 13th century, does not hint that they had their own language. Perhaps they already lost their ethnic identity.

There are about 200 inscriptions, (10) mostly votive and sepulchral, left by the Veneti near Este in the Italian province of Venezia. They are written in Etruscan alphabet. The language is distinctly not Slavonic but close to Italic languages. The inscriptions are dated in the 1st century B.C.

There is no doubt the language of inscriptions is different from the other languages of those times, but the question arises if it is an original Venetic language or an Italic dialect not used today.

Trying to dig out the Venetic language, the scholars had a close look at the names of the European rivers and lakes. They noticed that those names have no explanation in the languages of the people living there today, which means they must have been derived from the language in use before the languages of today developed.

H. Krahe, who did an enormous job (11) gathering and analyzing the names of the European rivers and lakes, found they are of Indo-European origin, archaic in form and are connected with "water determinations", like the Oka-aqua. He divided the names into two groups: one which roots in the word 'al' (a) similar to the Latvian 'aluots' — spring, (12) another rooting in the word 'vis', 'veis', similar to the Old Indo-European 'visam' — water.(13)

What made Veneti disappear? The only answer is that they were absorbed or destroyed by the later exodus of nations from the Eurasiatic steppes. It appears that the first is more presumable than the other. The Proto-Slavs absorbed the Veneti, giving the birth to Slavs; the Celts absorbed the Veneti in France, giving the birth to Gauls, and in the southern part of the Scandinavian peninsula

17

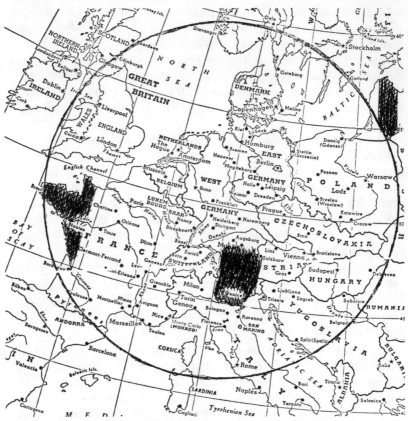

Map II. Peripherial Venetic settlements (black) in historic times.

appeared the Germans, after the Proto-Germans absorbed the Veneti who settled there.

When the Proto-Slavs came in touch with the Veneti about 2000 B.C., in the same period another Indo-European group reached its destination. The Proto-Greeks arrived in Greece and became Greeks. They fell under the strong influence of the Minoan culture which was in full swing in Crete Island. In Assyria Shamshi-Adad II was busy raising big temples to Assur, the great Assyrian deity and Anu and Abad. In neighboring Babylon, king Hammurabi watched the artisans engraving on a pillar of black diorite his famous Code, and in Egypt the biggest pyramid of Chufu (Cheops) pierced the sky for more than 500 years.

Back to Europe in southern Italy, particularly in south-east Sicily and Apulia, the Sentinello culture flourished, with the magnificent Maltese temples in their unique form of megalithic architecture. In

18

the Almerian province of south-east Spain the first farmers dwelt there in villages of oval huts, their floors sunk into the ground and roofed with wattle and doub.

In England the Windmill Hill farmers hoed plots for bread wheat and barley, and kept sheep, goats and pigs, but cattle were their main concern. In the Orkney Islands, under harsh climatic conditions, there were settled cattle-men who raised no crops.

In Denmark the Trichterbecher settlers lived peacefully as neighbors of the Ertebolle hunters-fishers down the centuries.

There were settlements of primitive farmers, called the Vardar-Morave people, the Danubians and Oltenians in the Balkan peninsula. The Tripolye peasants expanded their settlements over the plains to the north of the Black Sea, to as far as the Dnieper in Ukraine.

But of all those primitive farmers, the Swiss lakes dwellers, called the Cortaillod peasants, were on the highest level of culture about 2000 B.C.

NOTES TO CHAPTER III

1.**Bibliography:** Blesse E., 'Gedanken zur russichen and baltischen Fluss-and Ortsnamen,' BNForsch. 1954; Bujak F. 'Wendowie na wschodnich wybrzeżach Bałtyku', Gdańsk 1948; Dostal A., 'Venetove, Antove', Slavia 1950; Georgiev V. 'Die Herkunft der grössten Flusse der Balkanhalbinsel', Sofija 1959; Gerullis G. 'Die altpreusischen Ortsnamen', Berlin 1922; Kozłowski L., 'Wenedowie w źródłach historycznych i w świetle kartografii prehistorycznej', Lwów 1937; Laakmann N., 'Estland and Livland in frühgeschichtlicher Zeit', Leipzig 1939; Lehr-Spławinski T., 'O pierwotnych Wenetach,' Kraków 1946; Ravdonikas V.I., 'Plemena stepnych oblastej Vostocnej Evropy', Moskva 1956; Rozwadowski J. 'O nazwie Wenctów' Warszawa 1925 and, 'Studia nad nazwami wód słowiańskich', Kraków 1948; Vasmer M., 'Beiträge zur historischen Völkerkunde Osteuropas', SBPAWiss. 1932.

2. The exact account is: "Wendi autem humiles erant eo tempore et pauperes utpote a Winda repulsi, qui est fluvius Curonie, et habitantes in Monte Antiquo, iuxta quem Riga civitas nunc est edificata et inde iterum a Caronibus effugati pluresque occisi, reliqui fugerent ad Lethtos et ibi habitantes cum eis, garisi sunt de adventu sacerdotis. (Heinrici 'Chronicum Livoniae', Würzburg 1959, p. 64). It is worth mentioning that traces of the Veneti are still found in the Baltic countries. Besides the names of many rivers, the last census in Lithuania gives several names of places with the root ven, like Vendzeniskiu kaimas, Vendzgalin kaimas, Ventes kaimas and others.

3. According to T. Lehr-Spławiński, 'O pierwotnych Wenedach', p. 23, the original name was Veneti. The Germans changed the letter "t" to "d", and in their literature instead of Veneti exist Wenedi or Wenden.

4. L. Niederle, 'Slovanske' starożitnosti', Praha 1904, Vol. II, p. 88.

5. J. Schmidt, 'Die Verwandschaftsverhaltnisse der indogermanischen Sprachen', Weimar 1872, p. 27, also B. V. Gornung, 'Indoevropejskoe jazykove edinstvo i ego rospadenie', Sofija 1958; p. 194.

6. J. Perwolf, 'Polen Ljachen, Wenden', ASPhil. 1880, Vol. IV, p. 65. There is in Polish a word 'więcej' — more. M. P. Pogodin (1800-1875) tried to explain the word 'Veneti' through the Celtic language, in which 'Veneti' means white or bright.

7. R. Much, 'Die Deutung der germanischen Völkernamen', BGDSprach. 1895, Vol. XX, p. 18.

8. K. Müllenhoff, 'Deutsche Alterskunde', Berlin 1887, Vol. IV, p. 514.

9. This conception was presented by: G. Kossinna, 'Zur ältesten Bronzezeit Mitteleuropas III', Manus 1912, Vol. IV, p. 287-294; H. Krahe, 'Germanisch und Illyrisch', Heidelberg 1936, p. 571; A. Brückner, 'Starożytności słowiańskie', Lud 1925, p. 83.

10. 'Wielka Encyklopedia Powszechna', Warszawa 1969, Vol. XII, p. 178.

11. H. Krahe, 'Alteuropaische Flussnamen', BNForsch. 1948-1955.

12. To the group 'al' (a) belong: the river 'Ala' in Norway; 'Alara-Aller', the tributary to the river Weser; 'Alsa-Ausa', the river in the Venice district; 'Alsa-Als', the river near Vienna; 'Alapa-Alpe', the tributary to the Aller; 'Alantia-Elz', the tributary to the Neckar; 'Alunta', 'Aluo (n) ta', 'Alantete' etc., the rivers in Lithuania; 'Alento', the river in Italy; 'Alantas', two rivers in the Baltic countries; 'Aland', the name of some rivers in the Elbe basin in Wittenberg, Germany.

13. To the group 'vis', 'veis' belong: 'Viser — la Vis', the river in the French departments (districts) Gard and Hérault; 'Visera — Vézére, two rivers in the French departments Dordogne and Haute-Vienne; 'Visuria', the Anglo-Saxon 'Weor', English 'Wear', the river in northern England; 'Visurgis', 'Visara', 'Visura' — 'Weser'; 'Wisusia' — 'la Vezouse', the tributary to the Meurthe; 'Visantia-Visance', the river in the French department Orne; 'Visantia-Wiesaz', the tributary to the Steinlach in Wirtenberg, Germany; 'Visentios-Bisenzio', the tributary to the Arno in Italy; 'Visontia-Vesonza', the tributary to the Rhone in Valais, Switzerland; 'Visontion-Besancon', two rivers in the French departments Ain and Rhone; 'Viešinta', 'Viesita', two rivers in the Baltic countries; 'Vismund', the river in Norway; 'Vistla', 'Vistula' (Vistla), 'Wisła', the main river in Poland. It is worth mentioning that in Carpathian mountaineer's dialect in Poland the word 'wisły' (plural of the Wisła') still means a big water or a springtime flooding.

20

CHAPTER IV

SLAVS

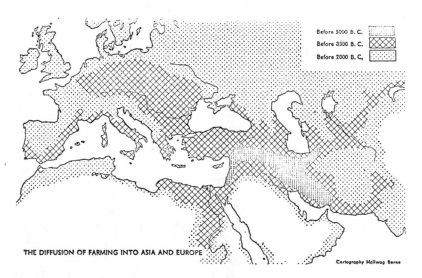

Before 5000 B. C.
Before 3300 B. C.
Before 2000 B. C,

THE DIFFUSION OF FARMING INTO ASIA AND EUROPE

Cartography Hallwag Berne

Map III. Diffusion of farming into Asia and Europe, after J. Hawkes, Prehistory, p. 327.

The linguists show (1) that the Proto-Slavs were in touch with the Veneti in the beginning of the second millenium B.C. They penetrated the thinly populated area and met no resistance. The coexistence between two ethnically different groups is evident since the newcomers took over the names of rivers and lakes from the natives.

The natives were on a higher level of culture than the newcomers. The question arises, how could Veneti have been absorbed by the Proto-Slavs? As the practice shows, the people on the higher level subordinate those who are on a lower platform. Why the reverse has been occuring? There seems to be some logic in it. the newcomers were more numerous than the natives. Since both groups were rather peacefully oriented the cooperation had been established which led to absorbing of the Veneti.

The process of absorption was a long one, and it might be accepted that it ended with the beginning of the Lusatian culture. The Proto-Slavs and Veneti ceased to exist, making room for the Ancient Slavs.

On what territory did this process take place? Where were the Slavs as a nation born?

The cradlelands of the 'Slavs is not known, and because of it, creates a very controversial problem.

There are four groups of theories. One group maintains that the big territory between the Baltic Sea and Black Sea and the rivers Volga, Don and Odra with the center in Volhynia could be the Slavic cradlelands. This group worked out the so called "Dneiper-Vistula theory".(2)

The second group developed the "Dnieper-Pripet theory", which accepts the possibility that the Slavic cradlelands were at the rivers Dnieper and Pripet.(3)

A different view is expressed by the third group. It maintains that the cradlelands were between the rivers Odra and Vistula (the "Odra-Vistula theory").(4)

The fourth group accepts a bigger territory, between the rivers Odra and Dnieper (the Odra-Dnieper theory).(5)

Viewing all these theories, it is impossible to determine the borders of the Slavic cradlelands. Perhaps it will never be done. Instead of trying to determine the borders it would be easier to find out where the center of the cradlelands could have been.

Deceased about 425 B.C., the Greek historian Herodotus, in his writings (6) naming nations north of Scythia in Europe, gives some account of the Neuri and Budini. No hint is given that they were of Slavic origin, but since they dwelt somewhere in Slavic territories, a big temptation arose among the researchers to see in those nations the forebearers of the Slavs.

After a lenghty arguing, the researchers are inclined to drop the Budini, but they strongly support the supposition that the Neuri were the Slavs.

The idea is not without a logical foundation. In the area where the Neuri might have lived are rivers with the names in which the letters 'ner' (nur) constitute the root. The names could be divided into two groups: one with the root 'ner' (nar — nor) which is Balto-Slavonic, another with the root 'nur' which is Slavonic. The first names are numerous in Lithuania. There are: the rivers 'Neris' and 'Narew', the Lake 'Narocz' and 'Naruszewicz' as a family name.(7) Then, there are two rivers, the 'Ner' and the 'Nerec' near the city of Łódź in Poland, the river 'Neretwa', a tributary of the Bug and the 'Noryń' a tributary of the Pripet.

The second group of names is exclusively in the Polish territory in the basins of the rivers Narew and Bug.

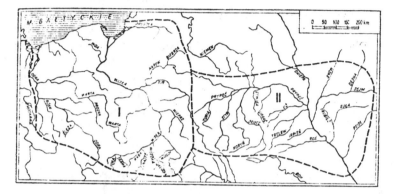

Map IV. Slavic Ethogenesis — a range of two zones of Proto-Slavic river names, after L. Leciejewicz, 'Mały słownik kultury dawnych Słowian, p. 441.

According to J. Otrębski (8) the word 'nur' (ner) derives from the 'neur' which means that all those rivers were named after the Neuri.

There is no such Slavic nation as the 'Neuri'. What is more, the root 'neur' is not of Slavic origin. The question arises, how could a nation which is not Slavic by name be counted as Slavic? The only explanation is, the Neuri must have been a part of the Veneti with their own name, and they were first absorbed by the Proto-Slavs.(9)

Herodotus was a conscientious historian. He checked all the written sources he had at his disposal, made a journey to Scythia and interviewed many Scythians before he wrote his history. Therefore the Neuri must have been quite a big nation not only in his times (10) but some centuries before.

It seems that their territory became the cradlelands of the Slavs.

There is no hint as to the real name of the Proto-Slavs when they met Veneti or Neuri as a Venetian branch. It does not seem that they had anything of the 'Slav' in it. The name 'Slav' must have been created when the Proto-Slavs met the natives.

23

How could it happen and what does it mean?

The most popular explanation in the past was that the name 'Slav' was derived from the 'słowo' — word, or 'sława' — glory. The first explanation accepts the idea that the name 'Słowianie' — Slavs appeared when the Slavs made contacts with the Germans. Meeting different tribes, the Slavs divided them into two groups: those whom they understood because they used the same 'słowa' — words, so they called them 'Słowianie' — Slavs; and those whose language was foreign, so they called them 'Niemcy' — mute people. Since the Slavs could not understand the Germans, they called them 'Niemcy'. Some Slavic nations (Poles) still call the Germans — 'Niemcy'.

The second Slavonic word is the 'sława' — glory, celebration. Some people again in the past have tried to use it in their explanation. According to them, the Slavs are good, peaceful, lovable people, and because of these virtues they are called the 'Slowianie' — the glory people or the gay people.

Both of those explanations are too naive to be taken seriously.

Some scholars tried to explain the word 'Slav' as deriving either from the name of some river or lake, called 'Slova' or 'Slava' (11) or from the word 'slovo' which is the Old Slavonic expression for mud,(12) because the Slavic cradlelands might have been in the marshy basin of the river Pripet. The Slavs liked marshlands for their settlements.

This explanation seems to be inaccurate. The Slavic cradlelands were not only the muddy region of the Pripet basin, but the dry land of central Poland. There are the names of the Slavic nations derived from the names of the rivers, but here are some rules which should be observed: namely, that the small nations could be named after the small rivers at which they settled, but the big nation was named after the big river (Moravians after Morava River, Vislans, after Visla (Vistula) River). There are some small rivers called 'Slova' or 'Slava', but not a big one. Since Slavs were a big nation this explanation doesn't seem to be proper.

More convincing could be the explanation (13) which admits that the word 'Slov'-'Slav' could be derived from the Slavic word 'swój' — fellow (countryman). After all, names of some nations mean 'our people', but this suppositon has been attacked.(14)

In light of all those highly controversial theories, it is difficult to find a satisfactory explanation as to how the Slavs got their name.

Ptolemy, in his 'Germania', for the first time introduced the Slavs under their own name into written records. Naming many nations

24

north to the Roman Empire, he mentions the 'Stavani'-'Suobeni', who lived in European Sarmatia and Scythia. Many scholars accepted the idea that those two expressions, also seeming not to be Slavic (15) are the names of the Slavs.

The first writer who made a distinction between the Veneti and Slavs was Jordanes, the Greek historian who lived in the 6th century.(16) He writes "per immensa spatia Venetharium natio populosa consedit, quorum nomina licet nunc per varias familas et loca mutentur, principaliter tamen Sclaveni et Antes nominantur" (a huge territory is inhabited by the rich nation called Veneti. Although they are divided into many tribes, each having a different name, they mainly call themselves Slavs or Antes).

Why did the Slavs appear first under the Veneti name?

As mentioned before, the westward marching Proto-Slavs came in touch with the Veneti, had been accepted, and in the course of time they absorbed the natives, giving birth to a new nation. The process was not observed by the neighboring Finns, Estonians and Germans.

According to Tacitus,(17) the Veneti made the booty expeditions against the Finns in this time. They must have been strong if the biggest river in Estonia is called 'Vente' after them. After all, they represented some power even in the 13th century, when the Teutonic Knights compelled them to embrace Christianity. It is possible that the Slavs supported the Veneti in their raids, but the Finns did not notice them as a new nation and they called them the Veneti, too. They could have given this name to the Proto-Germans marching north of the Eurasiatic steppes to Scandinavia. In this way the old name was transferred to the new nation in Finn, Estonian and German languages.

There is another possibility. The Finns borrowed some words from the Germans when the latter occupied Scandinavia.(18) It is possible that the Germans were in touch with the Veneti on the southern shore of the Baltic sea, who were not Slavicized yet. They called them properly the Veneti and informed the Finns across the Baltic about it. In this way the Slavs as Veneti appeared in the languages of the Baltic nations, and that is why Russia, is 'Vene' to Estonians, and 'Venaja', 'Venaa', Venat to Finns today.

Unfortunately, the ancient writers did not venture to travel to the Vistula to see that the new nation under the name of Slavs was born. It was too long, unsafe and unimportant a journey to them. After all,

25

it concerned a nation in 'Barbaria' — Barbaryland. So they relied on the information received second hand. As the Scythians were informers for the Greek scholars, so the Germans were to the Roman writers.

Slavs as Veneti perpetuated down the centuries. Jordanes was the first who spotted Slavs among the Veneti. He, as well as others, thought they were the eastern branch of Veneti. Since then the name Veneti is applied to the western branch of Slavs. The Germans, perhaps pursuing their national ambitions more than truth, still consider the Serbo-Lusatians in East Germany as 'Wenden', not Slavs, and the matter is even ridiculous in Austria. The Austrians call the Slovenes living in Austria as 'Wenden', and their cousins across the border in Slovenia (Yugoslavia) as Slavs.

NOTES TO CHAPTER IV

1. **Bibliography:** Antoniewicz W., 'Archeologia Polska', Warszawa 1928; Dvornik F., 'The Slavs in European History and Civilization', New Brunswick 1962; Hamp E. P., 'Venetic Isoglosses', American Journal of Philology 1959, Vol. LXXX; Henzel J., 'Ziemie polskie w pradziejach', Warszawa 1969; Kostrzewski J., 'Wielkopolska w czasach przedhistorycznych', Poznań 1914; and, 'Prasłowiańszczyzna', Poznań 1946; Meillet J., 'Le slave commune', Paris 1924; Mikkola J. J., 'L'avance des Slaves vers la Baltique', RESLav. 1921; Moszyński K., 'Badania nad pochodzeniem i pierwotną kulturą Słowian, RAFil. 1925; and, 'O Neurach Herodota', LUD 1954; Plezia M., 'Neurowie w świetle historiografii starożytnej'; Pic J. L., 'Die Urnengraber Böhmens', Leipzig 1907; Schwartz E., 'Goten, Nordgermanen, Angelsachsen', Bern 1951; Sulimirski T.', Najstarsze dzieje narodu polskiego', Londyn 1946; Szafarzyk P., 'Słowiańskie starożytności', Poznań 1842; Thomsen W., 'Über den Einfluss der germanischen Sprachen auf die finnish-lappischen', Halle 1870; Tymieniecki K., 'Neurowie-Veneci', PSLow 1957, Vol. VIII; Ułaszyn H., 'Praojczyzna Słowian', 'Łódź 1949.

2. P. J. Safarik was the author of the Dnieper-Vistula theory which he explained in his book, 'Slavanske starožitnosti', 1842, p. 36. His point of view shares W. Kętrzyński, and E. Bogusławski, 'Historia Słowian', Kraków 1888.

3. The second theory was developed by L. Niederle, 'Slovanske' starożitnosti', Praha 1902, p. 5. It was not new because K. Mullehoff in 'Deutsche Alterskunde', Berlin 1887, p. 89 points out possibility that the Vistula-Dnieper territory might have been cradlelands of Slavs. The same line of speculation shows J. Rostafiński in his deliberation 'O pierwotnych siedzibach Słowian', SAUm. 1908, Vol. XIII, p. 6-25. J Rozwadowski in 'Krytyczne uwagi o praojczyźnie Słowian', SAUm. 1906, Vol. I, p. 2 and K. Vasmer, 'Die Urheimat der Slaven', Breslau 1926, p. 118-143.

4. J. Kostrzewski was the author of the Odra-Vistula theory, which he explained in his book 'Wielkopolska w czasach przedhistorycznych', Poznań 1914, p. 155. He found a strong supporter in linguist T. Lehr-Spławinski.

5. This theory was developed mostly by the Russian scholars: P. N. Tret'jakov, 'O proischodżdenii slavjan', Moskva 1953, p. 44; A. J. Teremożkin, 'Prarodina Slavjan i lużickaja kul'tura', Kiev 1961, p. 7-10.

6. Herodote 'Histories', Paris 1949, Vol. IV, p. 268.

7. J. Hanusz, 'O dobie litewsko-słowiańskiej' w stosunku do prajęzyka indoeuropejskiego, RAFil. 1886, Vol. II, p. 268. There are many Polish words with the root "nar", "nor" or "nur", for instance: 'narowić' — to spoil; 'narów' — bad habit; 'nora' — burrow, den; 'nurkować' — to drive; 'nurek' — a diver; 'nurt' — a current; 'nurzać' — to dip. The words with the root "nur" are more frequent than others and all have some connection with water. T. Lehr-Spławiński in his 'O pochodzeniu i praojczyźnie Słowian', p. 13-14, writes: "The word 'Neuri' has the root "neur", which appears in the normal Slavic form "nur" — in such Slavic words, like 'zanurzyć', 'nurek' in Polish, in the side form as 'nyr' — in Old Church Slavonic 'nyriati', in Russian — 'nyriat', in Serbo-Croatian — 'ponirati', and in many names of rivers and lakes".

8. J. Otrębski, 'Beiträge zur baltisch-slawischen Namenkunde', BNForsch 1961, Vol. XII, p. 39-41.

9. H. Łowmiański, 'Początki Polski', Warszawa 1962, Vol. I, p. 118.

10. According to J. E. Powell, 'The History of Herodotus', Cambridge 1939, p. 60,66, the Greek historian wrote the part describing Scythia before 443 B.C.

11. The author of this theory was J. Rozwadowski.

12. J. Otrębski, 'Słowianie — rozwiązanie odwiecznej zagadki ich nazw', Poznań 1947, p. 35-53 and F. P. Filin, 'Obrazovane jazyka vostocznych slavjan', Moskva 1962, p. 56.

13. J. Otrębski, op. cit., p. 54-68. It is worth to mention that in Silesian dialect in Poland the people of the same family are called the 'swojacy' — fellows, relatives.

14. T. Lehr-Spławiński, 'Znowu o nazwie Słowian', JPol 1948, Vol. XXVII, p. 140-146.

15. "Unless we are to conjecture 'Stlavani' for Ptolemy's 'Stavani', or to insist on the resemblance of his 'Suobeni' to 'Slovene', the name Slav first occurs in Pseudo-Caesarius "Dialogues" early 6th century. . . The combination "sl" was difficult to the Greeks and Romans and they inserted "t", "tl" or most commonly "c", which continues to crop up. So too in Arabic "Saquliba", "Saqlab" — writes Encyclopedia Britannica, 1911, Vol. XXV, p. 229.

16. Jordanes, 'Gettica', AAnt. 1882, Vol. V. p. 62.

17. R. Much, 'Die Germania des Tacitus', Heidelberg 1937, p. 415.

18. E. Niemienen, 'Über einige Eigenschaften der baltischen Sprache, die sich in den, ältesten baltischen Lehnwortern der ostseefinnischen Sprachen abgespielt', Finnischen Akad., 1957, p. 185-206.

CHAPTER V

NEW LIFE

What economy did the Veneti represent when the Proto-Slavs met them on their way west? The answer seems to be simple: the Veneti as primitive agriculturists were on a higher level than the newcomers.(1)

How did they learn to farm?

According to archaeological findings, farming was not only the biggest revolution of the Neolithic, but perhaps of all time. It started somewhere around Jericho and Jarmo (2) in Asia Minor about (3) eight thousand years B.C. as a mixed economy: crop-sowing and animal-herding.

The new kind of economy travelled fast into all corners of the ancient world. It reached the Nile Valley perhaps 7000 B.C., Greece 5000 B.C., England 4000 B.C. and China 3000 B.C.

Farming used many roads to Europe. One led to Egypt down the Mediterranean shores to Spain, (4) by sea up to the Atlantic coast of the Iberian peninsula, to France and Britain. Another one starting from Anatolia reached Greece, (5) Crete, Sicily, northern Italy, and up the Rhone Valley to France and Britain.(6) The third led by Balkan (7) to Poland, Germany and Denmark.

There were settlements of the primitive farmers in Ukraine, called the Tripolye people. How they reached his region is not clear. They could have travelled along the western Black Sea shores or from Causasus.

The farming incomers practiced the mixed farming with barley and as many as three kinds of wheat (emmer, club and einkorn). Cattle were their main support, and from the first they seem to have relied very little on hunting to supplement their beef, mutton and pork. There is strong evidence to show how these newcomers

28

tackled the forests with axe and fire to open up pasture and arable land.

Nowhere has more been discovered of the impact between farming incomers and native Mesolithic peoples than in Denmark. The Trichterbecher settlers undoubtedly lived as neighbors to the Erthebolle hunters-fishermen during several centuries. They were in some kind of communication with one another, for odds and ends belonging to the Neolithic culture are found in the Erthebolle middens. Nevertheless the aborigines maintained their more primitive economy almost unchanged. What is interesting — and may well have happened elsewhere in forest regions — is that they actually prospered for a time, evidently increasing in numbers and founding new settlements.(8)

The primary farming way of life seems generally to have been a peaceful one, not given to warlike adventure. None of the Danubian villages, for instance, had defenses, and although in many regions Neolithic settlements were ditched and fenced, it was usually on a scale more appropriate to protection against marauding animals than against human enemies.

The Neolithic cultures, at least from Hungary to their western limits, were extraordinarily homogeneous down to the finest details. The peasants seem to have been almost as homogeneous physically as they were in their habits and manufactures.

Those characteristics of the Old Europeans found by the archaeologists are in accord with the written sources about the Veneti which constitute a big temptation to see Veneti as the only nation of the huge part of Europe in this time.

When the Proto-Slavs met their scanty settlements (9) in their way to the west somewhere between the rivers Pripet, Narew and Warta in Poland, they might have been startled seeing new economy.

There are no written records about it and the archaeological findings on the Polish territories referring to this epoch are extremely rare. Nevertheless, on reports how the Danubians, Morvava-Vardar people, Tripolye settlers, the Windmill Hill natives in England and Swiss Lake dwellers lived it is possible to picture how the Veneti lived, when the Proto-Slavs found them.

The Veneti lived in communes of 50 to 60 persons of close relatives, with grandparents at the top. Near to them were their married children, grandchildren, odd kinsfolk and sometimes adopted persons from outside. The Polish name of this social unit is the 'ród' — clan.

The 'ród' was a classless organization. The older people enjoyed a special respect but not special rights. "All ate from one kettle". Since in the earliest epoch of food-gathering and garden-farming the main bread-winner was the woman, communes have been of cognatic character, which means they derived from the common ancestor of the female line.(10)

The 'ród' was a typical self-supporting unit. Being insular in structure, it produced all that was necessary to sustain life. Its additional feature was close family ties which left traces in rich vocabulary.(11)

All problems concerning the commune were discussed during the dinner time or in free time after work. The decision had to be made unanimously. If there was opposition, the majority tried to gain approval by peaceful persuasion, very rarely by force.

No one had a special right in making decisions. The head of the clan presided over the meeting, but his voice was equal to the voice of any grown-up person of the 'ród'.

Fig. 1 Ancient clan house in Bulgaria changed into stable, after K. Moszynński, 'Kultura ludowa Słowian', Vol. I, p. 482

The clan occupied one big communal house, in Sweden even 85 metres long, perhaps which was shared with its livestock, especially in wintertime.(12) Cold and windy climate encouraged the sinking of house below ground level and screening of the entrance to the living-room with a porch or anteroom. Solid wind — and rain — proof houses built of local materials were essential in many parts of Europe.

The big house as well as land, inventory and livestock constituted the common property. The items of personal use, especially adornments, on the other hand, were counted to be private property and buried with the holder when he died.

If a member of a commune was killed or harmed by the member of another commune, all his kinsfolk demanded compensation for wrong doing. The process of justice, based first on revenge, then on compensation, was called the 'wróżda'.

The clan in its primitive form lasted down the centuries. The so called 'Niedziały rodzinne' were common in Poland in the 13th century; the Russian 'Mir' lasted until 18th century, and the Croatian 'Zadruga' survived even to our times.(13)

The glacial winds laid down vast beds of loess from Serbia to Poland and westward as far as Belgium. Loess soil is very well suited to primitive agriculture, for it is naturally well drained and lightly forested, and can be effectively cultivated with a hoe.

The economic basis of the Venetic farming was the cultivation of cereals and other food crops in little hand-hoed plots. Their main crops were inkorn wheat and barley, but they also grew emmer wheat, peas, beans and lentils. The numbers of cattle, sheep, and pigs kept seem to have been relatively small. Hunting and fishing had ceased for the Veneti to have any considerable importance. It seems generally to have taken anything from a decade to a quarter of a century for all plots within convenient reach of a village to become exhausted, and a move to be made to a fresh site.

The natives used the stone bowls and other vessels, or wooden ones if wood was abundant.

The essential cooking equipment of the house was the hearth and quern for corn-grinding. They were the saddle querns in use at the beginning.

It is not certain that, when the Proto-Slavs met the Veneti, basketing was known to the natives. What is more, it seems they did not make textiles.(14) If it is true they must have worn the skins as many other generations in the past.

The skin of goats could have been their first clothes. From the word 'koza' — goat derives the 'kożuch' — sheepskin, not from the sheep.

The newcomers from the Eurasiatic steppes must have been shocked to see so many strange arrangements of the Veneti. People for the first time had chosen the settled life, sacrificing the freedom of wandering, essential from the beginning of man. Instead of tents they had the solid huts and many implements, which constituted a burden for nomads. But they must have looked more healthy and happy because of the richness of their diet.

What could the Proto-Slavs have contributed to their common life with the Veneti? They were hunters, food-gathers and herdsmen.(15)

It seems not much. After all, the newcomers were on the lower level of civilization. It is possible that they introduced the dairy industry to farming economy. The beasts composing the early flocks and herds in the cradlelands of farming, and those later led into Europe, were usually much smaller than their wild counterparts. The cattle in particular (boslongifrons) were as diminutive as the modern Kerry. The usually accepted explanation is that, wherever possible, men selected the dwarf from among the wild stock, as they were best able to keep and to breed from the smaller, weaker and more docile animals, (16) for meat and skin more than dairy. Since the word 'daughter' means 'milkmaid' in almost all Indo-European languages, it might have been that the Proto-Slavs enriched the Venetic economy by introducing the dairy animals, especially milk cows.

Fig. 2. Saddle quern in use. Egyptian Statuette, after J. G. Clark.

Fig. 3. Honey gathering in Palaeolithic times, according to painting in Bicorp Cave in Spain, after L. Loth.

There was another economy in full swing. Since the climate did not help much to grow sweet fruit, the people found sweetness in honey produced by wild bees.(17) They made the 'barcie' — holes on the trees which served the wild bees as the beehive. The trees were marked, and when the time came, the 'bartnicy' — men gathering honey climed the trees and robbed the honey. This economy was so important that a special law had been established to regulate the matters.(18) The Veneti used honey to sweeten their meals and to produce very popular 'miód pitny' — alcoholic honey. The new economy and way of life were not difficult for the newcomers from the Eurasiatic steppes to adopt. They learned it quickly and enjoyed it. The Slavs appeared on the historic arena as a solid farming nation, not as brigands and pirates. The soil was sacred (19) to them, and there are many hints that the cult of Mother-Earth was deeply rooted in the Slavic soul.

Perhaps because of that the native Veneti accepted the migrating Proto-Slavs and called them the 'Swoi', 'Swojanie' (Slovyane — Slavs) — 'our people'.

NOTES TO CHAPTER V

1.**Bibliography:** Antoniewicz W., 'Archeologia Polski, Warszawa 1928; Burkitt Mc., 'Our early ancestors', Cambridge 1926; Childe V.G., 'The Dawn of the European Civilization', London 1947; Clark J. D., 'The Mesolithic Settlement of Northern Europe', Cambridge 1936; and, 'Prehistoric Europe', London 1945; Coon C.S., 'The History of Man', London 1955; Godlewski J., 'Dzieje i kultura dawnych Słowian', Warszawa 1966; Loth E., 'Człowiek przeszłości', Warszawa 1953; Keith A., 'The Antiquity of Man', London 1929; Krukowski S., Kostrzewski J., Jakimowicz R. 'Prehistoria ziem polskich', Kraków 1948; Mydlarski J.,'Pochodzenie człowieka', Warszawa 1948; and 'Jak wyglądała ludność Europy u schyłku epoki lodowej', Warszawa 1950; Okladnikov A., 'Palaoelithic and Neolithic in the USSR', Moskva 1959; Pigott S., 'Neolithic cultures in the British Isles', Cambridge 1954; Smith R. E., 'The Origins of Farming in Russia', Paris 1959; Weinert H. 'Ursprung der Menschheit', Stuttgart 1932.

2. The archaeologists found at Jarmo the first ground and polished stone axe and its variant, the adze. Other agricultural tools were sickles and simple grain rubbers or querns.

3. J. Hawkes, 'Prehistory', New York 1965, p. 307.

4. The Almerian people.

5. The Sesklo people.

6 The Windmill Hill farmers.

7. The Vardar-Morava people, the Danubians I, the Oltenians.

8. J. Hawkes, 'Prehistory', p. 337-338.

9. The Veneti were not the first people in the Polish territories. The first traces of human being are dated to 180,000 B.C. The Neanderthal hunters made their short-lived camps found by archaeologists at Piekary, near Cracow and Racibórz in Upper Silesia. The oldest human bones, discovered in 1951 at Franki Suchodolskie are dated 120,000 B.C. At the beginning of the last glacial period the hunters dwelled in caves near Zawiercie and Ojców. About 14,000 B.C. the hunters at Kamienna produced and exported ocher to paint dead bodies in red. It is the first trace of commerce in Polish territories. From the Mesolithic era, which lasted from 8,000 to 3,500 B.C. the hunters left on the plains many microlithic flints like arrow-heads.

10. J. Haukes, 'Prehistory', p. 356, writes: "A social anthropologist has written that there are facts pointing definitely to the close connection between communal ownership and mother-right on the one hand and invividual ownership and the father-right on the other hand. Now it has already been said that traces of matrilineal descent, and even of matriarchy, survive in the forms of Egyptian and Cretan civilizations. But in general the growth of urban life was extensively reduced by the Early Bronze Age upheavals just referred to, and may also have been weakened when land came to be in short supply. But there is every reason to suppose that under the conditions of the primary Neolithic way of life mother-right and clan system were still dominant, and land would generally have descended through the female line. Indeed, it is tempting to be convinced that earliest Neolithic societies throughout their range in time and space gave woman the highest status she has ever know. They way of life and its values, the skill demanded, were ideally suited to her.

11. Here are some examples of kinsfolk terminology: 'dziewierz' — brother of the husband; 'zełwa' — sister of the husband; 'jątrew' — wife of the brother; 'nieć' — son of the sister; 'snecha' — wife of the son etc.

12. J. Hawkes, 'Prehistory', p. 391, writes about the dwellings of the Neolithic Danubians who were either the Veneti or the people with a strong influence on Veneti, as follows: "The dwellings of the Neolithic Danubians seem to have evolved through three styles. The first (until recently believed to have been barns) were very imposing, long, rectangular houses sometimes as much as 32 metres in length. The central ridge of the steeply pitched roof was supported on a line of posts, flanked by a farther line on each side that presumably helped to support the sloping rafters. Those long houses were divided into two, parts, one end having a raised floor and walls of split logs sunk into sub-soil, the other lighter walling of wattle and daub. Perhaps the timbered end only was used for human living, the rest being handed over to the animals or used for stores. From these first houses, among the finest built in Neolithic Europe, the later Dnubians seem to have changed to a smaller two-roomed megaron type house, and then to a still smaller one-roomed form".

13. The Encyclopedia Slavonica, New York 1944, under the 'Zadruga' writes as follows: "It is a basic social, economic and familial institution still well preserved in the Croatian villages between the rivers Sava and Drava. A group of familes live in a common household called the 'hiza', possessing common fields, livestock, buildings, utensils and agricultural implements. It tends to be an economically self-sufficient community producing most of the life necessities for its members, food clothing, housing, medicine and recreation.

'Zadruga' is managed by a 'gospodar' and 'gospodinia' a male and a female chosen respectively by the male and female members of the 'druzina' — 'Zadruga' members. Their term is one year, but they may be reelected and often are.

Besides the common dwelling 'hiza' there are individual family dwellings 'komora' located around the 'hiza'. Next to common property 'skupcina' each member may own private property 'osebuniak', may work on it when the work for the common property is done.

The control of the 'Zadruga' affairs is vested in the hands of male and female adult members who discuss common affairs and make decisions about them each day at common meals, especially the evening meal, when all are home. A similar democratic organization prevails in the village 'selo' which may be composed of a number of 'Zadrugas'. Common affairs of the 'selos' or the commune 'opcina" — an administrative unit consisting of a group of villages — are discussed at the common gathering 'dekoncak'.

There is a detailed division of labor according to the age, sex, ability, interest and expediency, but there is no differential prestige placed on any kind of work. Everbody has some knowledge of every type of work performed in the 'Zadruga'. Some work is done by the women only, like gardening, spinning, weaving, embroidery, cooking, nursing and cleaning. Plowing, carpentry and carving are adult men's work.

Many tasks are performed in common by men and women. Girls and children engage in herding. The old people perform minor tasks and tend babies.

Both boys and girls are equally welcomed, no favoritism is shown in attitudes toward male or female children. An infant in the cradle 'dete' is shown great affection. Little boys 'dececi' and little girls 'deklice' are treated with moderation, respect and are taken seriously by all adult 'Zadruga' members. There is not much emphasis on competition in children's play, nor there is much praise for a special achievement of a child.

A child spends most of his time playing with other children. Older children are expected to take care and to be responsible for the younger ones. In this way the adult members or the parents seldom appear in the role of the disciplinarians.

There is remarkable respect for old age. Authority is accepted as long as it kept within defined limits.

As a result of such social organization, tension in the 'Zadruga' is limited. The 'Zadruga' view of life discourages aggressive, boastful, inconsiderate and self-seeking personalities, emphasizes cooperation, sociability and avoidance of violence. It favors equal distribution of power, of other values and unanimity in decisions on common issues, arrived at by persuasion and free deliberation, not by force.

There is a great emphasis on fairness and justice 'pravica' and belief that justice reigns everywhere, that "justice is stronger than God". In the past the 'Zadruga' peasants frequently rebelled in widespread uprisings against their feudal lords and in the name old justice 'stara pravica'.

In favorable circumstances anti-social behavior is kept at a low level, so are sorcery, mental diseases and beliefs in evil spirts. Protection against these spirits is not difficult. Hallucinations are also mild. There is a remarkable lack of suicides and also lack of fear of death. 'Zadruga' people may "see" heaven and believe in a gay and beautiful post-mortem life. In their told poetry the emphasis in on lyric and ritual songs. They play on single and double folk flutes and on many stringed (2-8) instruments.

The introduction of a money economy, the need to reorganize production to suit the needs of a market after the abolishment of feudalism worked toward disintegration of the 'Zadrugas' as self-sufficient economic units. This trend brought about a deterioration in interpersonal relations in the 'Zadruga' life. Consequently, many 'Zadrugas' split to form small family economies on a individualistic basis.

'Zadruga' culture was able to perpetuate itself throughout many centuries mainly because its democratic family organization, its system of self-sufficiency, which provided emotional, social, econimic security and stability''.

14. There is no evidence that the Windmill Hill people in Britain who lived in the same time, made textiles (J. Hawkes, 'Prehistory', p. 413).

15. Hunting, food-gathering and animal-herding as an exclusive economy were common in those times. In the Orkney Islands there were settled cattle-men who raised no crops.

16. J. Hawkes, 'Prehistory', p. 377, 378, 383.

17. The normal apiary system had been introduced on this area not earlier than in the 13th century.

18. Gallus Anonymous, the first Polish chronicler notes that Poland was ''a mellifluent country''.

19. According to 'Larousse Encyclopedia of Mythology', London 1959, p. 297, the pagan Slavs worshipped the Earth as a special divinity, which among the Russians was called 'Mati-Syra-Zemlya' which means ''Mother-Earth-Moist''. The Earth was supreme being, sentient and just. For centuries Slav peasants settled legal disputes relating to landed property by calling on the Earth as a witness.

CHAPTER VI
FLINT MINE

Fig. 4. Shaft in flint mine in the Góry Swiętokrzyskie — Holy Cross Mountains in Poland, after J. Bardach, 'Historia Polski', p.3

Man used stone tools from the dawn of civilization. They were rough and cumbersome at the beginning, made from the hard stuff, mostly flint and obsidian.

In the Mesolithic age the stone implements were highły refined.

(1) The hunters used flint for arrow heads and spearheads, knives and scrapers. All those tools were sharp but small, sometimes one inch long, hence the name of times — the Microlithic epoch.

The situation changed when farming developed. The farmers needed the strong, heavy and sharp equipment for forest clearance and for tilling the soil, as well as for carpentry and other specialized skills.

Patient labor was involved in their manufacture. First the flint and tough igneous rock, which were the preferred materials, were percussion flaked or pecked roughly into concrete shape. Then either the cutting-edge or (more usually) the whole implement was ground down and smoothed by rubbing it on the suitable rock such as sandstone, probably always with the addition of an abrasive. If the tool was to be perforated for the reception of the handle, this was first done by the crude method of drilling from both sides, probably with a bow-drill and abrasive; it was only in later Neolithic cultures that some kind of cylindrical drill was devised to get a clean, straight shafthole. Such straight perforations are found in the equipment of the "battle-axe" people, whose beautiful weapons brought the whole technique of the polished stone tool to its greatest perfection.(2)

Next to stone arrowheads, spearheads, knives and scrapers inherited from the earlier epoch, farmers had to develop axes, adzes, hoes, sickles and querns.

Two of these tools were particularly important in primitive farming — axes and adzes. The axe was set with its cutting-edge parallel to the haft, the adze, probably used also as a hoe, with it at right angles.

Tools had been used for many purposes. A typical example of a multiuseful implement, undoubtedly invented in the Neolithic but survived to our times, is the 'ciupaga' — walking cane of the Tatra mountaineers in Poland. It is a walking cane, axe, battle-axe and climbing tool.

The big demand for axes and adzes as hard as steel today forced the primitive farmers to look for special raw material. When they could not find it in the river beds and stone debris, they started to dig in the earth for it, first making quarries, then mines.

The knowledge of mining and quarrying, the first undertaking by man that can properly be called industrial, came very largely from Europe. The most highly specialized of these industries was flint mining by means of deep shafts sunk through the chalk to reach the flint nodules layered within it. Nodules obtained in this way were not only larger but fresher and more readily worked than surface flint. Mines had been organized in Sicily, Portugal, France, Belgium, England, Denmark, Sweden, Poland and Bohemia.

The process of flint mining is little known, therefore it is worth quoting J. Hawkes (3) on how this first industry worked in West Europe, to better understand the processing in Poland.

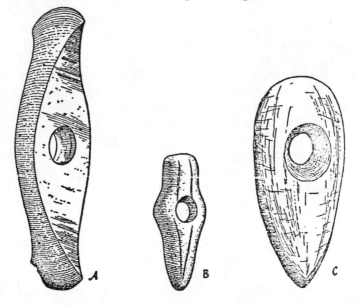

Fig. 5 Neollithic polished stone implements. A, B, C: doubleedged axes and hammer axe from France, after S. Wheeler

"Where it has been possible to recognize a chronological sequence, the earliest shafts have been simple pits, while later the miners learned how to drive galleries along the seams, leaving columns of chalk to support the roof in lieu of pitprops. The shaft might be as much as 12 metres deep; sump holes were sometimes sunk near their foot to collect rain water, and occasionally there were even such conveniences as wooden steps. The miners had their own kit bags; the commonest tools were picks made from the shaft and brow tine of red-deer antlers, shovels made from shoulderblades (ox, deer and pig,) and wedges from antlers tines. Flint axes were also used, and at Spiennes in Belgium rough flint picks. Antlers with tines left to make two-prong rakes were used for drawing back the rubble. The dark galleries were lighted by chalk-cut lamps, and the

38

nodules seem sometimes to have been bagged and then drawn to the surface with ropes. At some sites, such as the famous Grime's Graves in eastern England, there were hundreds of shafts, and each shaft involved shifting up to five thousand cubic feet of chalk. In short, this was a skilled and specialized industry.

Once mined, the flint implements were roughed out on the spot. Usually axes were flaked to approximately their final form, only the grinding and polishing being left to the purchasers; this reduced the weight and bulk of the goods to be transported. Occasionally (notably in Denmark) the working-up was not carried so far, and flint was traded in the form of shapless bars.

In some areas, such as the island of Rugen and in Denmark, excellent flint lay on the surface and workshops developed to exploit. This method of working is exactly paralleled by the known factories for stone axes, several of which have been identified in western Britain (Wales, Cumberland and northern Ireland). Here again the axes were brought up to the state at which only grinding and polishing was needed. Generally the workers do not seem to have undertaken any actual quarrying for their raw materials but used flakes struck from boulders. In Cumberland there is some evidence of the existence of "middlemen" working away from the quarries, who polished the axes before they were traded farther afield.

It is impossible to be sure of the social background of this specialized trade and industry. It is hard to believe that the workers of the more elaborate flint mines were not specialists, even full-time specialists. On the other hand it is not impossible that members of agricultural communities went to the mines in off-seasons to dig their supplies for the year. Really large hoards of axes such as would represent a professional merchant's stock have been found in Denmark and northern Sweden. In Britain there is evidence that the transport of the stone axes was in the hands of the native, pre-Windmill Hill people, who were not fully settled agriculturalists. Undoubtedly, however it was effected, the axes travelled far within the British Isles and beyond. Specimens from North Wales have been found in the Channel Islands, from northern Ireland and Cumberland, in considerable quantities in southern England.

Attention has been concentrated on the axe trade, because it is typical of the Neolithic economy. Other flint forms were rarely involved in specialized industry, for small tools could always be made by every family for itself. At Grand Pressigny in central France, however, a readily worked and pleasingly honey-colored flint was shaped locally into long, elegant flakes that were exported widely in western Europe. This trade began only towards the end of Neolithic times and reached its height as part of the expanding trade of the Bronze Age".

About 3500 B.C. on the Polish plains dominated a group of cattle-raisers, for whom farming was a side economy. Between 3000 and 2000 B.C. they created the culture of funnel cups. They used animal traction in farming and mined flint on a bigger scale in the Góry Świętokrzyskie — Holy Cross Mountains especially at Krzemionki Opatowskie.

Fig. 6. Stone axes and hammers mined and worked out in the Holy Cross Mountains in Poland.

Shafts were traced in 1922 at Krzemionki Opatowskie (4) near the city of Ostrowiec in the Góry Świętokrzyskie — Holy Cross Mountains. Archaeologists noticed a surface covered by more or less regularly placed hummocks and holes. Regularity was striking and intriguing.

After excavating one of those hummocks archaeologists were astonished to see that beneath the surface was a shaft with many underground corridors. Here, some thousands of years ago men mined flint.(5) The members of the digging party could not believe their own eyes.

The World War II and the restoration period following stopped excavation. It was not until the 1960's that archaeologists returned to their digging.

They found over 1200 shafts in this region and have managed to explore several of them.

How could miners in such remote times exploit it?

They dug a shaft about 20 feet deep in limestone and drilled underground corridors from it. Flint was in limestone like raisins in a cake, in the form of lumps similar to loaves of bread and about 7 inches thick.

Miners cut the raised lumps into flakes and made tools from them. Sometimes they worked in the shafts, sometimes on the surface. Waste flint and rabble gathered by digging the underground corridors were either brought to the surface and left heaped, making the characteristic hummocks today, or were thrown into old exploited shafts and corridors.

How did the primitive miners raise flint when they had no idea of bronze or iron tools? What sort of implement did they use?

Answers to these questions are found in the broken and forgotten tools left in shafts and corridors. Some 6 or 5 thousand years ago miners used hacks made of hard rock or deer horns.

There is an amazing story how they made those hacks. They softened horns by boiling then with sorrel leaves and then molded the horns into the proper shape and sharpness. Then they boiled them again in clean water. Thus the horns became even harder than they were at the beginning of processing. Tools made this way were quite good in breaking up the limestone.

When one shaft had been exploited miners dug out another at a distance of about a hundred feet. Sometimes corridors of the new shaft were connected with corridors of the old shaft. In this way miners could go down with one shaft and go out by another.

How well they developed the mining techniques in those remote times is proven by the fact that they even drilled ventilation shafts.

Miners worked 3 to 4 months in summertime. Thus, one shaft was under exploitation for over 300 years. The whole mining area could produce 26 tons of flint annually good for 20 thousand stone axes.(6)

Who could need such quantities of axes and other tools in those times when the population in Northern Europe was rather scarce?

The Holy Cross Mountains flint is pure silica, harder than steel and remarkably homogeneous. Furthermore, it was famous because of its beauty. The Holy Cross Mountains flint is the only flint in Europe and perhaps in the world with black streaks. This characteristic makes it easy to recognize.

For hardness and fine appearance the flint was in great demand. Archaeologists found axes made from it in excavations as far as the rivers Elbe, Danube, Dniester and Volga.(7) Their export when considering the primitive conditions of transportation is remarkable.

Now the question: Who worked in the mines — slaves or free miners?

All signs indicate they were free miners working on their own account. Society was not developed enough to use slave labor. Slavery came later, in the iron epoch.

It seems, other aspects played here a role, too. People on this level considered miners as men endowed with magical powers. To challenge them would be a foolish act. They were in constant contact with underground spirits.

The miners dug for long hours on their knees. After work they crept to the surface, covered with stone dust. Their appearances gave rise to panic among those who were not familiar with flint mining. Superstition had a splendid ground in which to flourish. There is the possibility that flint miners gave the start to many fairy tales about little people, dwarfs, Nibelungen and other creations of mind who according to the fables guarded treasures hidden beneath the ground.

When miners working on the surface were surprised by an enemy they usually jumped down into the shaft and took cover in long corridors. Thus, they made quite an impression. The enemy saw with his own eyes men disappearing under the surface. He could follow them, but he had to courage. Superstition made him flee. He was convinced he saw the spirits who dwelt underground. This is another motif of fairy tales — dwarfs suddenly disappearing beneath the surface.

It was safer to trade with flint miners than to rob them.

Not only other people regarded flint miners as men endowed with supernatural power but they believed it themselves, too. They believed that because of their offerings and magic spells the underground spirits cooperated and helped in mining.

In some shafts of the Holy Cross Mountains mysterious signs and drawings are found on the walls. Drawn with coal made of resinous chips used to illuminate the corridors in which they worked they might have been maps of mines and underground connections between them. But it seems to be rather a magic craft. On this level of civilization man strongly believed he was surrounded by a large number of supernatural beings called demons. Most of them were supposedly hostile to him. To appease those demons someone had to give offerings and make proper incantations.

Slavs were not the first to start flint mining in the Holy Cross Mountains. It was in progress when they arrived from Eurasiatic steppes. But it is possible they enlarged and perfected the mining.

42

Flint mining started about 4 thousand years B.C. continued to the iron epoch and perhaps longer.

The Stone age produced mining in many countries. Remnants of shafts and corridors are to be seen in France, Great Britain, Belgium, Holland and Denmark, but nowhere have they survived in such splendid condition as at Krzemionki Opatowskie.

Archaeologists in Poland have discussed opening the flint mines to the public.(8) They want to search as many shafts as possible to discover what might be the most spectacular for visitors to see.

NOTES TO CHAPTER VI

1. **Bibliography**: Forbes R. J. 'Studies in Ancient Technology', Leiden 1955; Godłowski K., 'Źródła archeologiczne do dziejów rolnictwa w Polsce', Warszawa 1960; Jirlow R., 'Pflugloser Getreidebau in Sweden', EAForsch. 1958, Vol. IV; Knowles F. H. S., 'Stone-worker's Progress', Oxford 1953; Kostrzewski J., 'Pradzieje Polski', Poznań 1949; Oakley J., 'Man the Toolmaker', London 1958; Sauce R. U., 'Primitive Arts and Crafts', Cambridge 1933; Tymieniecki K., 'Ziemie polskie w starożytności', Poznań 1951.

2. J. Hawkes, 'Prehistory', New York 1965, p. 421.

3. J. Hawkes, op. cit., p. 431-433.

4. Krzemionki Opatowskie is the name of the village where the flint mines from the Noelithic epoch were discovered. The name translated into English would be Flints of Opatów. Since the village existed in the remote past it is possible there is a permanent settlement from the Neolithic era when the flint mines flourished. Although the local industry ceased to exist and was forgotten, the name of the village remained and no one could guess its origin. Now the puzzle is solved.

5. J. Bardach, A. Gieysztor, H. Łowmiański, E. Maleczyńska, 'Historia Polski do r. 1466', Warszawa 1969; p. 4, 6.

6. Chapter VI is based on information delivered to the International Symposium of the European Neolithic Cultures held in 1969 in Warsaw, Poland. The Polish archaeologists took the delegates on tour to excavations. According to the press reports, after seeing the mines at Krzemionki Opatowskie the delegates were very impressed and stated that this is not only the largest area of flint mining in the world but in such condition that there is none comparable.

7. 'Wielka Encyklopedia Powszechna', Warszawa 1965; Vol. 6, p. 239.

8. The flint mines discovered at Krzemionki Opatowskie are under the control of the Museum of Archaeology in Warsaw, Poland. Prof. Tadeusz Żurowski heads the team of archaeologists exploring those mines.

43

B. ANCIENT SLAV EPOCH
from 2000 B.C. to the 6th century A.D.

After absorbing native Veneti the Proto-Slavs became Slavs and started their antiquity. The territory they occupied rendered good isolation. Two rivers — the Odra in the west and the Pripet in the east — with their tributaries and marshlands blocked the way from the east and west. The Baltic Sea in the north and the Carpathian Mountains in the south constituted barriers for invaders.

These characteristics led J. Kostrzewski and other scholars to develop the autochthonic theory, which maintains that the population between the rivers Odra and Vistula remained the same down the millennia, changing the way of life under the influence of civilization. There were no ethnic abruptions in this region, as the archaeological findings indicate.

Although the cradlelands of Ancient Slavs had natural borders, they did not keep the natives in splendid isolation. There were ethnic penetrations in Slavic antiquity, not counting short-lived Scythian invasions from the south.

The first penetration was made by some Illyric nations, which were absorbed by the Ancient Slavs quickly, but before submerging it left some traces, especially in onomastics, like the name of the city of Śrem in Poland. This fooled many scholars, leading them to develop the theory of Illyrian origin of the Slavs.

More impact was made by the second penetration by the Celts. There is no doubt about their arrival to the western territories of Poland in the 3rd century B.C. or even earlier. They played quite a role in the last century B.C. in this corner of the world before they were absorbed by natives probably in the 2nd century A.D. The traces they left in culture point out the peaceful co-existence between the Celts and Slavs before the former submerged.

The Germans made the third penetration. Starting with the beginning of our era they used the Polish territories as a transit route from the Baltic up the Vistula, down the Dniester to the Black Sea. Some centuries later the remnants of the Goths from the Black Sea used this thoroughfare in reverse, returning home to their Scandinavian cradlelands. They left traces in onomastics and language.

CHAPTER VII
LUSATIAN CULTURE

The fertile loess soil, very well suited to primitive agriculture, which runs in a wide belt from the Carpathian Mountains through middle Poland to the Baltic, lured many farmers from the south.(1)

The first group appeared about 4200 B.C. Their ribbon engraving ceramics indicate they must have migrated from the Danube. They prospered over 1500 years before the new group took over.

About 3500 B.C. the Polish plains were dominataed by a group of cattle-raisers for whom farming was a side economy. Between 3000 and 2000 B.C. they created the culture of funnel cups. They must have started flint mining in the Holy Cross Mountains and left especially in Masovia the big 'kurhany' — barrows, 300 ft long and 30 ft. long and 30 ft. wide, fenced by rocks 3-7 ft. high.

Then came another group, perhaps from the region of the lower Elbe and Odra, who created the culture of ball-shaped amphoras.

At the end of the Neolithic, about 2000 B.C., the settlement took insular form, the reason why many different cultures were found. The situation changed around 1700 B.C. First the Unietician culture embraced almost all of Silesia, western Poland, Slovakia and lower Austria. (2) It gave room for the new Trzciniecian culture.(3)

During the middle bronze epoch, around 1300 B.C. the Lusatian culture started to flourish. It spread all over the territories of Poland, then it embraced almost all of East Germany, Czechoslovakia and the region east of the river Bug. The name is derived from the typical burial place of this culture found in Lusatia (East Germany, today).

Long years of quiet, peaceful life helped to develop a genuine culture in some branches, especially ceramics and adornments in the most sophisticated manner.

The characteristic feature of the Lusatian culture, which at the beginning was amazingly unified on all territories, was the

47

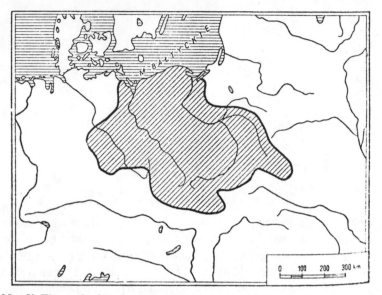

Map V. The reach of the Lusatian culture between the 7th and 5th century. B.C.

cremation. It constituted quite a novelty compared to the former Trzciniecian culture, when bodies had been buried in a crouched position. There is much controversy upon how the people of Lusatian culture came to the idea of burning the bodies of their dead.

The custom of cremation was not the Slavic invention. People burned bodies of their dead some 900 years before. The question arises who started practicing this custom among the Slavs. Neither Veneti nor new settlers from Eurasiatic steppes knew about it. It must have been some migration group who stopped in these territories a short period and showed the natives a new way of burial.

The quick spreading of this custom puzzled many historians. Had Ancient Slavs the same attitude towards cremation as the Romans did, considering it as the most dignified way of body disposal? As an example, the bodies of such emperors as Julius Ceasar, Pompeius, Augustus and Nero were burned.

After cremation the Ancient Slavs poured the ashes with bone remnants into a burrow if the dead was of humble stature.

If the dead was a chief or a person highly respected by all the remains were put into a cinerarium 'popielnica' and put into a grave richly endowed with tools and adornments.

Fig. 7. Typical implements of the Lusatian culture, after L. Leciejewicz.

Another feature of this culture was ceramics, one of the finest in northern and central Europe in those times. Some vessels, like amphoras, made without help of the potters wheel, had walls as thin as China today. What is more astonishing, the potters made beautiful imprints in the walls of amphoras by pushing special lumps from inside. The pots were painted in yellows and reds, and decorated with geometrical adornments in deep brown colors, sometimes yellow or red, very rarely white or black.

There are two typical vessels of Lusatian culture: the pitcher and the vase. The potter made pitchers in a highly sophistic form. With a stone in his hand he embossed the bellies from inside the vessel. This kind of ceramics dominated in the early epoch of Lusatian culture.

In times when this culture reached its peak other kinds of vessels appeared. They were vases and amphoras.

Object of art which this epoch presents, are exceedingly beautiful. Pins, buckles, and other luxury items are admired even today. Not one of the dressy women in New York, Paris or London would object to wearing bronze pin made by a craftsman at the Vistula River some 2.5 thousand years ago.

Next to flint implements, the people of the Lusatian culture used the bronze sickles, needles, axes, swords and adornments. Since there was no copper ore in the territory of the Lusatian culture, the implements had been imported from Hungary in ready form, or brought as metal to be hammered for use by the home craftsmen.

About 700 B.C., when the Lusatian culture reached its peak, iron had been introduced, but in a small way, and mostly in the form of adornments. It was imported from the south. The home production

49

of iron utensils started not earlier than in the 2nd century B.C.

The people of the Lusatian culture were the crop-sowers and cattle-raisers. They improved both economies.

As cattle-raisers, they kept the cattle on pastures close to their homes all year long. Then they started to gather hay and keep the cattle in wintertime in the same long communal house in which they dwelt. In time they began to build special shelters for the animals.

Fig. 8. Weapons and adornments of the Lusatian culture, after J. Lewański, 'Wrocław'.

There is a controversy about what forced those people to keep the cattle in their homes and to feed the animals with hay. It is possible that severe winters caused it, but it might have been that the cattlerustlers forced them to do it.

Having the cattle at home and watching them helped to develop the dairy industry.

The growth of population compelled them to enlarge and improve their farming. Since the open fields with fertile loess soil were taken under cultivation, it was necessary to seek a new farming land by forest clearance.(4) It must have been undertaken with the stone axes and adzes and with fire. The new 'gospodarka żarowa'' — fire farming left many traces in archaeology and onomastics.(5)

Using fire, the farmers learned to fertilize the soil with ashes. In this stage of cultivation, the main agricultural implements were the axe and adze. The farmers cut down the trees and bushes, and burned them and sowed the grain in the ashes without sacrifying the soil. In the cleared land they raised emmer, bread wheat, peas, beans, and lentils. They ate wild plums and apples. Cattle were more important to them than pigs, sheep or goats. Hunting was of no significance, but people living at the water's edge were naturally fishermen, using traps, net and fish-spears. They grew flax and wore linen, though it seems that skins and furs still made up their warmer clothing.

Fig. 9 Typical burial place of the Lusatian culture. The cinerary urn, with ashes of a woman is covered by a flat lid, and the urn with ashes of a man is covered by a bowl. Many small pots contained food given to the dead.

It appears that the people of Lusatian culture were first using animal traction in agriculture and the wooden plow. But the new improvement did not play a big role. They mostly hoed their plots when they learned to scarify the soil.

The people lived in communes as before, but owing to the new techniques in farming and dense population, the old social system was decaying making room for the federations of clans.

The social system revealed similar characteristics to the Croatian Zadruga. Every family had equal rights. The system of equality is spectacularly manifested in the fortified town at Biskupin. There were over one hundred family huts of the same size. It means the community was ruled not by a prince but by a council. The small place at the gate of the stronghold suggests it was a meeting place and perhaps a market place, too.

There is no sign of a temple. It does not suggest the inhabitants of the stronghold were atheists. They praised their gods not in temples but in sacred groves. Perhaps one was situated behind the walls, where the people prayed in peaceful times.

In this period the traditional system of social equality began to loose its power. Two groups had been emancipated: the bronze and iron craftsmen and the warriors on horses.

The first group emerged between 1100-900 B.C. in Saxony, between 900-700 in Brandenburg and between 700-400 in northern Poland. In the last period the group of warriors on horses came into existence, as the burial place in Gorszewice, Poland, indicates.

The burial places are sometimes imposing, pointing out that in the vicinity must have lived a numerous population down many generations. All bodies were cremated and the ashes deposited in cinerary urns.

The custom of cremation vanished about 600-500 B.C. in Upper Silesia, perhaps under influence coming from the south.

At the turn of the II and I millennium B.C., in the western part of the Lusatian culture, appeared fortified towns, which will be discussed in the next chapter.

Fig. 10. Reconstruction of the crate grave with "facial" urns.

In the 8 th century B.C. the Lusatian culture came in touch with the eastern region of the Alps and nothern Italy along the famous Amber Route, from the mouth of the Vistula to Italy. Many luxury items, traded for amber, were imported from northern Italy to the basin of the Odra and Vistula. Probably that amber lured some Illyric people from the south to penetrate the region of Lusatian culture.

The Lusatian culture grew up from two former cultures: the Unietician and Trzciniecian, and because of that it could be divided into two zones: the western and the eastern. Unified at the beginning, the Lusatian culture fell into many regional groups, distinctive especially in ceramics.

About 300 B.C. the Lusatian culture ceased to exist, replaced by new cultures: the Pomeranian and the Przeworskian.

Who was the author of the magnificent culture?

The answer to this question has caused a heated argument for over a century. Carl Schuchhardt (1859-1943) states that the Germans created the Lusatian culture. Alfred Gotze (1876-1946) came to the conclusion that this culture was of Thracian origin. George Kosinna accepts the possibility of Illyrian origin of the Lusatian culture. All those theories lost their strength, especially the last one, because the Illyrians never cremated their dead.

In recent years the autochthonic theory of Józef Kostrzewski has gained many supporters. According to it, the people who created the Lusatian culture were the Ancient Slavs who came into existence when the Proto-Slavs absorbed the Veneti.(6) They stayed on this territory down the centuries until the Middle Ages.(7) Many linguists support this theory, like the Poles: T. Lehr-Spławinski, M. Rudnicki and T. Milewski; the Russian V. Martynov and the Czech V. Machek.

NOTES TO CHAPTER VII

1.**Bibliography:** Durczewski J.,'Grupa górnoślasko-małopolska kultury łużyckiej w Polsce', Kraków 1948; Filip J. 'Pradzieje Czechosłowacji', Poznań 1951; Gardawski A., 'Plemiona kultury trzcinieckiej w Polsce', MStar. 1959; Gedl M., 'Kultura łużycka na Górnym Śląsku', Wrocław 1962; Kostrzewski J., 'Od mezolitu do okresu wędrówek ludów', Kraków 1948; and, 'Zagadnienie ciągłości ziem polskich w pradziejach', Poznań 1961; and, 'Kultura łużycka na Pomorzu', Poznań 1958; Rajewski Z., 'Osadnictwo ludności z kultura łużycką we wczesnym okresie epoki żelaznej w Biskupinie i okolicy', APol. 1958; Rudnicki M., 'Rzut oka na dzieje Słowiańszczyzny w czasach najdawniejszych', Archeologia 1953, Vol. V; Sulimirski T., 'Zagadnienie upadku kultury łużyckiej', SAnt. 1948; Wesołowski K., 'Zagadnienie metalurgii ludowej kultury trzcinieckiej', MStar. 1956; Żaki A., 'Początki rozwoju kultury łużyciej w Polsce', Kraków 1948.

2. The name Unietician culture comes from Unetice near Prague in Chechsłovakia.

3. The name Trzciniecian culture comes from Trzciniec near Lublin in Poland, where archaeologists found the typical settlement. The people of this culture buried their dead in a crouched position in burrows or flat graves, and used flint implements.

4. Nestor (1056-1114), the Russian monk in Kiev mentions in his chronicle that those Slavs who settled in open fields had been called "Polyani", and those in forest areas — 'Drevlyani'. It is possible that with the times, when new agronomy techniques of burning the forests and sowing crops in ashes was introduced came the distinction of Slavs. Those who farmed on the loess soil as before, which means 'pole' — open field got the name 'Polyani', 'Polanie', 'Polans' (Poles, today), but the new agriculturists, since they burnt the 'drewno'-wood, were named 'Drevlyani', 'Drzewianie', 'Drevlans'.

5. There are many localities in Poland with the names Żary, Żory. The word 'żar'-heat points out an area cleared by the fire.

6. W. Antoniewicz, 'Archeologia Polska', Warszawa 1929, p. 80 and A. Gardawski, 'Plemiona kultury trzcinieckiej w Polsce', MStar. 1959, p. 174, maintain that the Ancient Slavs were not only creators of the Lusatian culture, but the culture which preceded it, the Trzciniecian culture, which in 1500 B.C. dominated in central Poland.

7. J. Kostrzewski, 'Kultura prapolska', p. 19, writes: "Very ancient in its huge predominance native topographic onomastics of Poland postulates of the ancient colonization of our land by the Slavs, who settle here at least from the time when they separated (with the Balts) from their previous Indo-European linguistic community, which means about the half of the second millennium B.C.

CHAPTER VIII
BISKUPIN

It was in 1929 when Walenty Szwajcer, a young teacher in elementary school in Biskupin, Poland, swimming in the lake discovered the clandestine beams in the water. Sensing the remnants of the ancient settlement, like the Swiss lake town of Cortaillod, he informed the Department of Archaeology of the Poznań University about his discovery. The University sent Prof. Józef Kostrzewski to investigate. What he spotted surpassed the wildest dream. Thanks to the conservative action of water, the lake preserved in good condition the remnants of the huge fortified town built by the people of Lusatian culture around 550 B.C.

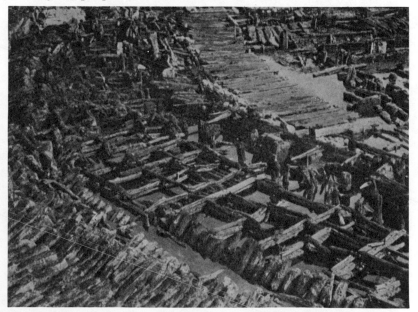

Fig. 11. Very impressive sight of the remnants of the fortified town Biskupin recovered by Polish archaeologists.

On an island which is a peninsula today, 600 ft long and about 500 ft wide stood a fortified town with one hundred huts built in 13 ranges along 11 streets paved with wood and connected by a circle street running along the bulwark.

The archaeological work, interrupted by the World War II, was completed in 1948. Since the lake belongs to the town of Biskupin, the remnants of the fortified settlement on its island has been called Biskupin, and now is an archaeological preserve in care of the state authority (1).

As mentioned before, the primitive farmers spread all over Europe around 3000 B.C. were peaceful people. They built open settlements. When their cattle were in danger from marauding animals or hustlers they fenced their settlements with the palisade or fosse. The entrenchment became deeper and stronger when the enemy grew in number.

The earth removed by digging the trenches had been used to build the bulwark. When the threat became bigger it was necessary to build bigger and more defensive dikes. Since the earth slides the people of Lusatian culture developed special techniques in building bulwarks. They strengthened it with layers of wood and wooden boxes filled with earth. To prevent the logs from rolling the builders used a hood structure. Logs with short cut boughs were laid across the top serving as hooks to keep the log layer beneath together.

The hook construction of the rampart is a typical feature used for Slavic strongholds through the centuries. It is to be found in remnants of almost all fortified settlements in Poland, as in Wolin, Kołobrzeg, Gdańsk, Santok, Wrocław, Gniezno, Poznań, Nakło, Ujście.

There are remnants of over 150 (90 in Poland) fortified towns raised by the people of the Lusatian culture between the 8th and the 5th century B.C. Some of them are larger than at Biskupin, but none was better preserved than in that place.

The fortified town at Biskupin had been raised on an island in the lake. It had been carefully planned and executed. A breakwater protected the settlement against flooding. Next the earth-wooden bulwark encircled it.

To build such a fortified settlement the builders used oaks from a forest area of 100 square miles. They brought the wood to the island floating the logs down the river Gąsawka to the lake.

There was only one access to the land and one gate to the fortified town. It was 24 ft long, 9 ft wide and had two wings upon which a

Fig. 12. The hook construction of the bulwark.

blockhouse stood. The incomer used the wooden bridge about 26 ft long connected the stronghold with the land and was checked by the guard at the gate before he could enter the town.

Fig. 13. Reconstruction of the gate of Biskupin

Inside the town there had been 13 long houses divided into family apartments. Every apartment had an ante-room, living room with the hearth situated in the middle and a special room behind it, which might have served as a sleeping room or a pantry or even both. All houses were equal, about 240 ft long. No trace of a bigger edifice points out that the social equality still prevailed in this stage of developement. It appears that 13 long houses sheltered 13 clans, every one constituting several families. Some 1000 to 1200 persons lived in the dwellings.

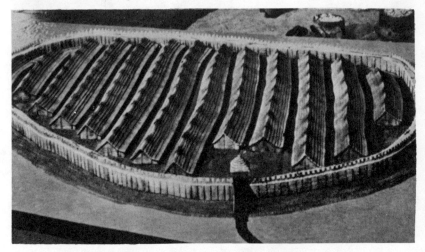

Fig. 14. Plan of the fortified town Biskupin, after L. Leciejewicz.

In front of every long house ran a parallel street. One street, circling along the bulwark, connected all the streets.

There is no sign of a sacral edifice. The builders of the fortified town must have praised their gods in sacred groves.

One little place at the gate served probably as town square, where the craftsmen traded their products and meetings took place.

It appears that the fortified town at Biskupin played not only a role of a fortress, but a trading post and a seat of local authority as well.

Why did the people of the Lusatian culture raise the fortified towns? The answer is simple: they had been threatened by other people, because no one in this primitive condition would build the huge fortress for no apparent reason.

Were those strongholds inhabited all the time or were they only refuge places used when the enemy invaded the country?

The size of the stronghold at Biskupin suggests that it was rather a refuge place. To feed over one thousand persons on a small place the big storerooms were necessary. None of them were inside the stronghold and archaeologists did not find any outside the ramparts. Perhaps they kept food in the stronghold in case of enemy sudden attack but not in large quantity.

How did they manage to survive the siege?

The enemy was not better supplied either. He lived on plunder and hunting. When the siege lasted longer than two weeks and there were no more animals to hunt or food to grab, hunger forced the enemy to end the siege and to go somewhere else.

Fig. 15. Reconstruction of the scene how Ancient Slavs had been strengthening with stones their bulwark in Biskupin.

Against whom did the people of Lusatian culturè build their strongholds?

There is a hot controversy among the scholars. T. Sulimirski (2) thinks the Scythian invasions destroyed the Lusatian culture. The fortified town had been raised against them. J. Filip (3) maintains that its fall was caused by attacks of the Pomeranians. E. Schwartz (4) is of the opinion that the German invasions ruined the Lusatian culture. Z. Rajewski (5) admits that the building of fortified towns could had been caused by the tribal wars of the people of the Lusatian culture, a conclusion also arrived at by J. Hawkes.(6)

It seems that those scholars are partially right. People of the Lusatian culture could had been threatened from the outside as well as from the inside.

The oldest fortified towns appeared in the south-western region of the Lusatian culture. It appears that the danger of invasion came along the Amber Route from the Alps by some Illyric nation.

The fortified towns in western Czechoslovakia could be explained as a defense line against the Celtic invasion. The deep penetration from Pomerania could have been caused, not by the Germans who appeared in this region around the turn of eras, but by the Veneti from Scandinavia who fled from the threat of the Germans marching down the Scandinavian peninsula. The refugees could have attacked their cousins on the other side of the Baltic Sea. This theory would explain, also, why the records are so strong about the Veneti on the southern shores of the Baltic. The invading Pomeranians built their own culture on the ruins of the Lusatian culture around 300 B. C.

The invasion of the late-coming Proto-Slavs from the east could have been a cause, also. Penetrating westwards, they met their cousins who earlier migrated, and by absorbing Veneti became the Ancient Slavs. Not liking intruders, the natives built fortified towns against them.

The tribal wars among the people of the Lusatian culture are not to be excluded. The archaeological findings indicate that some settlements were conspiciously rich and some poor. The later could have been the troublemakers.

Archaeological excavations revealed that inhabitants of the first fortified Biskupin cultivated two kinds of wheat (Triticum vulgare and Triticum compactum), poppy seed and linen. Judging by the skeletal remains they consumed meat of domestic animals in 98.9%, especially pork. They raised cattle, goats, sheep and dogs, and what is unusual, they ate dog meat.

The Biskupinians used the saddle quern and primitive wheel of two halves cut out of a board, with the whole in the center. The wheels rotated with the axles. The four-wheeled cart appears to have been an Ancient Slavs invention.

The archaeologists also found in Biskupin bronze needles, implements for wool combing, primitive looms, wooden plates and 'kabłączki skroniowe' — little bronze moons used as adornments of the women's head (7). It is worth mentioning that the Biskupinians developed their techniques of softening a horn by soaking it in water with sorrel before working on it.

The first town had been destroyed around 400 B.C. Then, the second fortified town had been raised and destroyed, too, its place being in an open settlement. From the 7th to 11th century A.D. appeared a stronghold again, but fenced with a palisade. Then the settlement on the island of the lake vanished for good. Perhaps the papal bulla— letter of 1136 refers to it, mentioning the village under the name 'Starzy Biskupicy'.

Settlement after settlement, fortified or open, but built on the same spot in the same way, gave archaeologist Józef Kostrzewski strong support for his autochthonic theory about the same ethnic people living here down the millennia. It would be impossible to continue the same forms with a shifting population.

NOTES TO CHAPTER VIII

1. **Bibliography:** Kostrzewski J., Lubicz-Niezabitowski E., Jaroń B., 'Osada bagienna w Biskupinie w powiecie żnińskim', Poznań 1936; Kostrzewski J., 'Gród prasłowiański w Biskupinie, w powiecie żnińskim', Poznań 1938; Malinowski T., 'Grodziska kultury łużyckiej w Wielkopolsce', FArch. Poznań 1954; Rajewski Z., 'Osadnictwo ludności z kulturą łyżycką we wczesnym okresie epoki żelaznej w Biskupinie i okolicy', APol. 1958, also 'Biskupin— wykopaliska', Warszawa 1960.
2. T. Sulimirski, 'Zagadnienie upadku kultury łyżyckiej', SAnt. 1948, Vol. 1, p. 158.
3. J. Filip, 'Pradzieje Czechosłowacji', Poznań 1951, p. 293.
4. E. Schwartz, 'Das Vordringen der Slaven nach Westen', SOForsch. 1956, Vol. XV, p. 91.
5. Z. Rajewski, 'Osadnictwo ludności z kulturą łużycką we wczesnym okresie epoki żelaznej w Biskupinie i okolicy', APol. 1958, Vol. II, p. 125.
6. J. Hawkes, 'Prehistory', p. 358, writes: "The general absence of weapons of war of Neolithic burials provides even more convincing proof of the absence of martial ideals in the hearts of the new peasantry. A striking contrast is provided in Late Neolithic and Early Bronze Age times when from the Caspian and the Russian steppes to Scandinavia and Britain, battle-axes, daggers and other arms appear in the grave of every adult male. Although it is rush to push economic explanation too far — many people have loved to fight their neighbors without any need for "Lebensraum" — it seems probable that the fact that good land was to be had for the taking and each succeeding generation could find a good living account for the peacefulness of early Neolithic communities. And similarly that the more warlike ideals of the succeeding phase were partly due to mounting populations and shortage of new land to feed them".
7. J. Kostrzewski, Kultura prapolska, Warszawa 1962, p. 156.

CHAPTER IX
AMBER

"After Phaeton had been struck by lightning, his sisters became changed into poplars, which every year shed their tears upon the banks of the Eridanu, a river known to us as the Padus. To these tears was given the name of 'electrum', from the circumstance, that the sun was usually called 'elector'. Such is the story, at all events, that is told by many poets, the first of were, in my opinion, Aeschylus, Philaxenies, Euripides, Satyrus and Nicander". This is a story recorded by Pliny the Younger (1) (62-113 A.D.).

What is it all about?

This heart-breaking story deals with amber which famous historian calls 'electrum'.

Pliny, who devoted a whole chapter to amber in his history, is angry with the above mentioned poets, who in his opinion twist all truth and make lies of it. To correct them, he gives this account: "Amber is produced from a marrow by trees belonging to the pine genus, like gum from the cherry, and resin from the ordinary pine. It is a liquid at first, which issues forth in considerable quantities, and is gradually hardened by heat and cold or else by action of the sea, when rise of the tide carries off the fragments from the shores of these islands". It is amazing how close Pliny was in his time to the truth.

Pliny was not the first historian who pays attention to amber. Herodotus in chapter 115 of the third book of his history tells what he knew about the precious item.

What was so good about amber that the ancient writers and poets paid so much attention to it?

Before answering the question it is necessary to find out what amber is.

About 40-50 million years ago the 'amber forests' grew on the south coast of the vast continent of Finnoscandia, which geologists define as the combined territories of Finnland and Scandinavia (2). Among other trees in these forests there grew a large number of resinous trees especially 'amber pine'.

Life in the animal and vegetable kingdoms of these forests was extremely extensive, and an ordinary observer can perceive various particles of plants and insects, 75 species of spiders, flies, ants, moths etc. (3). The trees damaged by lightning and storms secreted a large amount of resin to heal their wounds and safeguard their existence. It was this fossilized resin which became amber.

In the course of so many millions of years some parts of the Finnoscandia forests sunk, emerged and submerged again. In this process of change the masses of submerged, and in time, petrified amber became overlaid with other different strata. On the shores of Sambian Peninsula of the Baltic Sea in Poland, amber is the fourth layer to be found under layers of sand, lignite and brown coal.

Amber is one of the oxygenated hydrocarbons and its mineralogical name, succinite, emphasizes the presence of from 5 to 8 per cent of succinic acid. Its composition (4) is presented by formula $C40H64O4$.

The beds between Gdańsk and Klaipeda produce approximately 88 per cent of the world's entire amber yield. The second largest amber deposit is on the coast of Jutland. The deposits of amber in Sicily, Burma, on the shores of the Straits of Bering, in Thailand, Japan, and elsewhere, are almost negligeable compared to those in Poland.

There is also amber to be mined from near the Myszyniec Forest in Poland. It was carried there by the glacier from Scandinavia to the Vistula River in the Tertiary epoch.

How is amber harvested today?

Twice a year the Baltic Sea gives amber away: in autumn (October-November) and in springtime (February-March). In these months the water temperature is 36 to 40 degrees F. and the water is so thick that pieces of amber raised from the sea floor float on it.

The autumn and springtime storms on the Baltic Sea comb amber from the bottom and throw it on the shores. After every storm beaches are crowded. Hundreds of fortune hunters swarm to try their luck. Brought from the sea floor, amber is in the form of small pieces. Sometimes a chunk of two pounds is to be found which means big luck for the finder. The biggest piece recorded was over 20 pounds. The autumn and springtime crop gives 5 to 15 tons of amber.

Amber is usually light brown, but there are many shades of it, from pale-yellow to dark-yellow to brown and red. Chalk-white, violet,

Fig. 16. An insect 50 million years old preserved in a piece of amber

green, blue or black specimens as well as the crystal clear are rare.

People who lived on the Sambian Peninsula in ancient times were busy harvesting amber. They called it 'gentaras' or 'yantaras'. The Romans changed the name to 'gentarum' and the Slavs called it 'yantar'. But in the 18th century A.D. the Poles replaced the word with 'bursztyn' which is nothing else but a corruption of the German word 'Bernstein' for amber (5).

Already during the Stone Age amber was manufactured into ornaments which had a sacred significance. It was not until the Bronze Age that amber, in natural form, became a commodity that could be used for large scale trade with the West and the South (6). The both sources of amber were known and exploited. According to V. Gordon Childe (7) the forest folk discovered the amber of Sambian Peninsula and exported it to Western Norway, Central Russia and Finland in an era which ended 3,000 B.C.

Later on, the famous Vistula-Dniester route was established linking the Baltic Sea with the Black Sea. It served to export amber to the Aegean world (8).

Amber collected at the Jutland shores was sent down the 'amber river' Rhone to Massilia (Marseilles). This western route was better known in classical antiquity. Herodotus as well as Pliny mention it,

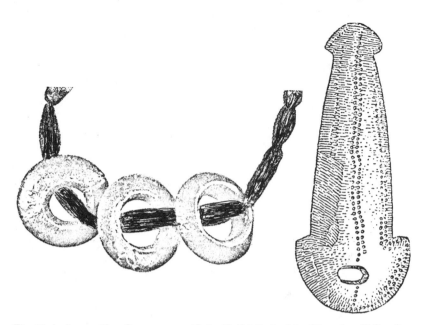

Fig. 17. Amber necklace from a grave at Lahn-Hallstatt, Austria, 6th century B.C., after F. Morton, 'Hallstatt und die Halstattzeit', and amber axe found in the River Vistula at Sandomierz, Poland, first half of the 2nd millennium B.C., after E. Sturms, 'Die neolitische Plastik'.

but they do not know about the eastern route Vistula-Dniester, or have a confusing ideas like Pliny.

When the amber deposits at the Jutland shores were exhausted the Sambian Peninsula became a main exporter of the precious commodity. Now, the eastern amber route had three forks: one to Athens, two to Rome.

The main route would appear to have passed up the Vistula until somewhere in the neighborhood of the first big bend in that river. Here started the first fork. It turned south-west and crossed Noteć near Nakło threading its way between the lakes that lie between the river Warta, it struck the latter stream probably near Obornik. South-west of Obornik lies the Early Iron Age cemetery of Gorszowice. The route itself appears to have passed up the Warta and struck across the south region of Poznań through Zaborowo (another Early Iron Age site where amber occurs in large quantities) possibly reaching the Odra near Głogów. It probably passed up this stream as far as Wrocław where it turned south eventually crossing the Kłodzko Pass (9) to Vindobona (Vienna, today), where the Romans had a big trading post.

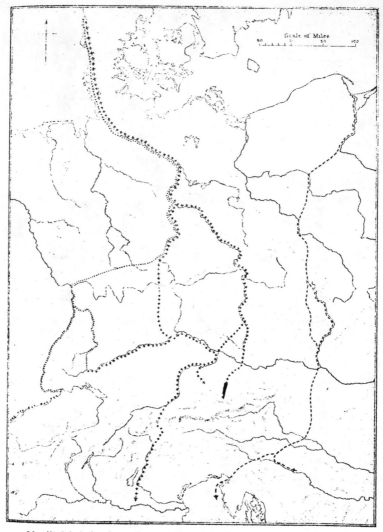

Map. VI. Principal amber trade routes. From J. M. de Navarro, *Prehistoric routes...*
++++ the central route
· · · · · the western route
– – – – – the eastern route

The second route from Kalisz City ran along the Odra River crossing it near the city of Opole, then through the Moravian Gate aimed to Carnuntum (Petronell, today) where the second Roman trading post was.

Finally, the third amber route ran along the Vistula River and through the Carpathian passes down to Acquincum (near Budapest, today) where the third Roman trading post was.

Archaeology helped a lot to discover these routes. There were many Roman coins, imported goods and even some amounts of hidden amber on the way.

And so, under the remnants of a hut built in the 1st century A.D. near the city of Wrocław over one ton of the worked up amber was found.

In Wrocław three deposits of amber weighing 5200 pounds were recently discovered.

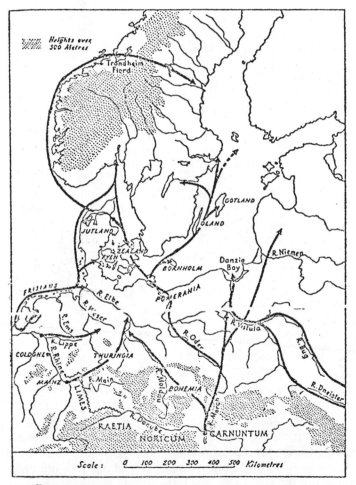

Map VII. Principal European trade routes. From Sir Mortimer Wheeler, *Rome beyond the Imperial Frontiers.*

In Basonia near the city of Lublin the treasure consisted of 400 pounds of natural amber and 60 pounds of amber beads.

The last hidden deposit was discovered near Szamotuły and Rzeszów.

Fig. 18. Hiding place of amber discovered at Wrocław

As is now evident, there were workshops of amber on the Polish territories. Beads in Basonia are not the only proof of it. Archaeologists discovered the proper workshop in Jacewo near Wrocław. They found there a big amount of raw material, scraps and tools. In Jacewo there were the beautiful articrafts of amber like combs, beads and others showing how high was the art of craftsmen.

The hidden amber proves that it travelled by stages. Tribes placed along the route traded the precious commodity among themselves. It appears, the Roman traders took over amber at the Polish border or in their trading posts like Vindobona, Carnuntum or Aquincum. It explains the strange concidence why the Roman writers knew so little about Slavs. They relayed information obtained from the merchants. Since they did not chance to reach the Baltic shores they had not much to tell about the life of Ancient Slavs. They reported only what they had heard so the writers got some confused and even absurd information.

It was during the times of the Roman Emperors that amber was most widely used for ornaments and jewelry in the classic countries. Judging by the coins found in graves east of the Gulf of Gdańsk it was reached in the second half of the second century A.D. (10).

Amber was one of the five commodities of a Rome's foreign trade (11).

There were two reasons why the amber was so greatly esteemed in the Ancient World: superstition and its use as an adornment.

When rubbed the amber becomes strongly electrified and attracts light bodies to itself. This quality was probably the main reason why the ancients attributed so many mysterious virtues to the mineral.

Amber in the Stone Age was connected with the cult of the sun. Pliny mentions that the precious item was considered as an extract from the rays of the sun and because of that it was called 'electrum', which derives from 'elector', the sun. The Greek appelation for amber, 'electron' means in fact 'substance of the sun'. The first Greek philosopher known to us, Thales of Miletus (640-546 B.C.) declaes that amber has a soul.

Based on these beliefs amber took a strong position in classic antiquity. Its function as a talisman, or charm, especially when worn as a necklace was considered to protect the wearer from secret poisons, and to be effective as a counter-charm against sorcery and witchcraft. The ancients solidly believed that it was capable of arousing love. There were even people asserting that if a slave girl administered amber in the proper way to the king, the monarch would not only fall madly in love, but make her a queen, too.

How much magic power Romans attributed to amber is indicated by the fact that gladiators wore charms made from it and bearing the inscription 'I win'.

No wonder, the demand for amber was unusually high in ancient Rome. In the time of Nero, an expedition sent from the eternal city to the Sambiam amber beds returned with 13,000 pounds of the precious commodity.

The use of amber in medicine lasted through antiquity and almost into modern times before it was dethroned (12). Nevertheless, the precious mineral retains its status as an adornment in the world markets. As necklaces or bracelets it can be seen on the necks and arms of the most fashionable ladies in New York, London, Paris, Tokyo, just as it was on the necks of Penelope, Cleopatra, Poppaea.

Amber played a bigger role in making Slavdom than many

69

historians can account for. It was no sheer coincidence that the region where the amber routes forked at the bend of the Vistula River formed the strongest Ancient Slavs center. The trade with the precious commodity brought inhabitants many advantages. Others who settled farther away were not so fortunate (13).

On the other hand, amber routes also played a negative role. They destroyed ethnic homogenity of the Slavs. Before the trade expanded Slavic people constituted quite a uniform group. After cutting their lands by the routes three separate groups started to form: West Slavs, East Slavs and South Slavs.

NOTES TO CHAPTER IX

1. **Bibliography:** Andree, K., 'Der Bernstein und seine Bedeutung in Natur un Geisteswissenschaften, Kunst und Kunstgewerbe, Technik, Industrie and Handel', Königsberg 1937; also, 'Der Bernstein, das Bersteinland und sein Leben', Kosmos 1951; Birkat-Smith, K. 'Primitive Man and His Ways', Toronto 1963; Buffum, W. A., 'The Tears of the Heliades; or Amber as a Gem 1900; Charlesworth, M.P., 'Trade-routes and Commerce of the Roman Empire', Cambridge 1924; Novarro, J., 'Mode, Prehistoric Routes between Northern Europe and Italy defined by the Amber Trade', The Geographic Journal. Vol. LXVI, 1925; 'Pliny — The Natural History of Pliny', Bonn's Library, Vol. VI, p. 397-404; Spekke, A., 'The Ancient Amber Routes and the Geographical Discovery of the Eastern Baltic', Stockholm 1957; Sturms, E., 'Der Ostbaltische Bernsteinhandel in der vorchristlichen Zeit', Bonn 1953; Williamson, G. Ch., 'The Book of Amber', 1932.

2. K. Andree, 'Der Bernstein, das Bernsteinland und sein Leben', Kosmos 1951; p. 28.

3. G. Ch. Williamson, 'The Book of Amber', p. 133.

4. Encyclopedia Americana, New York 1944, Vol. 1, p. 471.

5. A. Brückner, 'Słownik etymologiczny języka polskiego', Warszawa 1957, p. 50.

6. A. Spekke, 'The ancient Amber Routes and the Geographical Discovery of the Eastern Baltic', Stockholm 1957, p. 48.

7. V. Gordon Childe, 'The Dawn of European Civilization', p. 200.

8. A. Spekke, op. cit., p. 27, writes: "Amber statuette of Ahur-nasir-apel, King of Assyria (885-880 B.C.) was found on the banks of the river Tigris where the Assyrian town of Kalhn (Calah in Genezis) was once situated. The amber of this statuette has been chemically tested and was found to be the Baltic amber. Amber of the same period was found also in the graves of the Kuban region in the Northern Caucasus. In the capitals of Assyria, Ashler and Babel, amber beads were found in the foundations of temple towers. Amber is also mentioned in Assyrian jewelers' list dating back to approximately 1st millenium B.C."

9. A. Spekke, op. cit., p. 61.

10. Ed. Sturms, 'Der Ostbaltische Bernsteinhandel in der vorchristlichen Zeit', Bonn 1953, p. 168-178.

11. Mortimer Wheeler, 'Rome Beyond the Imperial Frontiers', 1954, p. 176, writes: "Roman trafficking with lands outside the Empire was founded primarily on the supply of five commodities: amber from Poland, ivory from tropical Africa, incense from Southern Arabia, pepper from India and silk from China.

12. The functions of amber according to the well-known unfinished Ersch and Gruber Encyclopedia (1818-1850) embraced almost the entire field of medicine.

13. A. Spekke, op. cit., p.49, writes: "The poverty of the Estonian Bronze Age culture is not surprising. A similar state of affairs exists in most countries where the primary metals for making bronze, lead and copper were not discovered. The only exception to the rule among the countries near Estonia was East Prussia, which, although deficient in metal ores, enjoyed a rich Bronze Age culture. She was in a position to obtain these in exchange for her own amber, an article in very great demand in those days".

CHAPTER X

LUGIAN ALLIANCE

According to the ancient writers a Lugian Alliance existed on the Polish territories.(1) It was created not later than in the last century B.C., by people who were recorded as 'Lugiones'.

Who were these 'Lugiones'? Why did they organize an Alliance? To answer these questions it is necessary to explain the name first.

Some historians maintain the word 'Lugiones' (Lugians) is derived from the name of a Slavic tribe 'Luhy' or 'Lugi' which settled in the region of Lusatia now in East Germany (2). Others accepted the possibility the name might have come from the Irish Celtic word 'Luige' (3) which means oath. There are some who say the name came from the Illirian expression (4) describing people living on marshland. Others say the name is based on a Proto-Slavic word 'ląg' or 'lug' which also meant the marshland.(5)

The name of Lugians, therefore, can be explained in terms of many Indo-European languages (6) which indicates it is a very old expression.

The most proper explanation seems to be based on the Irish Celtic word 'Luige' (7). It tells about an oath which, from remote times, was a binding force of many alliances. To guarantee cooperation people used a solemn form of promise.

Thus, Lugian Alliance was a sworn alliance (8).

If the oath was the basic requirement for organizing alliances there was no need to publicize the fact by giving a special name to an organization. Perhaps it was so in many instances but not in this case. Members of the Lugian Alliance were tribes of different ethnic origin who lived along the amber routes. To keep them together the validity of oath must have been emphasized. Anyone who dared to break it was the subject of the gods wrath.

What tribes were members of the Lugian Alliance?

Everything indicates that in the 300 years of the Alliance existence, its membership kept changing. Some tribes joined, some left it. That is the reason the ancient writers differed so in naming the tribes.

Nonetheless, after careful consideration, it may be accepted that in the first century A.D. the tribes living along the amber routes from North to South were as follows: the Harii, Helveconi, Helisii, Manimi, Naharvali and Duns (9).

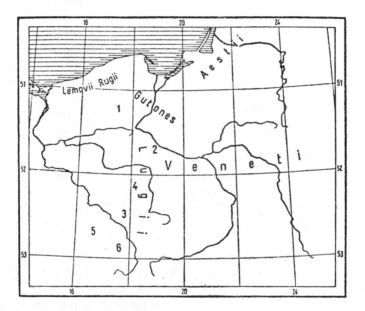

Map VIII. Tribes living along the amber route after Tacitus: 1. the Harii; 2. Helveconi; 3. Manimi; 4 Helisii; 5. Naharvali; 6 Duns.

What was the ethnic background of these tribes?

According to sources, the Harii might have been Germans. Their tribal name supposedly is derived from the old German word 'Harja' which means a military force 'Heer' in German today (10). The Helveconi looked like Germans (11), too. The Helisii probably were Slavs who occupied the center of the amber route (12). Around the city of Wrocław dwelled the Manimi and south of them at the Sobótka Mountain were the Naharvali (13). Both of these tribes probably were Celtic mixed with the Slavic people. The last member of the Lugian Alliance to the south were the Duns who settled in Upper Silesia. They were probably Celtic (14).

It appears the Lugian Alliance was Celtic in the south, Slavic in the middle and Germanic in the north, although organized by the Celts.

Why did the Celts organize and lead the Alliance? They were famous warriors with many conquests from Ireland to the Volga River. In a short time most of the Europe was in their hands. Why did they not try to conquer the amber routes by force?

The only explanation is their unit in contact with the Slavic tribes was too weak to engage in warfare. Since according to the Roman writers the Celts were 'the cleverest of Barbarians' they tried to profit by peaceful cooperation with the natives. For this purpose they organized the Lugian Alliance and led it.

They had no other choice. The Slavic Helisii were a strong tribe. No German invaders could conquer it. The Vandals, Burgunds and others, after they settled at the mouth of the Vistula River tried their luck in vain. They had to go around the Helisii lands when they decided to migrate south and west. Their fate was shared by the Goths, newcomers from Scandinavia. As it was not possible to conquer the Helisii, they left their temporary settlements at the Vistula and went down along the famous Baltic-Black Sea Route to live on the shores of the Black Sea.

How could Celts lead the Lugian Alliance composed of ethnically so different tribes?

The oath binding the members of this organization must have been supported by a strong belief that breaking it would draw a horrible wrath from the gods. To support this idea the Celts must have imposed their religious beliefs upon the other tribes. This would explain why the Sobótka Mountain was religiously such a famous center in those times. Celts probably built the capital of the Lugian Alliance at the 'Holy Mountain (15). On top of the Mountain religious rites were performed down through the centuries. Celts asked the leaders of other tribes to come and partake in their celebrations. Games, lavish feasts and merrymaking must have impressed the guests so deeply that the rites on the Sobótka Mountain continued until the 18th century A.D. long after the Celts vanished from this region. Religious bond is sometimes much stronger than the tribal tie.

How did the Lugian Alliance operate?

It appears that one tribe traded amber with another down the amber route. Collected at the Sambian Peninsula the precious merchandise wandered from the hands of German Harii to the hands of Slavic Helisii and to the hands of Celtic Manimi. At the Sobótka Mountain, or even south of it the Roman traders took over the costly commodity.

It explains two facts: Why the ancient world had such poor

74

information about Slavdom and why the Roman merchants often mentioned the Limian Grove.

If the Roman merchants had crossed the Polish territories as far as the Baltic shores, they would certainly report the situation on this land. They must have gone as far north as the Sobótka Mountain, where the Limian Grove supposedly was located so they only mentioned it. There were the big religious festivities combined with trading of all kinds of merchandise giving traders opportunity to come and see the place.

For amber and other items the members of the Lugian Alliance received luxurious rather than practical objects.

In the 1st century B.C. the bronze objects made in famous casting workshops in Capua, Italy, were brought to Polish lands. Next to it came ornamented ceramics, such as pitchers, amphoras and bowls. Glass and silver wares were imported, too, and even the object of Roman religious cult, like the Mercuri statue, found in Kołacinek in Brzeziny county or a statue of the Egyptian goddess Isis discovered in Małachów near Gniezno (16). Presumably the Roman merchants convinced the Slavic clients that these were the objects of good fortune and traded their gods for amber. It is very unlikely that there were missions of Roman or Greek religions on Polish territories.

Roman coins appeared on Polish soil, also. The oldest ones dated from the times of the Republic. The whole number of coins left is unknown. In Great Poland over 15,000 pieces were found. Archaeologists dug out a treasure of about 2,000 coins near the city of Kalisz and 500 near the city of Piła.

Most of coins are from the time of Emperor Antonius Pius (138-161) and Emperor Trajan (98-117), when the Roman Empire was at its peak. The Polish territories flooded with silver denars. The establishment of the Roman Province Datia south of the Carpathian Mountains was one reason for this.

In the 2nd and 3rd centuries A.D., the silver denars vanished but the gold areus appeared. Five of them minted in the 2nd and 23 minted in the 3rd centuries A.D. were found (17).

Roman coins played a role with the chiefs of tribes who were engaged in trading, although adornment was the only value for the people.

Besides amber the Lugian Alliance sent furs, honey, wax, slaves and small children to Rome. Later on the export was enlarged by iron products such as knives and swords.

Goods probably were shipped in boats made by Ancient Slavs in a

Fig. 19 Objects imported from Rome in the 1st century A.D.: a lamp, bronze fibula and glass bottle.

simple way as a doug-out canoe. Some of them were found by archaeologists in the bed of the rivers Vistula and Odra. Using doug-out canoes the Slavs went down to the sea and, with the Avars, attacked Constantinople in 626 A.D.

The Lugian Alliance developed in the first century A.D., when the German tribes in the Polish territories were weak. When the Vandals

Fig. 20. The 'terra sigillata' found in Goszczynno near Łęczyca.

76

left, their place was taken by the Rugians, the next German invaders from Scandinavia. Then came the Goths who pushed the Rugians out and took their territories at the mouth of the Vistula. However, they did not become a member of the Lugian Alliance.

The Goths left their territories, too, and migrated to the shore of the Black Sea. Then, the Slavs took advantage of it and pushed the rest of the German tribes out of the Lugian Alliance. Since the Celts had left Polish territories more than 100 years before, the organization was Slavic all the way at the end of its existence.

The Lugian Alliance was not a trade institution only, but a political force as well. Margod (8-19 A.D.), king of Marcomans, a German nation, was an aly of the Lugians (18). The situation changed in 91-92 A.D. (19). The Lugian Alliance sided with the Roman Empire against the Marcomans. This is the only evidence that the people in Polish territories were in confederacy with ancient Rome.

The Lugian Alliance was the first political organization on Polish lands recorded by history.

NOTES TO CHAPTER X

1. The Lugians were known to Strabo, Tacitus, Ptolemy, Cassius Dio, Zosimas and the author of Tabula Peutingeriana.

2. P.J. Szafarzyk, 'Słowiańskie starożytności', Poznan 1842; Vol. 1, p. 535.

3. M. Schonfeld, 'Wörterbuch der altgermanischen Personen und Völkernamen', Heidelberg 1911; p. 157.

4. H. Krahe, 'Germanisch und Illyrisch', Heidelberg 1936; Vol. 2, p. 572.

5. L. Niederle, 'Slovanske starožitnosti', Praha 1919; p. 51.

6. K. Mullenhoff, 'Deutsche Alterskunde', Berlin 1887; Vol. 4, p. 484, maintains that the name Lugfiones is of German origin. Like Goti-Gutones or Frisii-Friscones so were Lugii-Lugiones.

7. There are many Celtic names with the root "Lug" either as geographic names or personal ones. Even the Celtic god had had the name Lueg. H. Hubert in 'Les Celtes depuis l'epoque de la Tene et la civilization celtique', Paris 1932, mentions that there were four cities historically founded with the root "lug". J. Cramer writes about Lugudunum, and Macdonald in Luigi mentions a tribe Lugi in England. E. Simek in 'Velka Germanie Klaudia Ptolemaia', Brno 1935; p. 161, accepts the idea that Lugians were the nation or an alliance of Celtic tribes at the beginning, but in course of German penetration and Celtic migration they were Germanized keeping the Celtic name only.

8. Tacitus in 'Germania', cap. 43 expresses his opinion of the Lugians as a big nation in words: "latissime patet Lugiorum nomen".

9. The names of these tribes are accepted after Strabo and Ptolemy.

10. Tacitus calls the tribe Harii, Ptolemy — Charini. R. Much, Harii, RGAlt. 1915; Vol. 2, p. 450, thinks they were warriors. To the same conclusion comes Schwarz in 'Germanische Stämmeskunde', p. 67 and O. Hofler in 'Kultische Geheimbunde der Germanen', Frankfurt 1934; p. 3.

11. H. Łowmiański, op. cit., p. 236.

12. G. Schutte, 'Ptolemy's Atlas', p. 67; maintains that Calisia (city of Kalisz today) was a capital of Helisi. H. Łowmiański, op. cit., p. 133, thinks that the name Helisi might had been of Venetic origin which Germans changed into Calisi and Ptolemy might had used it freely to name the capital of Helisi.

13. The presence of Celts in Silesia has been stated by many scholars. M. Hahn in 'Die Kelten in Schlesień', Leipzig 1931, finds two groups of Celtic settlements south of Wrocław between the town of Głupczyce and the Odra River. One belonged to Boii, which according to the author were conquered by Vandals about 100 B.C. Another group in Upper Silesia existed one century longer. J. Filip in 'Pradzieje Czechosłowacji', Poznań 1951; p. 63, maintains that the Celtic settlement in Bezdzieków in Upper Silesia was an oppidum. H. Łowiański, op. cit., p. 190, writes: "The presence of Celts appears most distinctively on fertilous regions in Upper Silesia, from the 4th and 3rd century B.C., because south of the city of Wrocław rather numerous Celtic graves (over 50) were discovered, and in Nowa Cerkwia and Cieszyn there should have been two Celtic oppida . . . The treasures of Celtic coins and single coins found in Little Poland as well as in Silesia might have been brought there by merchants and warriors. As a serious archaeological evidence of Celtic presence in Little Poland there are two Celtic graves in Iwanowice, county Miechów, from the turn of 2nd and 1st century B.C." A. Żaki, 'Z badań nad kulturą celtycką w Małopolsce', ARozhl. 1935, p. 799-803, states that for a short time it was a Celtic oppidum in Tyniec and castellum at Poznachowice, near Kraków in Poland.

14. Their names was probably Dunoi. E. Simek, 'Velka Germanie Klaudia Ptolemaia', Brno 1935; p. 161, maintains the Lugians were at the beginning a Celtic nation or an alliance of mostly Celtic tribes Germanized by the German invaders in the later times. E. Schwarz in 'Germanische Stammeskunde', p. 68, is of the same opinion stating that the names of the Lugian tribes are rather Celtic than Germanic.

15. There is some evidence that the Lugian alliance could have been based upon religious cult. M. Schónfeld in 'Luigii', REnc. 1927; col. 1715-1717, maintains the Lugians were not an alliance of tribes, but an alliance of cult. H. Cehak-Hołubowiczowa i 'Śląski Olimp', Warszawa 1953; p. 1-18; 'Kamienne kręgi kultowe na Raduni i Ślęży', Warszawa 1959; p. 51-97 and in Monumentalne zabytki kultowe na górach Ślęży, Raduni i Kościuszki', Kwartalnik Opolski 1960; p. 49-61, states that at the Sobótka Mountain was a big religious center in times of the Lugian alliance.

16. S. Trawkowski, 'Jak powstawała Polska', Warszawa 1961; p. 41-46.

17 H. Lowmiański, 'Początki Polski', Warszawa 1963; Vol. 1, p. 335-340.

18. Strabo III C. 290, Tacitus, Annales XII. cap. 29, 30 mention that when in 50 A.D. Vannius, king of Quadi was expelled from his country then the Lugians and other nations attacked him to get riches which Vannius brought from his country.

19. Dionis Cassii Cocciani, 'Historiarum Romanorum quae supersunt', Berolini 1901; Vol. 3, p. 179.

CHAPTER XI

RUDKI AND IGOŁOMIA

In the years between World Wars I and II ironworks in the 'Góry Świętokrzyskie' — Holy Cross Mountains in Poland bought blocks of iron slag weighing 110-200 pounds from local peasants. These slags contained over 50% iron, indicating they were richer in metal than the local iron ore and consequently they melted well with ore.

Peasants found no problem in obtaining and delivering the slags. There were many in the fields sticking in the ground close together. The peasants dug them out, loaded their carts and brought them to the foundry (1).

Who put those slags into the ground?

No one gave a lot of thought to it at first. But then came the archaeologists and they discovered some possible reasons.

When Julius Caesar fought the Gallic wars there existed the big iron works in Europe east of the Alps. They could be compared to Pittsburgh, Sheffield or Ruhr of today.

As stated before, six thousand years ago there were the biggest flint mines in Europe in the same Holy Cross Mountains. The famous streaked axes made in this region became widely demanded export items. No doubt the flint mines provided the beginning of metallurgy in this area.

The first attempts to melt iron of the local bog iron ore in Slavic territories took place in the 5th century B.C. Metallurgy spread in the second century B.C. owing to the fact that this kind of ore was common. In the turn of eras they began to use iron from mine ores in the Holy Cross Mountains. Its center was the town Rudki Opatowskie just as Krzemionki Opatowskie was the center of flint mining. Both places are located in Opatów county.

The local rock played a dominant role in developing iron mining. It is a hard quartz. Slavs made not only hacks of it but hammers as well. It was easy to break iron ore into pieces ready to melt on quarts slabs.

Iron ore in Rudki Opatowskie is a hematite. Silver denars of caesars Vespasian and Trajan found in old shafts indicate the mine was in operation in those times (2).

As it might be seen, miners using quartz hammers and granite hacks mined the ore. They broke it on granite slabs into small pieces (3).

Mining and melting operations were located five miles apart from each other. The iron ore had to be transported from one place to the other. Transportation caused some problems because of the mountain terrain. Workers carried ore in baskets.

Founders melted iron in a small kiln called a "dymarka' — blast furnace (4). It was of a cylinder shape but a little wider at the bottom being 30-12 inches in diameter and 15 inches high.

Founders put ore and charcoal in layers into it. After ignition they pressed the air into it with bellows to obtain the higher temperature. Under the heat some chemical processes followed which caused the iron to separate from the ore. Because of the low temperrature the iron was not in liquid form as it is now in the foundry but in a paste form richly polluted with slag.

The 'dymarka' was used only once. Founders did not bother with the slag. Since the product they wanted gathered on the top they collected it and left the slag in the earth where it remained for over two thousand years. Metallurgists assume that the founder used 400 pounds of iron ore and 450 pounds of charcoal in one blast furnace.

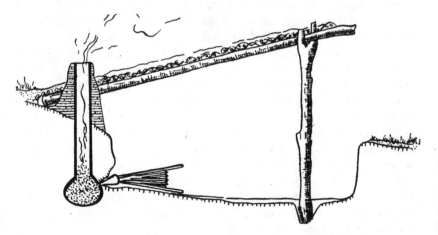

Fig. 21. Reconstruction of 'dymarka' — iron kiln

80

As is shown, in the area of 300 square miles the Ancient Slavs used over 20,000 'dymarkas' annually in the autumn and every one produced 20-30 pounds of iron (5).

Founders had a specific way of building 'dymarkas'. They placed them in two or three close ranges.

Who taught the the Ancient Slavs how to melt the iron ore?

It is known that the Celts were settled on the Polish lands for some time. They are accredited with two iron epochs in Northern and Middle Europe. But inhabitants of these territories produced this metal from bog iron ore. Is it possible that the Slavic founders independently deveoped this process (6)?

The mining ore is richer in iron than the bog iron ore. No wonder the Holy Cross Mountains basin became so important in a short time. It was the largest iron producing center in Europe east of the Alps, between the 1st and the 4th centuries A.D.

After obtaining iron from the ore, founders gave it to hammersmiths who crumbled out slags with quartz hammers on granite slabs.

The Holy Cross Mountains basin began the start of iron production on a bigger scale. By melting the bog iron ore, everyone could produce iron to his own needs. The technology was a simple one. The bog iron ore was easy to melt. It produced metal in the form of a paste at a temperature of 1500 F. degrees. If there were winds the founder could produce iron without using bellows.

Now the process became more refined and craftsmen were needed. So, the new technics caused the need for miners, founders and smiths.

The iron production must have been a very popular occupation among the Ancient Slavs. Based on linguistics it is easy to find out that the most common family names derive from the word 'kowal' — smith (Kowal, Kowalski) as well as from 'ruda' — ore (Rudnicki). There are countless names of places from those two occupations such as Rudki, Rudniki, Kuźnice, Kowalów etc.

Many tools and implements had been made from iron in the Polish territories. According to archaelogical findings ancient blacksmiths hammered knives of many kinds, axes, sickles, scissors, hammers, razors etc.

At the end of the last century B.C. blacksmiths started to make iron swords, arrow and javelin points and spurs. All these items were produced mostly for export. They were purchased by the German warriors and probably by Roman legions stationed near the Polish lands.

81

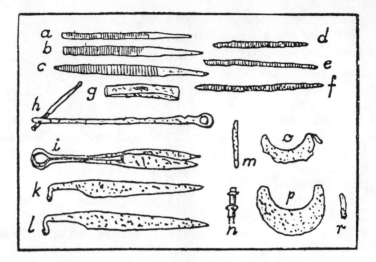

Fig. 22. Iron implements found in a blacksmith grave from the last century B. C. at Rządz in northern Poland: a-c rasps, d-f files, g hammer, h an implement of unknown use, i scissors, k-l knives, m n r fragments of bronze objects, o-p razors.

Germans needed swords which, according to Tacitus (7), they did not make.

Slavic blacksmiths were excellent craftsmen. Archaelogical findings indicated they knew the technics of carburation using the charcoal or burned bones and horns. They learned to make a bar from two or more bars by covering a soft bar with a hard one.

In 1967 at Nowa Huta near Cracow workers dug the ground for new ironworks. They were amazed when their ditchers uncovered pottery kilns full of pots. They called archaelogists and excavation revealed more than anyone could dream of (8).

On the left bank of the Vistuala near Cracow in the area of villages Tropiszów, Igołomia and Kościelnik there was a big pottery center. Archaeologists excavated over one hundred kilns. Some of them were full of pots ready to use but nobody took them away. Over 1500 years they waited for someone to take them.

The same pots are to be found in graves and settlements dated from the 4th and 5th centuries A.D. (9).

The greatest shock for scientists was the size of production. In one kiln in 8 hours 2,000 pots could be fired. It is possible that a kiln working without stoppage could produce three times in 24 hours 6,000 pots. Even if we assume that not all kilns worked day and night the number of fired pots must have been at least 10,000 a week.

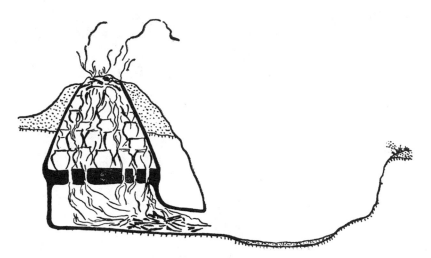

Fig. 23. Reconstruction of pottery kiln at Igołomia

It seems that from the beginning of the 3-rd century A.D. there developed the new technique of pottery, called the ceramics of the gray clay (10). There were pots of different shades of gray color, but sometimes there was also brown, red and yellow. There were two kinds: one had a flat surface made on a potter's wheel, another which was made by hand had a rugged surface. The same vessels of daily use of both kinds pots, bowls, jugs were produced.

What was the purpose of production on such a large scale? Was the pottery export-oriented like the foundry products?

It looks like the production was directed to local markets. During the 1st century A.D. fine ceramics and glass wares were imported from Rome to please the rich people as archaelogical findings indicate (11). The unfavorable political situation halted import and forced the development of the ceramic industry on the Polish territories with the help of craftsmen trained abroad.

This supposition is supported by the fact that in the kilns of Igołomia were 80 percent of the vessels with rugged surfaces and 20 percent had fine surfaces. It means the potters produced their wares mostly for the use of common men. Only one-fifth of the production went into the houses of leaders in the form of fine pottery.

The ceramic center at Igołomia was not the only one on Slavic territories. There were others in Poland and in the regions of the the East Slavs, but the one at Igołomia was on the biggest scale (12).

Excavated kilns are in the shape of a ball. They are wider at the bottom and narrower at the top, and consists of two chambers divided

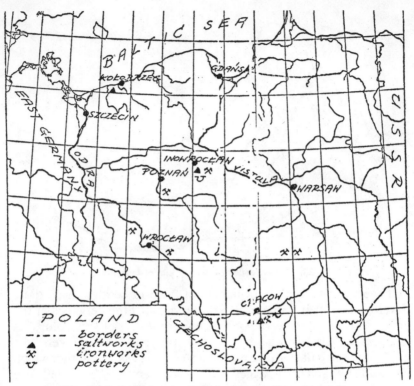

Map IX. Industrial centers in Poland in the 4th century A.D.

by a crate. The lower area served as the hearth and in the upper chamber the potters placed their pots.

As the pots in the kiln indicate something unexpected must have happened. Probably, there occured a sudden enemy attack for capturing the skillful craftsmen who had a high price on the slave markets (13).

The kilns of Igołomia, Tropiszów and Zofiepole are the second largest in size in Europe. Only the concentration of kilns in Rhineland, Germany, were larger.

Next to the ceramic kilns archaeologists found the iron furnaces of the 1st and 2nd centuries A.D. As the findings indicate, this industrial center at Igołomia was 4 miles long. The iron kilns ran in three ranges.

The iron-ceramic center at Igołomia must have been played quite a role in the first centuries A.D. Its size speaks for itself. Placed on the left bank of the Vistula, which in those times flowed in this area before turning a few miles south, was a splendid commercial route for merchandise produced by the local craftsmen and shipped to other territories.

Iron and ceramics were not the only industrial products of the Ancient Slavs. Salt was another important product.

Slavs obtained salt from brackish springs. The mining of salt in some areas came later, about the 13th century A.D.

The process was a simple one. People heated the salty water and after evaporation the sediment of salt coated the bottom of the vessel. There are some people around the world who obtain salt in this primitive way even today.

The biggest centers of brackish springs rich in salt were near the city of Kołobrzeg on the Baltic coast and east of Cracow around the city of Bochnia. Only the springs near Inowrocław could compete with them, although they are not as rich in salt (14).

Now the question arises, was it possible that the Ancient Slavs obtained salt from brackish springs around Bochnia? Today, the city is famous for salt mines. No installations exist to produce salt from the brackish springs because there are no such springs in this area.

But the archaeological findings indicate that in the remote past there were brackish springs around. They must have disappeared because mining cut off their underground water supply. Besides, the names of some localities show traces of a connection with salt production in the remote past (15).

Three main salt centers met the demands of almost the entire Slavic population on the Polish soil. Moreover, salt produced by those centers was an export item as well as amber and iron. This is sufficiently proved by finding the Roman coins in the vicinity of old salterns (16).

According to the archaeological findings there were three blacksmith centers in this period. The biggest one was located at the middle part of the Warta River and two smaller were situated in the center of Silesia and at the lower Vistula. All those centers located along the Amber Route indicate that iron melted in the Holy Cross Mountains basin had been transported quite a distance and forged into products at places close to the trade routes (17).

NOTES TO CHAPTER XI

1. Bibliography: Bardach J., Gieysztor A., Łowmiański H., Maleczyńska E., 'Historia Polski do r. 1466', Warszawa 1960; Bielenin K., 'Staropolskie zagłębie żelaza', Dawna Kultura 1956; Gajewski L., 'Badania nad organizacją produkcji pracowni garncarskich z okresu rzymskiego w Igołomi', APol. 1959; Godłowski K. 'Źródła archeologiczne do dziejów rolnictwa w Polsce', Warszawa 1960; Gumowski M., 'Moneta rzymska w Polsce', PArch. 1958; Kazimierczyk J., 'Osada hutnicza w Groszowicach', DKult. 1954; Lańczyk G., 'Wyniki dotychczasowych badań na Tyńcu', MStar. 1957; Łęga W., 'Handel między państwem rzymskim a Pomorzem nadwiślańskim', PArch. 1958; Malinowski T., 'Narzędzia kowalskie okresu późnolateńskiego i rzymskiego w Polsce', PArch. 1953; Rauhut L., Studia i materiały do historii wczesnośredniowiecznego hutnictwa żelaza w Polsce', Wrocław 1960; Sedlak W., 'Milenijne refleksje świętokrzyskie', ZNauk. 1962.

2. W. Sedlak, 'Stanowiska żużla starożytnego na tle lokalnych zasobów rudy żelaznej na na odcinku Łysica-Łysa Góra', PAN 1957.

3. According to K. Bielenin, S. Holewiński, 'Rudki— starożytny ośrodek górniczy w Górach Świętokrzyskich', Przegląd Geograficzny 1961, Nr. 3. p. 134-138, there are many blocks of stones in Holy Cross Mountains with signs that man worked iron on them.

4. M. Radwan, 'Ważne odkrycie', KwHKM 1960, Nr. 4, p. 561-564, and S. Holewinski, 'Uwagi o procesie redukcji żelaza z rud w kotlinie świętokrzyskiej', KwHKM 1960, Nr. 4, p. 569-571.

5. W. Sedlak, 'Milenijne refleksje świętokrzyskie', p. 61.

6. J. Kostrzewski, 'Ze studiów nad wczesnym okresem żelaznym w Polsce', SAnt. 1953, Vol. IV, p. 27, writes that iron appeared in Polish territories at the end of the bronze period, as a competition to the bronze adornments. The same author in 'Wielkopolska w czasach przedhistorycznych', Poznań 1923, p. 133, maintains that in the Hallstatt period iron was imported to Polish territories from the south, then the inhabitants of northern Poland started to mine the iron from iron bog ore. J. Piaskowski, 'Metaloznawcze badania wyrobów żelaznych z okresu halsztackiego i wczesnolateńskiego, znalezionych na Śląsku', PArch. 1960, Vol. XII, p. 135, gives a lot of thought to how the Ancient Slavs learned to mine the iron ore in Holy Cross Mountains and founder it. Since it was too early for Celtic penetration of Polish territories, although they might had contributed to iron industry in later times, the Slavs could learn metallurgy from the Neuri, who produced this metal at Kamienka at the Dnieper River or from Scythians.

7. Tacitus, 'Germania', cap. 43, mentions that Germans south of the Carpathian Mountains treated the Celtic Cotini with disdain, because Cotini were busy with iron industry. It means, the Germans in this region did not bother to make spears or swords which they needed in numerous battles.

8. L. Rauhut, op. cit., p. 252, writes about two other centers of iron production in Poland. One was at Tarchalice in Silesia and judging by the size it must have had a large output, the other one was located at Witów in Piczów county.

9. S. Trawkowski, 'Jak powstawała Polska', Warszawa 1963, p. 40.

10. L. Gajewski, 'Badania nad organizacją produkcji pracowni garncarskich z okresu rzymskiego w Igołomi', APol. 1959, Vol. III, p. 121.

11. B. Rutkowski, 'Terra sigillata znaleziona w Polsce', Wrocław 1960, p. 108, maintains that fine Roman pottery found in Polish territories are from 41 to 96 A.D.

12. T. Reyman, 'Problemy ceramiki siwej', p. 171.

13. It is worth mentioning that the word 'Igo' is often found in Roman records, as names of Celtic war leaders. In Ancient Slavonic 'Igo' meant a yoke. The question is which one of two words could be a base for the name of Igołomia? The next question— had Igołomia any connection with the tribe of 'Igyllones' placed by Ptolemy somewhere between the rivers Odra and Bug?

14. S. Trawkowski, op. cit., p. 84-86.

15. According to A. Brückner, 'Słownik etymologiczny języka polskiego', the name 'Bochnia' is derived from the root 'boch' or 'bech', popular in the names of many localities. There id 'Bochyn' nad 'Bohatnica' in Czechoslovakia. The root is difficult to find out what its original meaning was. The same linguistic problem exists in the name of 'Wieliczka' another salt city in the vicinity. In it is the ancient Slavic adverb 'wieliki' which is common in East Slavonic but was shortened to 'wielki' in Polish. It proves that the city of Wieliczka is a very old settlement and so well known through the centuries that linguistic changes could not twist it.

16. M. Gumowski, op. cit., p. 87-149 and W. Łęga, op. cit., p. 51.

17. T. Malinowski, op. cit., p. 268-269.

CHAPTER XII
SOCIAL DIFFERENTIATION

When the Proto-Slavs absorbed the Veneti and the new nation was born, the population expanded. The loess fields became less abundant, forcing people to look for new land for cultivation. There were dense and big forests in those times.(1) Hence men started to clear wooded areas by burning the trees.

It gave not only a new acreage for cultivation, but the soil was richly fertilized by the ashes. Farmers sowed grain and corn without necessity of rousing the soil. The new economy which used axes to cut down trees called it 'gospodarka żarowa' — fire farming. It was excellent for millet cultivation.

The new economy strengthened the old one, the garden farming, which used hoes as implements.

People noticed that by rousing the soil with ashes they could grow better crops than before, when they sowed grain into the ashes only. The hoe technique was expanded on the burnt areas as well.

The burnt areas were usually bigger than gardens, and to cultivate it all with hoes made the labor tiresome. Women who started farming found a solution. By dragging the fallen trees with the sharp cut branches, they rouse the soil. Rousing was not as deep and thorough as by hoeing, but much more acreage could be cultivated in less time.

A new farming implement had been invented: the 'radło' — plow, in its crudest and most primitive form was used to break soil and to throw it to both sides.

It had not happened in the Slavic cradlelands. The implement similar to the plow is found in the drawings of ancient Egypt and Babylon (2). 'Radło', as well as farming, wandered from Asia Minor through the Balkan peninsula to Poland. The soil-breaking plow had been called an 'ard in Sweden and Germany, marking its way from

Poland, because there is little difference between the 'ard' and the 'radło'.(3)

'Radło' became a very popular implement of the Ancient Slavs, as the Slavic names of its parts indicate.

The Slavs east of the Vistula had been using the 'socha' — another kind of primitive plow. It appears to have been a Slavic invention made by improving the forked hoe.(4) The name is derived from the 'rozsocha' — branching (forking) tree.

The plow, which is an improved 'radło' with braces, moldboard, share and wheels, came late to Poland (5).

It appears that women not only started farming, but invented the farm implements as well. They hoed and they had driven 'radło', also. Traces of this working method among the Slavic women are left in Russian ritual.(6)

Men, who were busy with cattle-hearding, noticed that using oxen as the 'radło' or 'socha' traction gave better results because animals are stronger than women, so they applied oxen in farming. Therefore, men took over the land cultivation from the women. The use of animal traction in farming revolutionized not only the economics, but all walks of life. Next to cattle-raising, the corn-sowing became the second wealth of the Ancient Slavs.(7)

Introduction of animal traction in farming changed the social system, also. The clan lost its economic strength.

In former epochs the clan consisted of 50 to 60 persons of kinsfolk needed to meet all the needs of the individuals. Now the smaller unit was able to satisfy the wants. Father working with the oxen in cornfields, mother gardening and housekeeping, and children tending the cattle and sheep and gathering fruit, berries and mushrooms, could produce enough food and other necessities to sustain life. The family became a production and consumtion unit.

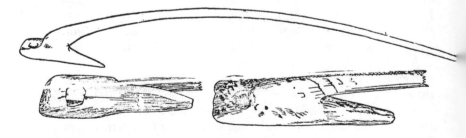

Fig. 24 Primitive wooden 'radło' — ard found by the archaeologists in 3 1/2 feet deep in earth at Wiewiórki in northern Poland, after K. Moszyński, 'Kultura ludowa Słowian', Vol. I, p. 162.

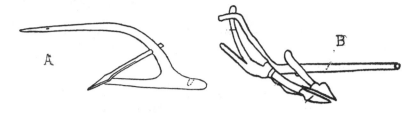

Fig. 25 'A' Slavic 'radło' with blade found at Dabergatz near Berlin, Germany, after K. Moszyński ludowa Słowian', Vol. I, p. 163, and 'B' the 'socha' — forked plow, after S. Trawkowski, 'Jak powstawała Polska', p. 29.

The big communal house lost its purpose, too. It was divided into small one-family apartments, as the excavations in Biskupin revealed (8), and in time the common roof disappeared. The people started to build huts standing separately. They no longer used one big kettle to feed the whole clan. Each family cooked meals for itself.

In this epoch the sense of land property started to form. Pastures and woods remained the common property as they were before, but cornfields became the matters of appropriation. If one family had a cornfield under cultivation for some years and left it after soil exhaustion, they protested when another family tried to take this cornfield under cultivation. So, next to personal and mobile things, developed the property of real estate.

Families worked differently. One produced more than another. In this way began the social differentiation in settlements. The rich and poor families appeared. Those who worked efficiently lived in better huts and enjoyed better living and social standing. Equality, a typical characteristic of the earlier epochs ceased to exist.

Decision-making changed, too. In earlier epochs the clan discussed the problems and made decisions during the lunch-time or evenings after work. Now this system no longer worked. Families lived separately. A new institution had to be invented to summon all grown up people in one place and time. This institution was called the 'wiece' — gathering, and has played an enormous role in the history of all Slavic nations.

It is possible that at the beginning the gathering took place during the many festivities in which all inhabitants of the settlement participated. The place of meeting must have been the sacred groves.

Next, the sex differentiation followed.

In earlier epochs the woman was mostly a breadwinner. The clan had a cognatic structure. Even when men started to play a leading role

89

in society, women had equal rights in meetings, discussions and making decisions.

Now the situation changed. Men, as producers of both wealth and livelihood, substantially improved their standing in the family as well as in society.

The cognatic clans began to disintergrate. They were replaced by the agnatic clans with the 'starosta' — elderly man as the head.

It is possible that women took part in meetings at the beginning. But the main topics of discussion were problems of cattle-raising and crop-sowing, not very much familiar to women, so they became less interested in participation.

It appeares that women lost their right to participate in gatherings when military democracy developed. Discussions about war were considered an entirely manly subject in which no woman should participate.

Family huts caused the establishment of villages in circular form or in lines along the rivers, depending upon safety needs. If there was danger of molesting the settlers by cattle-rustlers or marauding animals the 'okolnica' — round village had to be built. Huts stood close together forming the circle. There was only one gate to get in, closed at night. Inside the 'okolnica' the cattle were herded for the night. When the danger was imminent the villagers strengthened their habitat by raising the palisade around the village. This form of settlement gave the start to fortified towns and cities. Biskupin was based on it the archaeological findings indicate.

The 'ulicówka' — one street village along the river led to forming a territorial unit. A long stretching village came in contact with another village which belong to different clan. Since between villages were the 'pola' — cornfields of both villages, the Poles found a special name for this territorial unit, the 'opole'. It started in Slavic cradlelands but developed after Slavic migrations.(9).

The 'opole' consisted of several neighboring villages, sometimes belonging to different clans. The close existence caused many problems which had to be solved. The 'opole' gathering evolved.

NOTES TO CHAPTER XII

1. **Bibliography:** Brackmann J., 'Die Anfänge des polnischen Staates', Berlin 1934; Bratanic B., 'Nekolko napomena o technickoj konstrukciji starog slovenskog pluga', EP 1960, Vol. III; Broda J., 'Gospodarka zrębowo-wypaleniskowa w Beskidzie Żywieckim', Slant. 1932; Chotek K., 'Kopanicovy a zdarovy zposob pripravy pudy v

Ceskoslovenskych Karpatech', Ar. Roz. 1961; Dziekoński T., 'O częściach pracujących pługów i soch na ziemiach polskich w XIX wieku', HKM 1954; Hołubowicz W., 'Opole w wiekach X-XII', Katowice 1956; Kostrzewski J., 'Kultura, prapolska', Warszawa 1962, also, 'Pomorze średniowieczne', Warszawa 1956; Marinov W., 'Die Pflugformem in den Gebirgsgegenden Bulgariens-Balkan and Rhodopegebirge', LISL 1938; Moszyński K., 'O początkach i pochodzeniu wyrazów pług i płużyca', JP 1956, Vol. XXXVI; Tymieniecki K., 'Społeczeństwo Słowian lechickich', Lwów 1928; Urbancova V., 'Klasifikacia slovenskoho orneho naradia', SN 1961; Wojciechowski Z., 'Ustrój polityczny ziem polskich w czasach przedhistorycznych', Lwów 1937.

2. Encyclopedia Britannica 1972, Vol. IX, p. 29, accepts'possibility that the use of plows dates as far back as 3600 B.C. in Mesopotamia and back to 3000 B.C. in Egypt.

3. J. Kostrzewski, 'Kultura prapolska', Warszawa 1962, p. 28-29, states that the word 'radło' derives from the Slavic 'orać' — to plow. For the Ancient Slavs the 'artaj' was the plowman, because he used the "ardło" — plow. 'Ło' as the ending of the word is typical for Slavic implements, like 'szydło' — awl, 'kowadło' — anvil etc. Thanks to transposition of letters in words in Old Slavonic between the Baltic and Adriatic perhaps in the second half of the 8th century A.D., the word 'artaj' took form 'rataj' and the word 'ardło' — 'radło'.

4. K. Moszyński, 'Kultura ludowa Słowiań', Warszawa 1967, Vol. I, p. 177.

5. K. Moszyński, po. cit., p. 186-187, writes that the plow according to written sources had been introduced in the 12th century in Russia, in the 13th century in Poland and in the 14th century in Bohemia and Serbia. Pliny mentions the plow as a Celtic invention in Swiss Alps. Its name derives (according to Pliny) from the word 'plaumorati' — farming by plow.

6. Larousse Encyclopedia of Mythology, New York 1966, p. 298, states that when the Russian peasants wished to preserve their village against the epidemic of plague or cholera, they sent their women to drive the plow at midnight to furrow the village. The ritual was common in Russia before World War I.

7. S. Trawkowski, 'Jak powstawała Polska', Warszawa 1961, p. 34, writes, that the word 'imienie' in Old Slavonic ment the cattle at first, then the wealth as the Polish 'mienie' — wealth indicates. The same meaning has the Serbian and Croation word 'blago' — cattle. The Polish word 'zboże' — corn has a root 'bog' which derives from the word bogactwo-wealth. It means the cattle-raising and corn-sowing constituted base of Ancient Slavs livings.

8. See chapter VIII Biskupin. It is worth mentioning that at Tripolye in Ukraine the communal houses had many hearths which shows that the differentiation started in the big house, and the cause was not the need for privacy, but to prepare separate meals. The clan, composed of several families, lived in the communal dwelling, but the families no longer ate from one kettle. The next step was to divide the communal house into small one family apartments.

9.Hence different names in Slavic languages. It was 'opole' for the Poles, the 'okolina' for the Czechs, the 'vierw' for the Russians and the 'żupa' for the Serbs.

91

CHAPTER XIII

MIGRATION TO THE EAST

For fifteen centuries or even longer Ancient Slavs lived together in geographic isolation. Despite Celtic and German penetrations they clung to their cradlelands. No attempt was made to abandon territories between the Baltic Sea and Carpathian Mountains, rivers Odra and Bug (1).

After all they had little chance to do it.

Among West Germans, rather colonially minded people, were groups of brigants. They placed themselves at the Roman Empire borders and operated in the moments of weakness by organizing booty expeditions.

In the east the Roman Empire borders blocked the East Germans who left the Polish territories to settle at the shores of the Black Sea. At the end of the 3rd century A.D. both groups met. German cordon was sealed. At the northern borders of the Roman Empire were camped the Hermanduri, Norsists, Marcomans, Quads, Gepids, Longobards, Visigoths and Ostrogoths.

Nations making this cordon paid little attention to the cultural accomplishments of Rome. They did not even try to accept it but took advantage of booty expeditions, Roman tributes and trade with slaves.

The German cordon blocked the path of Slavic migration to the west but the path to the east stood open. Enormous territories were thinly populated. Slavs at the river Pripet basin moved to the Dnieper and north before the Hunnish invasion.

Ancient Slavs formed a homogenous ethnic group which was divided by the Amber Route and the Baltic-Black Sea Route.

By organizing the Lugian Alliance to safeguard the Amber Route Celts cut the Polish territories in the middle. Contact between the two halves of Slavs almost ceased to exist. Both halves started to develop separately. Thus, the turn of eras found two groups: West Slavs and East Slavs.

Gothic invasion and the establishment of the Baltic-Black Sea Route caused a further division. East Slavs were divided into East and South Slavs.

How do we know that the Ancient Slavs inhabiting the Polish territories formed three groups?

The answer to this question is given in linguistics. There were changes in the Ancient Slavonic which led to the formation of Slavic languages (2).

There is little doubt that Goths played some role in Slavic migration to the east. Drifting along the rivers Vistula and Dniester German tribes on their way made booty expeditions against the Slavic settlements. Thus, they forced the native population to move east where places were safer. Moving east the Slavs absorbed some small tribes and reached the river Oka (3).

About migration to the east Nestor writes: "And the Slavs, too, settled along the Dnieper and were called the Polyane; others, the Drevlyane because they lived in the depths of the forests; others, again, settled between the Pripet and the Duna and were called Dregovitches; others settled along the Desna were called Polotchane, after the Polota, a stream which joins the Duna. And the Slavs who settled round Lake Ilmen kept their own name of Slavs and built a city which they called Novgorod. And others settled along the Desna, the Sejm and the Sula were called Severyane" (4).

The following Slavic tribes took part in the march to the east: Dregovitches (Dragovitches), Krivitches, Severyans (Severyane), Slovens, Dulebs and Sclavens (Sclaveni). Later on new tribes appeared on the scene: Vyatiches, Tivercis, Radimitches, Ulitches, Volhynians, Polyans and Drevlyans (5).

The name of Severyans is derived from 'sever' which like 'Serb' was a common name for a tribe used in singular number. It is difficult to find out the meaning of this word. Some linguists maintain the name comes up from 'sever' — north (6) or 'swoj' — our, mine (7) but reasoning is not convincing.

The Severyans occupied the area along the rivers Desna, Sejm and Sula. There are some places in Poland named 'Siewierz' but they might have been settlements of prisoners of war established during the wars of Polish kings Boleslas the Great and Boleslas the Bold with the Russian state of Kiev. As a military group the Severyans migrated from the Dnieper to the Balkans and settled at the river Tsierna in Banat (8). The Polyans of Kiev were their branch.

The Krivitches, called by Latvians 'Krevs', derive their tribal name from a prince Krive but there is not much proof to justify such supposition (9). Their settlement was in two periods, the first at the river Wielika and Upper Dvina and the second in the area from Smolensk to Nowogródek and the river Niemen. Thus, the periphery names originating from tribal Krivitches are to be found from Pinsk to Slonin and Nowogródek. Krivitches did not partake in the Balkans invasion (10).

The Dregovitches colonized the marshland of the river Pripet. Hence their name which is from the word 'dryg' or 'dreg' ('dreha' in Byleorussian) which means a bog (11). Dregovitches took part in the Balkan colonization as the record of 620 A.D. mentions. Two small groups of Dregovitches settled down, one at Salonika and the other at the river which was called after them Dragovitsa (Dragovtsa) and is a tributary of the Maritsa. Dregovitches who settled here were named Drugovits (12). They migrated from the Pripet River basin as archaeological findings indicate (13). Those Dregovitches who remained were absorbed by the state of Kiev in the 9th century A.D.

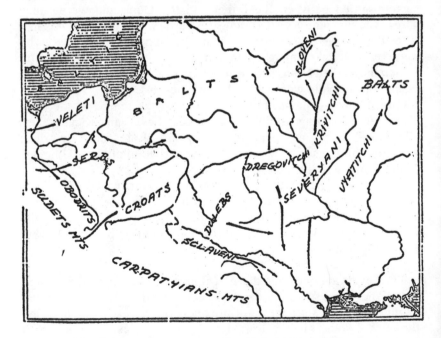

Map X. Migrations of Slavic nations from the Polish territories

94

Drevlyane lived south of the river Pripet. They colonized the area between rivers: Horyn, Slutch, Uz na Teterev. They had their own state in the 9th century A.D. with the capital located in Iskorosten (now Korosten). In 883 the prince of Kiev forced them to join his state.

Slovenes migrated from the south in the 4th century A.D. They colonized the area at Lake Ilmen and assimilated local Finnish tribes. As the Sclavenes marched at the head of the Slavic migration to the south so the Slovenes marched to the north. Names of both groups are the consequences of contact between them and non-Slavic groups they met on their way. In the 8th and 9th centuries A.D. Slovenes organized their own tribal state with the capital at Novgorod Vieliky.

No princely tombs of the 1st and 2nd centuries A.D. are to be found on territories inhabited by the East Slavs. Nonetheless, discovered treasures of Roman coins indicate three political centers (14). One existed at the Upper Dniester along its left bank at the tributaries Zbruch and Seret, where salines were. Probably it was the Sclavene groups who inhabited this area before they migrated to the Balkans in the 6th century A.D.

The second center was situated at the Central Dnieper, between Kiev and Ros. Archaeologists found about 400 Roman coins in Kiev and among them the latest one dated from the time of Emperor Marcus Aurelius. The treasure was hidden before the Goths invasion.

The third center was near the city of Vladimir of Volhynia as a golden medalion found there, indicates.

The East Slavs created two material cultures: the Zarubiniecian and the Czerniakhovian cultures.

NOTES TO CHAPTER XIII

1. **Bibliography:** Bazylew L., 'Historia Rosji', Wrocław 1969; Carr E.H., A History of Societ Russia' 1950; Clarkson J.D., 'A History of Russia from the Ninth Century', London 1962; Dowżenok W.J., 'Zemlerobstwo drewnioj Rusi do seredyny XIII st.', Kyiw 1961; Grekov B., 'La Culture de la Russie de Kiev', Moscow 1947; Juszkow S.W., 'Obszczestwiennyj stroj i prawo kijewskogo gosudarstwa', Moskwa 1949 Karoluk W.D., 'Zapadnyje Slavianie i Kijewskaja Rus', Moskwa 1964; Paszuto V.G., 'Wnieszmaja politika drewnej Rusi', Moskwa 1968; Rybakow B.A., 'Pierwyje wieka russkoj istorii', Moskwa 1965; Tichomirow M.N., 'Drewnierusskije goroda', Moskwa 1956; Vernandsky G., 'A History of Russia', New Haven 1959.

2. According to Z. Klemensiewicz, T. Lehr-Spławinski, S. Urbańczyk, 'Gramatyka historyczna języka polskiego', Warszawa 1965, p. 26-32, when Ancient Slavs as a group came into existence about 2000 B.C., their language was homogeneous. During this time came the first palatalization. The rear lingual consonants 'k', 'g', 'ch' became

soft 'c', 'z', 's' before the old front vowels, for instance: 'ręka', 'ręczyć'; 'mogę', 'możesz'; 'słuch', 'słyszeć'. When the Amber Route and the Baltic-Black Sea Route divided the Slavs into two halves, there followed the second palatalization. In this time it ran unevenly. The eastern half which in later times started the East Slavic and South Slavic languages changed the consonants 'k', 'g', 'ch' into 'c', 'dz', 's', for instance: Polish 'kwiat' — flower, Russian 'cvet'; Polish 'gwiazda' — star, Russian 'zvezda' etc. Next to these changes in the East Slavic languages 't' and 'd' before 'l' vanished, for instance: Polish 'mydło' — soap, Russian 'myło'; Polish 'płótł' — he plaits, Russian 'plel'. In this way came the first division of homogeneous Ancient Slavs language. When the Slavs settled in the Balkan the second division became a fact. In the combination of vowel and consonant 'or' and 'ol', the vowel 'o' was put before 'r' and 'l' in the West, East and South linguistic groups, but the Southern Slavs changed 'o' into 'a'. In this way we have: Polish 'równy' — equal, Russian 'rovnyj', Croatic 'ravan'; Polish 'łokieć' — elbow, Russian 'Loket', Croatic 'lakat'. According to A. Meillet, 'Le slave commune', Paris 1924, p. 2, the Slavic languages started to form shortly before the 7th or 8th century B.C., but the differences between them must not have been serious ones, since SS. Cyril and Methodius, could preach the gospel to all Slavic nations in the 9th century in their Slavic language used at Saloniki, Greece, without dificulty.

3. Jordanes, 'Getica', cap. XIII.

4. 'Povest vremennych let', p. 19.

5. There are three writers enumerating the East Slavic tribes. First the Bavarian Geographer in the 9th century A.D. mentions Bugans and Ulitches. In the next ·century Constantine Porphyrogenitus, 'De administrando imperio', cap. 9,37, besides Ulitches knows Krivitches, Dregovitches, Severyans and Drevlyans. Then Nestor (1056-1114), 'Provest vremennych let' next to the above mentioned enumerates the new ones: Polyans, Tivercis, Slovenes, Radimitches, Vyatiches, Polotchans, Dulebs and Volhynians. Of all these tribes H. Łowiański, 'Początki Polski', Vol. 11, p. 89 considers as the original East Slavic tribes only: Dregovitches, Krivitches, Severyans, Slovenes, Dulebs and Sclavens.

6. M. Vasmer, 'Russisch-etymologisches Wörterbuch', Vol. 2, p. 600, and A. Brückner, 'Wzory etymologii', Slavia, Vol. III, p. 214.

7. J. Otrębski, op. cit., p. 89.

8. H. Łowiański, op. cit., p. 105.

9. H. Łowniański, op. cit., p. 94-96.

10. M. Vasmer, 'Die Slaven in Griechenland', p. 163; and R. Trautman, 'Die elb — und ostseeslawichsen Ortsnamen', Berlin 1949, p. 30.

11. J. Perwolf, 'Slawische Volkernamen', ASPL., Vol. 594, p. 574.

12. L. Niederle, 'Slovanske starożitnosti', p. 428.

13. J. Werner, 'Slawische Bronzefiguren aus Nordgriechenland', Berlin 1953, p. 8.

14. V.V. Kropotkin, 'Lukasevskij klad bronzovych rimskich monet IV veka', Moskwa 1960, p. 215-222; and H. Łowiański, op. cit., p. 391-395.

CHAPTER XIV
MIGRATION TO THE SOUTH

Loaded with spoils conquered at the battle of Nedao the Goths at the Black Sea were decimated, tired and frustrated. They left their habitat and moved west. Some remnants decided to return to their old homeland, Scandinavia (1) through the Polish territories.

After three centuries of wars in the south the Goths changed their attitude and became more settled people but the Huns shattered their future. Returning to Scandinavia they paid their passage with silver denars, gold solids, medallions or other valuables (2), and tried to cross the Polish territories as quickly as possible.

Marching warriors told many stories about the wonders of the fascinating world in the south. They sang songs of heroes and famous battles. Slavic imagination began to work. There were questions asked: "If the Goths had such big spoils, why don't we? We can fight, too. Courage and bravery are not alien to us".

The long cherished fear which Ibrahim ibn Jacob mentions, that Slavs were afraid to go south because the heat might cause the blood to boil in their veins, troubled them no more. Since some of them had fought at the walls of Constantinople and Rome together with Goths and survived the others could do the same.

The Slavic youth were incensed by the idea of war adventures. Armament was no problem. There were three big ironwork centers. But who would instruct and lead the youth?

As the Vandals had asked the Celts to train them in battle procedure, the Marcomans and Huns had asked the Romans, so it is possible the Slavic youth asked the returning Gothic warriors to do the same. Probably they met refusal at first. The old Gothic warriors were weary of wars. They had enough of booty expeditions and camping. All they wanted to accomplish was to return safely to the old country and to live a quiet life.

The Gothic youth might have looked quite differently. All their dreams of conquering Rome, Constantinople and other cities were shattered. Owing to the lack of human reserves they had no chance to fight.

Now, the opportunity knocked at the door. There were many young men in Polish territories eager to fight. The door to the huge reservoir of human resources stood open. Dreams of gates of Constantinople and Rome became vivid again.

Military training of the Slavic youth must have begun.

Not all the Slavic tribes were bitten by war fever. The great majority could not even have had an idea what was going on. Tribal relationship was rather poor. Many tribes lived in isolation.

The war temptation and migration overwhelmed those who lived near the Baltic-Black Sea Route. The first were the Dulebs.

Since the 'Povest vremennych let' is the only source mentioning Dulebs some historians doubt if such a tribe existed.(3) Their suppositions support the fact that the name Dulebs was out of use long before the 9th century A.D. Neither the Bavarian Geographer nor Constantine Porphyrogenitus mention it. Besides, the 'Povest vremennych let' states twice the existence of Dulebs, but places Dulebs and Buzhans on the same territory. The peripherial names of villages and small streams on this territory indicate that the tribe of Dulebs must have existed.

Dulebs had their habitat between the rivers Bug and Slutch.

It is difficult to explain what the word 'Dulebs' means. (4)

Most probably the word 'Duleby' — Dulebs is a Gothic loaned word (5). The name 'Dietleib' was common among the Goths. It might be that a certain Gothic warrior called 'Dietleib' trained the Slavic youth at the river Bug and then led them as a troop. It might be, too, that a small Gothic tribe under the name of 'Dietleibs' invited by the Slavic tribes to settle down, took over and Slavicized.(6)

Dulebs were the first Slavic tribe who went south. One group settled on territories belonging to Hungary today. Thus, one district between the rivers Mura and Lake Balaton is called 'Dudleipa'. Another group under the name of 'Dudleby' found a habitat in Bohemia. The rest migrated to Carinthia and settled at the Upper Drava River.

Next to the Dulebs the Gothic instructors probably trained their neighbors, the 'Sclaveni' — Sclavens in warfare.(7) The name was given to them by Byzantinians. Sclavens occupied the territories between the rivers San, Upper Dniester and Carpathian Mountains in the 5th century A.D. They moved southward and took over territories on both banks of the Danube. In this time they entered into close contact with the Byzantinian Empire and became the object of interest of many writers especially Jordanes.(8) They marched at the head of Slavic migration down the Balkan peninsula in later times.

NOTES TO CHAPTER XIV

1. **Bibliography:** Hrabec S., O polskiej gwarze wsi Duleby w b. powiecie buczackim, Łódź 1955; Jabłonowski A., 'Ziemie ruskie — Wołyń i Podole', Warszawa 1889; Jorga N., 'Epoque et caractere de l'etablissement des Slaves dans la Peninsule des Balkans', RHist. 1930; Kucharski S.M., 'Stosunki polsko-ruskie do schyłku w. XIII', Sl. Or. 1958; Labuda G., 'Du(d)lebowie' SSSlav. 1961; Moravcsik G. 'Byzantinoturcica', Berlin 1958; Paszkiwicz H., 'The Origin of Russia', London 1954; Stieber Z. 'Toponomastyka Łemkowszczyzny, 'Łódź 1948; Tichomirov M.N., 'Drevnerusskie goroda', Moskva 1956; Vasmer M., 'Die Slaven in Griechenland', Berlin 1941.

2. M. Gumowski, 'Moneta rzymska w Polsce', PArch. 1958, Vol. X, p. 125.

3. R. Jakimowicz, 'Szlak wyprawy kijowskiej Bolesława Chrobrego w świetle archeologii', Równe 1933, p. 15; and S. Kupczyński, 'Stosunki, polsko-ruskie do schyłku w. XII', Sl. Or. 1958, p. 227.

4 The nearest Slavic expression to it is 'dulęba' — a stupid, crazy or mentally ill man which gives no explanation. Attempts were made to derive the name from the musical instrument 'dudy' — bagpipe or 'dudek' — hoopoe (A. Bruckner, 'Wzory etymologii', Slava 1924, Vol. III, p. 211-213) but without success.

5. J. Vasmer, 'Russisch-etymologisches Wörterbuch', Vo. I, p. 379; and T. Lehr-Spławiński, 'Dulebowie', SSSlov.

6. According to Jordanes 'Getica IX', p. 70, it was a common practice in those times to accept the foreign names for tribe and person.

7. It appears that the Gothic word 'cunning' — war leader had been accepted by the Slavs in this period. It took different forms like 'knięg', 'kunigas', 'kneź', 'kniędz' and 'książę', 'kniaź' — the prince at the end. H. Łowmiański 'Początki Polski', Vol. I., p. 382, states that looking closer at Gothic words loaned by the Slavs it is not difficult to discover that most of them center around the 'cunning' as tribal chief of Goths was called. A 'kniędz' — prince lived in 'chyza' — house upon the 'chełm' — hill which on one side had a 'tyn' hedge and on the other side a 'pergyni' — ravine. In his garden he grew 'luk' — chieve or onion and he kept 'muto' — cattle. He wore a 'szelm' — helmet, could 'goneznąć', — heal people and 'gonozic' — solve their problems. The 'Wolch' — Roman paid him 'żelsti' — tribute. Those words highly support the theory that the Germans were the military instructors and leaders of the Slavs at the beginning of the Slavic heroic epoch.

8. H. Łowmiański, op. cit. Vol.II, p. 112.

99

CHAPTER XV
MIGRATION TO THE WEST

After the Hunnish defeat, the German Thuringians created a strong state at the rivers Elbe and Saal. It reached as far as Magdeburg and the Danube having in its territories the German Varnas and Saxons. Between them and the Slavs was a large belt of empty spaces.(1)

West of the Thuringians stretched the vast domains of the Romanized Frankish monarchy. The Germans invaded and plundered it.

When it became too much the Franks marched against them and in 531 in the battle at the river Unstrut defeated Thuringians. Moreover, they started the expansion along the Danube River. In the same year the Franks made an agreement with the Slavic Serbs who appeared in the empty belt between the Germans and Slavs. In this way they forced the Varnas and Saxons to pay them tribute.

The Serbs had their habitation in north western Poland.(2) They were known as 'Sorni' (3), 'Spory' (4), 'Serbi (5) and 'Sorabi'. The linguists tried to explain the name by using words such as: 'pasierb' (6) — stepson; 'serbać' (7) — to drink loudly through the teeth, and many others.

The root of the word 'Serb' is not characteristic to the Slavic languages. It can be traced in Mesopotamia, Gaul, Mauretania and many other countries of the ancient world. Recorded by Pliny and Ptolemy Serbs at Caucasus could have had nothing in common with the Serbs in northern Poland.

The name of Serbs is the oldest among the names of Slavic tribes. Its archaity rests in the way that the singular form describes plurality. Originally, they said 'Serb' not 'Serbs' when they mentioned the whole nation.(8)

From northern Poland the Serbs migrated to Lusatia and from there one group moved toward the Elbe (9) and another south to Bohemia and Dalmatia later on. Their descendants live now in Serbia which is one of the six republics of Yugoslavia. One group of Serbs remained in Lusatia (East Germany, today) and survived to our times. They are sometimes called 'Sorbs'.

In 556 the Saxons evoked an uprising against the Franks. Following their example the Thuringians revolted in 561 and the Varnas did the same in 595.

The Franks found themselves in a difficult situation. To check the rebellious Germans they asked the Serbs to help them. Attacked from two sides the revolting Varnas suffered a painful defeat and dispersed in 595. Their territories were occupied by the Serbs with the agreement of the Franks.(10)

Following the Serbs, the Obodrits their neighbors in western Poland moved to the west. Their name is explained in many ways, too. Some linguists maintain, it is derived from the word 'bodr' (11) — alert. Thus, the stronghold at the Danube took the name 'Bodrok'. Some others think it is derived from the word 'bodry' (12) — brave. There are some who insist the name is from the 'odra' (13) — water. Thus, the Obodrits were people who lived on both banks of the big river (water).

It seems the most convincing explanation comes from the name of the Odra River.(14) Like 'domovit' meant a man who lived in a 'dom'-house so the Obodrits might have been people who lived on both banks of the river Odra.

Obodrits divided themselves into two groups. One group migrated to the district of Mecklenburg (Germany, today) and lived there for many centuries until it was Germanized. The second group went south and settled at the Tissa River in Hungary. It disappeared in the course of time. Probably it was absorbed by the local people.

There are no descendants of the Obodrits today.

The German Rugians were never on the island Rugen. After arriving from Scandinavia they settled at the mouth of the Vistula. Pushed away by the Goths they occupied the Slavic territories between the rivers Vistula and Wierzyca. Here they dwelt for sometime. Tempted with booty expeditions they went south with other German nations. They could not denationalize all Slavic natives who remained in primordial regions. But the name of 'Rugians' stayed. They Slavs modificated it to 'Rujans' or 'Ranians'.

The Slavic Rugians migrated west to an island and gave it their name — 'Rugen Isle'.
How do we know it?
The names of Rugian places prove it. They have the same ending 'evy', 'ovy' or 'evo', 'ovo' (Ciecholevy, Ciecholevo, Jazdrovo, Kocievo) as the places between the rivers Vistula and Wierzyca (15). There are no descendants of the Slavic Rugians today.

NOTES TO CHAPTER XV

1. **Bibliography:** Bulin H., 'Podunajśti "Abodriti"', Praha 1960; Dobrovsky J., 'Geschichte der böhmishen Sprache und altern Literatur', Prag 1818; Fritze W.H., 'Probleme des obodritischen Stämmes and Reichsverfassung', Giessen 1960; Hauptmann L., 'Kroaten, Goten and Sarmaten', Germanoslavica 1935; Knoor H.A., 'Die slawisce Keramik zwischen Elbe und Oder', Leipzig 1937; Lehr-Spławiński T., 'Obodriti-Obodrzyce', Kraków 1947; Lintzel M., 'Untersuchung zur Geschichte der alten Sachsen', Magdeburg 1937; Natanson-Leski J., 'Nazwy plemienne w Polsce', Wrocław 1959; Pliny, 'Naturalis historia'; Polaschek E., 'Veltae', REnc. 1955; Ptolemy, 'Geographia'; Taszycki W., 'Najdawniejsze polskie imiona osobowe', Wrocław 958; 'Thietmari Merseburgensis episcopi Chronicon', Berlin 1935; Trautmann R., 'Die elb-und Ostseeslawischem Ortsnamen', Berlin 1948; Tymieniecki K., 'Wiślanie', Kraków 1961; Zierhoffer K., 'Nazwy miejscowe północnego Mazowsza', Wrocław 1957.
2. H. Łowmiański, 'Początki Polski', Warszawa 1963, Vol. II. p. 69.
3. Pliny, 'Naturalis historia', Vol. II, p. 19.
4. J. Szafarzyk, 'Starożytności słowiańskie', Vol. I, p. 143.
5. Ptolemy, 'Geographia V', cap. 8, 13.
6. J. Szafarzyk, op. cit., Vol. II, p. 253.
7. F. Miklosich, 'Etymologisches Wörterbuch der Slawischen Sprachen', Wien 1886, p. 192; and A. Brückner, 'Wzory etymologii', p. 209.
8. H. Łowmiański, op. cit., Vol. II, p. 53-58.
9. According to H. Łowmiański, op. cit., p. 317, the Slavs migrated to the river Elbe in the first half of the 6th century A.D., about 50 years before the Avaric invasion. It means that the Slavic migration westward coincides with the migration of the East Slavs to the river Danube and the Black Sea.
10. H. Łowmiański, op. sit., p. 330-336.
11. J. Szafarzyk, op. cit., Vol. II, p. 656.
12. J. Lelewel, 'Slawia dziesiątego i dwudziestego wieku', Poznań 1853.
13. J. Perwolf, 'Slawische Völkernamen', ASPhil. Vol. VII, p. 595.
14. H. Łowmiański, op. cit., Vol. II, p. 77.
15. E. Kamińska-Rzetelska, 'Nazwy miejscowści typu Tuszkowy, Ciecholewy na Pomorzu', Wrocław 1963, p. 69-86.

CHAPTER XVI
HERITAGE

Ancient Slavs dwelt in Polish territories for over 2000 years before they split into seperate nations to shape their own destinies beyond the borders of Poland.

What had they learned during this long stay?

Written records tell very little, but with the help of linguistics, ethnology and archaeology one can get rather a good picture on what cultural level the Slavs were when they left cradlelands in Poland (1).

Here linguistics play an impressive role. When some Slavic nations parted between the 5th and 7th centuries the communication among them was poor and broke off completely when the Hungarians and Bavarians cut off the Western Slavs from the Southern Slavs in the Balkan. However, in their languages remain about 1700 common words unchanged or slightly changed in sound, form and meaning. It points out that this vocabulary constitutes their cultural heritage from the time when they lived together (2). The number is impressive if we consider that well educated people today use about 8000 words.

Of the 1700 common Slavic words, 1400 describe all aspects of human life and facts surrounding man, and about 10% or 170 refer to religious and spiritual beliefs.

Before they left the cradlelands in Poland Ancient Slavs knew parts of the human body: head, leg, arm, forehead, chin, hand, elbow, mouth, side, rib, back, chest, lung, heart, liver, stomach, belly, hip, womb, ear, eye, heel, palm, finger, foot, thigh.

They knew phenomena around them: earth, mountains, shore, ravine, pit, cave, field, meadow, rock, stone, flint, clay, water, sea, river, lake, brook, stream, torrent, current, whirl, swamp, mud, puddle, ice.

They used metals: lead, sulphur, silver, gold, copper, iron.

They discerned facts of weather and time: scourching, heat, cool, frost, foul weather, rain, snow, white frost, hail, glow, shine, dark, shadow, cloud, fog, rainbow, wind, storm, thunder, light, sun, star, sky, autumn, summer, winter, spring, month, day and night, dawn, daybreak, moon, evening, yesterday, tomorrow, mourning.

They gave names to trees: oak, beech, hornbeam, maple, linden, poplar, yew, ivy, birch, aspen, alder, fir, willow, hawthorn, juniper, lilac, apple tree, plum tree, nut.

They cultivated the crops: rye, wheat, barley, oats, millet, flax, hemp, corn.

They recognized the animals: bear, bison, wolf, fox, stag, rabbit, heron, woodpecker, crow, oriole, beetle, mosquito, fly, spider, fish, snake, lizard.

They knew how to: plow, sow, reap, mow, sheaf.

They used implements: rake, shovel, flail, axe, hammer, quern, plow, hoe, harrow, scythe, sickle, fork.

Their dairy products were: milk, cheese, cream, butter.

They lived in: house, hut, room; which had: threshold, hallway, window, gate, table, bench, bed.

Among the people were: father, mother, daughter, uncle, sister, brother, grandfather, grandmother, aunt, stepmother, father-in-law, mother-in-law, son-in-law, daughter-in-law, woman, man, widow, grandson, match-maker, servant, peasant, neighbor, guest, enemy, friend, guard, landlord, landlady, plowman, shepherd, war leader, deputy, judge.

They used as weapons: arrow, bow, mace, spear; and they knew: quarrel, battle, war, pillage, slavery, freedom, army.

They knew: life, death, beginning, end, time, mark, name, order,

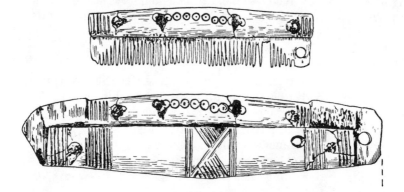

Fig. 26. Combs in horns, after J. Kostrzewski, 'Kultura prapolska' p. 176.

truth, dignity, respect, glory, fame, rumor, wisdom, knowledge, old age, youth, strength, power, labor, creation, spirit, soul, mind, feeling, will, thought, memory, wish, faith, hope, love, favor, hate, anger, fear, gay, sorrow, shame, error, guilt, punishment.

They believed in: gods, paradise, hell, devil, miracle; and they prayed and sang.

They brought with them implements and arrangements and used them down the centuries, even when they were forgotten in the cradlelands like the 'zadruga' (3), fire-farming (4) and wheat pan (5).

Fig. 27. The 'prażnica' (przula) — pan to fry unripe wheat used in Yugoslavia today, after J. Kostrzewski.

Since the Ancient Slavs lived along rivers and lakes, they gave names to almost all fish and they developed means to catch them. They knew how to build bridges, dams, ferryboats, boats, doug-out canoes.

The linguists have come to the sensational conclusion that the Ancients Slavs were forerunners of the seafaring Northmen.

According to J. Kostrzewski ('Kultura prapolska', p. 295), the Slavic word 'prom' — ferryboat, was taken from the Slavs by the Germans and introduced to Scandinavia and England. H. Falk ('Altnordisches Seewesen', p. 88-89) thinks that the Scandinavians learned from the Ancient Slavs how to build boats which they called 'ledja', 'laedia' from the Old Slavonic 'aldija', which in Polish has a form 'łódź'. M. Rudnicki (Sl. Occid. Vol. XIV, p. 232) maintains that the 'korab' — ship, received its name because the Ancient Slavs built it from the 'kora' — bark, as the North American Indians did their canoes. Again, the Scandinavians added 'i' to the name, which they changed into 'karfi'.

Ancient Slavs cared about hygienics. They whitened their huts with slack lime (6), washed the furniture with horsetail, and produced soap from ashes and fat. The word 'mydło' — soap has an old ending 'ło' which in Old Slavonic meant 'the implement'. They bathed and took steam baths in special houses called 'łaźnie'. Many fine combs found in ancient fortified towns show that the Ancient Slavs took good care of their hair. Men had long hair to their shoulders and mustaches, but no beards. The oldest razors discovered by archaeologists are from 1110-900 B.C. in areas of Lusatian culture (7).

It seems that when the Ancient Slavs parted, they were culturally developed enough to compete with the nations of Ancient Rome and Greece. No wonder they adapted themselves in a short time to the conditions with which they had to cope. What is amazing is the fact that they lived in isolation down the millennia, having almost no steady connection with the centers of the antic culture, which means they had to develop their own way of better life.

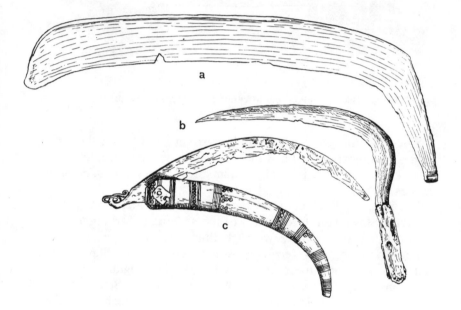

Fig. 28. The a-small scythe; b-iron sickle; c-iron sickle with horn case found by archaeologists in north-western Poland, after J. Kostrzewski.

NOTES TO CHAPTER XVI

1. **Bibliography:** Bruckner A., 'Słownik etymologiczny języka polskiego', Warszawa 1970; Filin F.P., 'Obrazowanije jazyka wostocznych Sławian', Moskva 1962; Geogiev W., 'Bałgarski etimologiczen recznik', Sofija 1962; Jagić N., 'Entstehungsgeschichte der kirchenslawischen Sprache', Berlin 1913; Lehr-Spławiński T., Kuraszkiewicz W., Sławski F., 'Przegląd i charakterystyka języków słowiańskich', Warszawa 1954; Machek V., 'Etymologicky slownik jazyka

ceskeho a slovenskeho', Praha 1957; Malecki M., 'Najstarszy literacki język Słowian', Kraków 1947; Moszyński K., 'Pierwotny zasięg języka prasłowiańskiego', Wrocław 1957, also, 'Kultura ludowa Słowian'; Stieber Z., 'Zarys gramatyki porównawczej języków słowiańskich', Warszawa 1971.

2. T. Lehr-Spławinski made up the list of the common Slavic words.

3. Common work and life was the basic social and economic system of the clan in earlier epochs. Remnants of it survived in Poland until the 13th century as the 'niedziały rodzinne'. But, brought from Poland in the 6th century, the system was transferred to the Balkan and managed to stay in Croatia almost in pure form to our times under the name of 'zadruga'.

4. According to Ch. Vakarelski, 'Sledi na ednopolnata zemedelska sistema u B-lgarite', EP 1960, Vol. III, p. 408-418, the fire-farming economy long forgotten in Poland had been in use in the Rhodop Mountains in Bulgaria until 1912.

5. Polish archaeologists found remnants of the rectangular clay pans 2-3 feet long with walls 2-3 inches high in many excavations. For what purpose were those pans used? No one in Poland uses such big pans today. Researchers tried to find an explanation but their reasoning was not convincing. The riddle was solved in one word by a Yugoslav folklorist, who visiting Poland found the "mystery" pan in a museum. He said it was the prażnica' — pan in which the peasants of Yugoslavia parched the unripe wheat for the tasty 'prażmo' — dish. The Polish researchers were surprised with this explanation. So there would be no doubt, the Yugoslav scholar, after returning home, sent his Polish colleages the authentic 'prażnica' used by Yugoslav peasants today. It fit almost completely the description of the pans found in archaeological excavations. Linguists helped here, too, finding that the prażmo as a meal was widely appreciated by the Ancient Slavs. It survived in Poland only in the family name Prażmowski. So, when the forefathers of Yugoslav nations left their homeland in Poland in the 6th century they brought with them the prażnica' and used it even now (J. Kostrzewski, Kultura prapolska, Warszawa 1962, p. 133).

6. The archaeologists found recently near Biskupin in Poland the remnants of the calcier which had been in use 4000 B.C.

7. J. Kostrzewski, Kultura prapolska, p. 178.

CHAPTER XVII
NEW CULTURES

The Lusatian culture, considered as the first Slavic material culture, came to an end in the 3rd century B.C. New factors and influences caused a new culture to develop commonly known as the culture of pit graves.(1) There were two centers of this culture in the West Slavs' territory: the Oksywian and Przeworskian cultures; and two in the East Slavs' lands: the Zarubiniecian and Czerniakhovian cultures.

The Celtic penetration reached the Vistula bringing new improvements and inventions. As in former cultures, the basic metal was copper, but now iron took its place. The progress degraded copper and bronze to a material good for making adornments, like pins, bracelets, clasps and others.

The West Slavs' territory underwent two influences; one coming by land from the Roman northern provinces from the south, another by the Baltic Sea from the west. There is a reason why the culture of pit graves (2) produced two separate centers, one in the north and another in the south of Poland.

Archaeologists found the characteristic features of the northern center at Oksywie near Gdańsk at the Baltic Sea. Hence the name: the Oksyvian culture. Graves in the earlier phase of this culture were endowed with old ceramics, and the new ones were adorned with geometric motifs. Weapons were produced almost entirely in bronze.

The people of this culture participated in amber trade along amber route.

Starting with the 1st century A.D. weapons disappeared in the graves but the bodies were richly endowed with adornments in bronze, amber (combs and beads), glass and utensiles of everyday life like knives and razors.

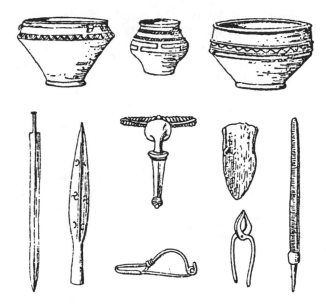

Fig. 29. Typical objects found in the pit graves, after L. Leciejewicz, 'Słownik kultury dawnych Słowian', p. 128.

Fig. 30. 'Princely tomb' at Gosławice in Silesia from the 1st century A.D., after S. Trawkowski, 'Jak powstawała Polska'.

At the end of the 1st century the burial rite has changed with inhumation beginning to replace cremation. The skeleton graves returned (3) marking the social differentiation. New ceramics and iron products bear the signs of the influence coming from the Bornholm island and Jutland.

The Oksywian culture reached its peak at the end of the 3rd century A.D., when it covered northern Poland. In this time the traces of the Roman influence appeared coming by sea from the Rhone Valley.

Who was the author of the Oksywian culture? German scholars like G. Kosinna, J. Peisker and others are convinced that the Goths, invading territories at the mouth of the Vistula, brought the Oksywian culture from their Scandinavian home country and transplanted it into natives of Pomerania. J. Kostrzewski rejects the idea (4) stating: "In old times scholars maintained that the newcomers from Scandinavia introduced the skeleton graves, until it appeared that: a) the anthropological features of the dead buried in these graves does not correspond to the anthropological features of the Swedish people in the Roman period; b) the skeleton graves are unknown in Sweden in the late of the La Tene period, but they are to be found at the lower Vistula.

Kostrzewski does not undermind the influence of the Gothic invaders upon the natives (5), and he comes to the conclusion that the Oksywian culture is the joint product of the natives which he calls the Veneti, and the Goths, with the natives playing the leading role. The archaeological findings seem to confirm this opinion.(6)

Since the Veneti are identified with the Slavs, it appears that the authors of the Oksywian culture were the more-or-less Slavicized native Veneti, with a little help from the Gothic invaders.

The other center of the pit graves culture developed in southern Poland with the typical settlement near the city of Przeworsk, hence the name, the Przeworskian culture. It developed from the former Lusatian culture under the Celtic influence at the beginning, and the Roman after.

Characteristic to this culture were big cemeteries with graves richly endowed with ceramics, weapons and utensiles (hammers, axes, knives, needles, keys and others). Next to the urn graves skeleton graves, started to appear, meaning that inhumation began to replace cremation.

Settlements in this culture were open and rather small, with the rectangular huts sometimes lowered into the ground.

110

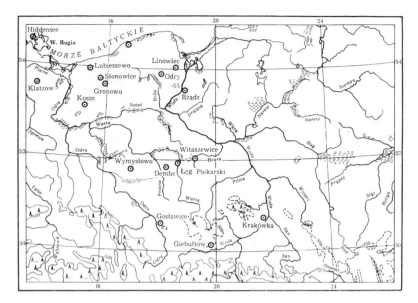

Map XI 'Princely tombs' from the 1st and 2nd centuries A.D. in Poland.

Farming with cattle-raising was the basic economy as the archaeological findings indicate. Hunting and fishing played a minor role. Iron production, especially foundry and smithery, reached a high level as well as the so called 'grey ceramics' made by using the potter's wheel.

'Princely tombs' appeared at the end of the 1st century A.D. in Silesia, southern and middle Poland, marking the development of the inter-tribal political organizations, the proto-types of the state. The richly-endowed graves, next to the poor ones and some with no endowment at all, suggest the far-reaching social differentiation of rich leaders, a middle class and perhaps slaves.

The Marcoman wars deminished trade with Roman provinces in the south, but there are traces of contacts with the Rhine Valley and the Black Sea shores down the Baltic-Black Sea route.

At the beginning of the 4th century A.D. the inhumation of the dead became a common feature. It appears that in this time the inter-tribal 'states' took more stable form.

Similar to the Lusatian culture, which left its evidence in magnificient remnants of the stronghold at Biskupin, the characteristics of the Przeworskian culture are archaeological findings of a big iron-ceramic center at Igołomia near Cracow and the iron basin at Rudki Opatowskie in the Holy Cross Mountains.

111

The Przeworskian culture ceased to exist in the first half of the 5th century A.D. because progress introduced new elements of the culture.

The Oksywian and Przeworskian cultures are two variants of the pit graves cultures on the Polish territories which in those times were the West Slavs territories. Next to it developed the Zarubiniecian and Czerniakhovian cultures in the East Slavs lands.

W.W. Chwojka, the finder of remnants of the settlement near Zarubince in Ukraine called the new culture the 'polja pogriebienij' — funeral fields culture.(7) The people cremated their dead, and ashes with burned bones and food were poured into pits. No cinerary urns were in use.

The funeral fields culture is divided into the older, Zarubiniecian, from the 2nd century B.C. to the 2nd century A.D., and the younger, Czerniakhovian, from the 2nd to the 5th century A.D.(8)

The settlers at the upper and middle Dnieper, southern Pripet and Desna created the Zarubiniecian culture. They were strongly influenced by the Przeworskian culture coming from the west.

Farming and cattle-raising became strongly supported by hunting and fishery. Implements had been made of iron; adornments of bronze. Ceramics made by hand had no decoration. The people built small open settlements, the huts with suken floors. There were some strongholds in the north. The social differentiation showed little progress over the clan communes.

The center of the Zarubiniecian culture moved to the east, crossed the Dnieper in the region of Kiev and expanded into new territory. The typical findings were at Czerniakhov near Kiev, hence the name of this culture.

The people of the Czerniakhovian culture developed ceramics on the potter's wheel and iron production to a high degree. Their bi-ritualism is evident in cemeteries. Next to pit graves with ashes of cremated bodies are skeleton graves richly endowed with ceramics, silver and bronze adornments, glass beads and occassionally with Roman coins.

W.W. Chwojka finder of the 'funeral fields' culture as well as A.A. Spicyn, his continuator, maintain (9) that the East Slavs created the Zarubiniecian and Czerniakhovian cultures and that the Czerniakhovian culture is the sequence of the Zarubiniecian culture.

Some German scholars (10) without hesitation ascribe both variants of the pit graves cultures — the Oksywian and Przeworskian — to German wandering nations, and state that the Zarubiniecian and Czerniakhovian cultures are German creations, too. This opinion is not shared by many other historian. They corrected W.W. Chwojka and A.A. Spicyn that the Czerniakhovian culture is not the continuation of the Zarubiniecian culture although the first gave the birth to the second one, because from the 2nd to the 5th centuries both cultures developed independently.(11) The East Slavs created the Zarubiniecian culture, but the Czerniakhovian culture could be ascribed to different ethnic groups with the Slavic Antes in the leading role (12).

What did cause the Oksywian, Przeworskian, Zarubieniecian and Czerniakhovian cultures to decay?

H. Łowmiański (13) maintains that the Hunnish attacks on the Antes territory and north of the Carpathians were the main cause, since the Czerniakhovian culture ceased to exist in the 5 century almost in the same time when the fall of the Przeworskian culture followed. This opinion is shared by W. Hensel (14). But G. Labuda (15) arrives at other conclusions. Since the Oksywian culture, at the lower Vistula, and the Zarubiniecian culture, at the middle Dnieper, came to a halt at the same time is impossible that they were destroyed by the Huns, because there are no signs of Hunnish invasion so deep in the north at all. The beginning of the great migrations brought changes in political, social and cultural life in Europe as well as the end of the pit graves culture.

NOTES TO CHAPTER XVII

Bibliography: Eber M., 'Südrussland', Reallexikon der Vorgeschichte, Berlin 1929; Chwojka W.W., 'Polja pogriebienij w Sriedniem Pridnieprowije', Kiiv 1901; Jażdżewski K., Z zagadnień ciągłości kulturalnej i osadniczej na ziemiach Słowiańszczyzny pierwotnej', Łódź 1958; Kozłowski L., 'Zarys pradziejów Polski południowo-wschodniej', Lwów 1939; Kucharenko J.W., 'K woprosu o proischożdienij zarubinieckiej kulturi', Moskva 1960; Ljapuszkin I.I., 'Dnieprowskoje lesostiepnoje lewobierieżje w epochu żeleza', Moskva-Leningrad 1961; Machno E.W., 'Ranniesławjanskije (zarubiniecko-korczewatowskije) pamiatki w Sriedniem Podnieprowije', Moskva 1955; Nosek S., 'Materiały do badań nad historią starożytną i wczesnośredniowieczną międzyrzecza Wisły i Bugu', Lublin 1951; Rudenko S. I., 'Kulturnaje nasielenije gornogo Ałtaja w Skifskoje wriemia'', Moskva 1953; Simonowicz E.A., 'Pamjatniki czerniachowskoj kulturi stiepnogo Podnieprowija', Moskwa 1955; Smiszko M., 'Kultury wczesnego okresu epoki cesarstwa rzymskiego w Małopolsce Wschodniej', Lwów 1932; Spicyn A.A., 'Polja pogriebalnich urn',

Moskwa 1948; Tackenburg K., 'Zu den Wanderungen der Westgermanen', Mumms 1930; Talbot Riece T., 'Les Scythes', Paris 1958; Wielowiejski J., 'Przemiany gospodarczo społeczne ludności południowej Polski w okresie późnolateńskim i rzymskim', MSt. 1960.

2. When the custom of body cremation was well established among the Slavs during the Lusatian culture there were two ways of handling ashes and burned bones of the dead: to put them into cinerary urns and deposit them in the cemetery with some small urns containing food or to pour the rest of the ashes from the funeral pile over the cinerary urn. The new culture simplified the rite. Cinerary urns disappeared. The people threw burned remnants of the body with the rest of funeral pile, food and adornments into one pit, sometimes covered with stones. Hence the name of the new culture: the culture of the pit graves.

3. The custom of body cremation was introduced in a period of the Lusatian culture. The people buried their dead mostly in crouched positions in all epochs before. Now, during the Oksywian culture they returned to the old custom. The question arises: Why did they revive the old rite? G. Labuda in 'Fragmenty dziejów Słowiańszczyzny zachodniej', p. 45, maintains possibility that it was the custom of the natives of Pomerania accepted by the Gothic invaders. This explanation could be possible for the region of the Oksywian culture, but since the skeleton graves appeared in all Middle Europe in this time the question is still open what caused the people to revive the old custom.

4. J. Kostrzewski, 'Zagadnienie ciągłości zaludnienia ziem polskich w pradziejach', Poznań 1961, p.41.

5. J. Kostrzewski, 'Ślady archeologiczne', p. 100-102.

6. G. Labuda, 'Fragmenty dziejów Słowiańszczyzny zachodniej', p. 29-30.

7. W.W. Chwojka, 'Polja pogriebienij w Sriedniem Pridnieprowije', Kiiv 1901, p. 182.

8. G. Labuda, 'Fragmenty dziejów Słowiańszczyzny zachodniej', p. 39.

9. A.A. Spicyn, 'Polja griebalnich urn' p. 53.

10. M. Ebert, 'Südrussland in Altertum', p. 352; G. Muller-Kuales, 'Die Goten', p. 1166. Some German scholars even state that the Bastarns and other German nations created the culture of the 'funeral fields', Here are: P. Reinecke, 'Aus der russischen archaologischen Literature-Graberfelder vom Ende der La Tene-Zeit und aus jungeren römischen Kaiserzeit in Government Kiev', p. 43-50; K. Tackenberg, 'Zu den Wanderungen der Wesgermanen', p. 268-295.

11. I.I. Ljapuszkin 'Dnieprowskoje lesostiepnoje lewobierieżje', p. 352.

12. H. Łowmiański, 'Antowie nad Dnieprem i Rosią', p. 55-56; B.A. Rybakóv, 'Poljanie i Siewierjanie', p. 105.

14. W. Hensel, 'Szkice wczesnodziejowe', Slava Antiqua 1952, p. 291.

15. G. Labuda, op. ci., p. 103-104.

114

CHAPTER XVIII

SLAVS AND CELTS

From all nations penetrating the Slavic cradlelands the Celts made the biggest impact upon the natives (1). The presumptive origin of those people seems to lie partially in the inhabitants of north-Alpine Europe, designated by archaeologists by reason of their burial as 'Urnfield' people. They cremated their dead and buried the ashes in urns placed in cemeteries known to archaeologists as Urnfields. They lived in villages and were bronze-using agriculturalists. Their culture is spread over many centuries from about 1300-700 B.C. (2).

The Celts were a restless, mobile people at the time of their ascendancy in Europe, having little concern for permanent settlement. The partially pastoral aspect of their economy forced them to move around. They never established a stable, large political body like the Romans, but being bright, the Celts acquired cultural achievements from the Mediterranean area and transplanted them into middle and northern Europe, rendering the natives a great service.

The Celts are creators of the Hallstatt (3) and La Tene (4) cultures.

From about 450 B.C. the Celts started expanding into the Italic peninsula and, in 390 B.C. they battled the gates of Rome. Others pushed further east, into Asia Minor, down into Macedonia. The Celtic traces in Britain are dated as early as 600 B.C., but the main influx can be detected at about 250 B.C.

The Celts were organized into tribes, but it is clear, and Caesar makes it explicit, that the Gauls knew themselves to belong to the wider group known as 'Celtae' or 'Keltoi' according to the Greek form. The Romans called them 'Galli' from which the word 'Gaul' derives, and the Greek writers knew them also as 'Galatae' of Asia Minor.

After the fatal attack on Delphi in 299 B.C. the fortunes of the Celts began to change. The Romans defeated them and established their supremacy throughout Galia Cis-Alpina in 255 B.C.

How did the Celtic influence affect the Slavic cradlelands?

There is no doubt about the Celtic presence in the Slavic territories. The question is how big their influence was. Archaeological findings indicate that it was much bigger than the scholars maintained.

In chapter IX we tried to establish that some Celtic tribes organized the Lugian Alliance in Poland along the Amber Route, the first political body known in this region in the turn of eras.

Tacitus mentions that the Celtic Boii supposedly occupied the region of Bavaria and western Czechoslovakia. Hence that land was called 'Boihaemum'. Part of the Boii left their country around 60 B.C. under pressure from German Marcomans, but the rest remained and Slavicized in later times. Because of this the Czechs, were known as 'Bohemians' and their country as 'Bohemia'.

It appears that the Celts from Czechoslovakia reached the Polish territories and left many traces.

In 1959 archaeologists discovered the Celtic shrine of great importance near Libenice, not far from Kolin in Central Bohemia (5). Another Celtic shrine was at Krusza Zamkowa near Inowrocław in the middle of Poland, on the ancient Amber Route. Excavating under supervision of Poznań University started in 1974. It is the second Celtic cult place found in Poland. The first one was at Janikowo in the same region.

According to L. Leciejewicz (6), the Celts built the ceramic centers at Nowa Cerekwia in Silesia, Wyciąż and Igołomia near Cracow, and some strongholds called 'oppida' at Poznachowice, Tyniec and Cieszyn.

Celtic words loaned to the Slavs indicate that the Celts brought to the Polish territories the better farm implements like the iron plow, scythe, handmill, iron and ceramic kilns and the potter's wheel.

The Slavs learned from the Celts how to produce iron from bog iron ore and to make the iron implements.

The Celtic society was clearly differentiated, in its peak epoch, with aristocracy composed of leaders, the Druids as priests and the rest as common people. There are many burial mounds built between the 6th and 5th centuries B.C. at the Upper Danube and Rhine and in Czechoslovakia. Scholars call it the 'princely tombs' in which the Celts buried their leaders on wagons. This means the burial rite was changed, and inhumation of the aristocracy at least began to replace cremation.

There are several mounds around Cracow and Przemyśl in Poland, among them the best known are the 'Kopiec Krakusa' — Krakus Mound and the 'Kopiec Wandy' — Wanda Mound. According to the legends, the people raised those mounds around the 7th century A.D.

to commemorate their heros 'Krakus', or 'Krak', who supposedly killed the dragon, and his daughter Wanda, who committed suicide by drowning herself in the Vistula to save her country from German bondage.

Prof. Janusz Kotlarczyk contradicted this legendary view. Lecturing at the Polish Academy of Science in Cracow in 1974, Kotlarczyk concluded that the Celts, not the Slavs, raised the mounds in Poland, which served the Druids as astronomic observatories primarily, and as places of religious observances secondly.

The Krakus Mound and the Wanda Mound constitute a pair with the Krakus Mound being bigger. The distance between them is 28,000 ft. If someone stands on the top of the Krakus Mound on May the 1st at 4:18 A.M., he sees the rising sun behind the top of the Wanda Mound.

Two mounds at the city of Przemył play the same role but on another day of the year. Like the mounds at Cracow one is bigger and the distance between them is also 28,000 ft. If someone stands on the top of the bigger mound on November the 1st in the morning, he sees the rising sun from behind the smaller mound.

There were four main feasts in the Celtic year. The year began on what is now the first of November with the feast of 'Samain'. Three months later on the 1st of February was 'Imbolc' followed by the feast of 'Beltine' on the first of May. The fourth feast was that of 'Lugnasad' on the first of August. Of these four, 'Samain' and 'Beltine' were the more important and in the myths many important events took place on those days. (7)

Being more pastoral than agricultural, the Celts marked their Calendar Year by putting their cattle to pasture on the first of May and bringing them back on the first of November. The Celtic temple in Libenice, Czechoslovakia, was also oriented on those days as the findings indicate.

Prof. Kotlarczyk thinks that even in the 7th or 8th centuries A.D. the Slavs were not on such a level to build elaborated mounds, but the Celts were some centuries before when they left mounds and temples in Bavaria and Czechoslovakia. There is no doubt that the Celts occupied almost entirely the region of southern and western Poland in the turn of eras.

Two mounds at Cracow have their names: the bigger (48 ft.) is the Krakus Mound; the smaller (39 ft.), the Wanda Mound. Prof. Kotlarczyk tries to explain these names with the help of Celtics. In his interpretation the name 'Wanda' might derive from the Celtic word 'Ven'-relative and 'Don' — the name of goddess. From those two words might derive the none-Slavic name 'Wanda'. 'Ven-Don' could have meant the 'relative, helping goddess'. Since animal and human sacrifices were of common practice among the Celts, the priestess with the same name as the goddess (Ven-Don) might have been sacrificed by drowning in the Vistula every year to draw away all mishaps from the country.

Prof. Kotlarczyk is not certain about the name of the bigger mound although he maintains that the legend of a hero slaying a dragon is typical for the Celts.

It is possible to explain the name 'Krakus' or 'Krak' with the help of Celtics. On the top of the bigger mound was a sacred circle marked with stones. The Druids stood inside and at dawn of the first of May watched the sun rising behind the Wanda Mound to give the signal to start the big festivities of the year. The circle in Celtic was 'Krk' or 'Kirk'. Hence, there is not much change in transformation 'Krk' to 'Krak' or 'Krakus'.

What did happen to the Celts in this region of Europe? The common belief is that they had been chased from Czechoslovakia by the German Marcomans. Rather it appears they remained and Slavicized since their Celtic name 'Bohemia' lasted down through the centuries to describe the Slavic Czechs.

The same event might have occured on the Polish territories. The Celts disappeared not by being chased or destroyed but Slavicized. Even today the people around Cracow practice the Celtic rites like the 'Siuda-Baba' and others. (8) Assuming the shifting population, it is impossible to accept that the Celtic customs would endure for such a long time. It could be that the names of many Polish cities are of Celtic origin. (9)

Fig. 31. The Krakus Mound at Cracow.

118

NOTES TO CHAPTER XVIII

1. **Bibliography:** Filip J. 'Keltove ve stredni Europe',, Praha 1956; Hoppe W., 'Kelten', München 1958; Jahn M., 'Die Kelten in Schlesien', Leipzig 1931; Kendrick T. D., 'The Druids', London 1927; Kostrzewski J., 'Pradzieje Polski', Poznań 1949; Kossack G., 'Studien zum Symbolgut der Urnenfelder und Hallstattzeit Mitteleuropas', Berlin 1954; Leeds E.T., 'Celtic ornament', Oxford 1933; Łowmiański H., 'Początki Polski', Warszawa 1963; McCulloch J.A., 'The Religion of the Ancient Celts', Edinburgh 1911; Moreau J., 'Die Welt der Kelten', Stuttgart 1958; Piggott S., 'Barbarian Europe', Edinburgh 1965; Powell T.G.E., 'The Celts', London 1958; Rosen-Przeworska J., 'Zabytki celtyckie na ziemiach polskich', 1948; and, 'Problem pobytu Celtów w Małopolsce', 1957; Rybova A., and Suedsky, 'Libenice', Prague 1962; de Vries J., 'La Religion des Celtes', Paris 1963; Żaki M., 'Z badań nad kulturą celtycką w Małopolsce', 1955.

2. A. Ross, 'Pagan Celtic Britain', New York 1967, p. 9-10.

3. The Hallstatt culture is traditionally known as the iron-using culture. The graves which gave their name to this phase were found at Hallstatt in the Salzkammergut in Austria and were excavated in the last century. It lasted between 700 and 500 B.C. The changes in custom were manifold and fundamental. The burial rite has changed, inhumation beginning to replace cremation. The weapons are elaborate, iron now appearing as well as bronze.

4. The Hallstatt culture is supposedly Celtic, but there is no question concerning the La Tene culture. This second is typically Celtic as the ritual deposit of metalwork in the lake at La Tene on Lake Neuchatel in Switzerland indicate. It combines new and exciting features, inspired by Greek and Etruscan designs.

5. A. Ross, 'Pagan Celtic Britain', New York 1967, p. 40-41.

6. L. Leciejewicz, 'Mały słownik kultury dawnych Słowian', Warszawa 1972, p. 61.

7. Larousse Encyclopedia of Mythology, London 1966, p. 243-244.

8. The 'Siuda-Baba' is the boy maskarading the woman with the face besmeared with soot and trying to smear anyone on his road. Another Celtic ritual is carrying the little cart around the village with the statue of Christ now (Christianized rite) on it. The custom of throwing rolls from the top of the Krakus Mound in springtime festivities had been practiced even in the second half of the 19th century.

9. There are cities with the ending 'lin' — Lublin and Dęblin in Poland; Berlin in Germany; and Dublin in Ireland. There is the city of Cieszyn (Tessin pronounced by the Germans and Czechs) in Poland and Tessin in Switzerland. Is it possible that these cities are of Celtic origin?

CHAPTER XIX

SLAVS AND GOTHS

The Roman source notices that the Goths (1) appeared in wars for the first time at the lower Danube 248-251 A.D. They seized the Greek city of Philippopolis and Olbia, Tyras and other cities at the mouth of the Danube and Dniester in later times (2). They were a German nation, the cousins of those Germans in the west whom the Romans fought since the beginning of our era. The writers noticed that the West Germans left their cradlelands in Scandinavia, marched up the river Rhine and settled at the upper Danube using their settlements as a base against the Roman border cities.

How did the Germans appear in the eastern part of the Roman Empire? What route did they follow?

No written records give account of this event. It appears that the Germans followed the famous Baltic Sea-Vistula-Dniester-Black Sea route as the archaeological findings indicated (3). They left Gotland, their homeland in middle Sweden, and traveled through Kattegat and Sund arriving by sea at the mouth of the Vistula in the 2nd century B.C. These small groups were militarily oriented and some historians (4) consider them as military units.

Arriving at new lands, the Germans looked for a proper place to settle down. Armed men marched in front, shielding the way for women and children who carried their meagre possessions. They were too weak to confront the natives. Avoiding the struggle, they settled deep in forests. Women, children and old folks stayed at home and farmed, and young men were busy with booty expeditions.

Since there were no signs of damage to the native villages in the vicinity, it could be accepted that the Gothic incomers used tricks of the fox, robbing settlers who lived farther away rather than neighbors.

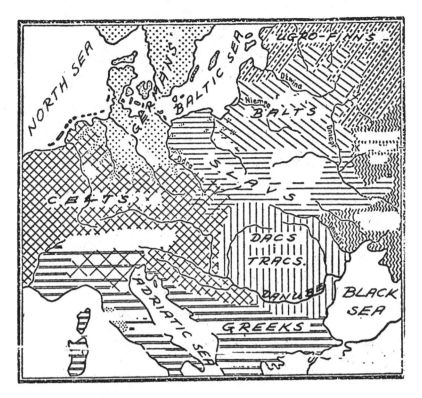

Map XII. European nations in the 1st century A.D., after S. Trawkowski.

The archaeological findings reveal the territory infiltrated by the Goths. They settled first near the lower Vistula and with time moved farther west to the Parsęta River and south to the Noteć River. Their cousins, the Gepids, who arrived later to the Polish territories, settled east of the lower Vistula (5).

A typical Gothic settlement was at Węsiory, county Kartuzy (6). It was completely isolated from the neighboring native settlements with some 250 Goths dwelling there. Burial places were arranged in the 'juridical circle' with the most important in the center, similar to many found in Scandinavia. Here the judge, sitting on the stone marking the grave of one powerful forebearer, pronounced sentences upon criminals.

Gothic settlers at Węsiory represented lower levels of economy compared to the natives. They were cattle-raisers and farmers using primitive techniques of fire-farming.

It is possible that the small groups of Gothic incomers lived in

121

isolated settlements at the beginning, but when their number grew, they subordinated the native Veneti without destroying them. The burial places, made long before the Germans arrived were continously in use during the Gothic stay at the Vistula and after they left these territories (7).

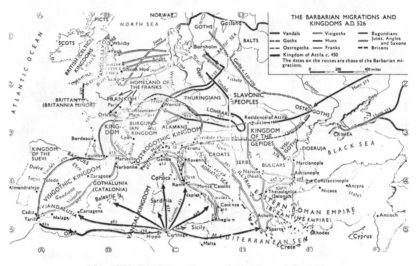

Map XIII. The Migrations and kingdoms A.D. 526.

The coexistence between the natives and incomers produced a new type of culture. The Goths and Gepids adopted Veneti ceramics like vases and bowls as well as burial procedures not practiced in Scandinavia. Next to 'skeleton' graves are graves with cremated bodies which means people of two rites were buried there. Weapons were no longer placed in graves. Adornments of iron, numerous in former epoch, had been replaced by adornments of bronze, silver and gold.

In the first half of the 3rd century, the Goths and Gepids suddenly vanished from this territory. Since they appeared almost simultaneously at the lower Danube, they must have moved. Their spies in the south must have observed that there were better conditions for settling at the Roman borders in the south-east. So, the Goths and Gepids, with a quick march, left the Polish territories along the Baltic-Black Sea route.

122

The Goths first subjugated the Scytho-Sarmatian nations dwelling at the Roman borders in the east, then from 248 to 332 harassed the north-eastern territories of the Roman Empire. Suffering heavy losses, they drew volunteers from Scandinavia (8). Defeated by the Emperor Constantine II in 332, the Goths turned against their neighbors to the north and east. They created a big but short-lived kingdom with Hermanric as their ruler (9). At this time the Goths came in touch with the Slavs again. Jordanes (10) records: "Quos constat morte Hermanrici regis sui, decessione a Vesegothis divisos Hunnorum subdicios dicioni, in eadem patria remorasse, Vinitharis tamen Amalo principatu sui insignia retinente. Qui avi Vultulfi virtute imitans, quamvis Hermanrici felicitate inferior, tamen aegre ferens Hunnorum imperio subiacere, paululum se subtrahens ab illis suaque dum nititur ostendere virtute, in Antorum fines movit procinctum, eosque dum agreditur prima congressione superatus, deinde fortiter egit regemque eorum Boz nomine cum filiis suis et LXX primatibus in exemplum terroris adfixit, ut dediticit metum cadavere pendentium geminaret".

This historic event happened in 367. Vithimir, the war leader of the Ostrogoths, warred with the Slavic Antes (11) under King Hermanric. He must have been victorious because he is better known to historians as Vinithar, the conqueror of the Slavs (12)

The fortunes of the Ostrogothic kingdom changed when the Huns appeared. Hermanric suffered a painful defeat and committed suicide. Vinithar, his successor, took over but he had been forced to accept the Hunnish supremacy. It appears that the Antes tried to profit from the Ostrogoth's defeat and rebelled against them. Thus, Vinithar crashed the rebellion and crucified their leader Boz with his sons and 70 lieutenants.

The Huns felt endangered by this victory. Not wanting the Ostrogoths to regain power, they defeated them and Vinithar lost his life in the battle.

This episode indicates that the Goths settling at the Black Sea were in touch with the East Slavic Antes only. Archaeological findings are in accord with this opinion.

The last contact between the Slavs and Goths took place, when the remnants of the Goths returned to their old homeland in Scandinavia. They used the Baltic-Black Sea route again.

Being in touch with the Slavs for many centuries, the Goths and other German nations must have left some traces in the language.

Linguists found 26 Gothic words in the Slavic languages (13):

123

a) names of buildings: 'chlew' — piggery; 'chyz' — hut; 'tyn' — fence;

b) names of livestock: 'nuto' and 'skot' — cattle; 'osioł' — ass; 'wielbłąd' — camel;

c) names of food articles: 'luk' — chive; 'chleb' — bread; 'lek' — medicine;

d) names of implements: 'nabozez' — borer; 'stklo' — glass; 'bljudo' — meal; 'kotel' — kettle;

e) names of arms: 'selm' — helmet; 'plk' — regiment;

f) names of authority; 'knędź' — prince; 'cesar' — emperor;

g) names of trade: 'kupiti' — to buy; 'kusiti' — to taste; 'lichwa' — usury; 'lst' — sly; 'chąsa' — theft;

h) adjectives: 'chodog' — skill; 'tjud' — alien;

i) other names: 'Dunaj' — Danube; 'Volch' — Roman; 'shelm' — hill.

There are some linguists who believe that these words had been loaned from Gothic in three different epochs (14), when the Goths stayed at the Vistula (150 B.C.-200 A.D.); when they settled at the Black Sea (200-400 A.D.) and when they returned to Balkan (400-600 A.D.). This is especially true of words like 'ass' or 'camel' because those animals are unknown in northern Europe.

How many words did the Goths borrow from Slavonic? It is difficult to tell since the Gothic vocabulary is small. One word, 'plinsjan' (plęsati in Slavonic) — gambol, and dance is for sure (15). It appears that the Goths accepted some kind of Slavic dance unknown to them.

NOTES TO CHAPTER XIX

1. **Bibliography:** Cross S. H., 'Gothic Loanwords in the Vocabulary', Harvard Studies 1934; and 'Slavic Civilization through the Ages', Cambridge, Mass. 1948; Jażdżewski K., 'Atlas pradziejów Słowian', Łódź 1946; Kiparsky V., 'Die gemeinslawischen Lehnworter aus dem Germanischen', Helsinki 1934; Kmieciński J., 'Niektóre zagadnienia wędrówki Gotów w świetle dotychczasowych badań oraz w świetle wykopalisk w Węsiorach, pow. kartuskim', Zeszyty Naukowe Uniwersytetu Łódzkiego 1958; and 'Zagadnienie tzw. kultury gockogepidzkiej na Pomorzu Wschodnim w okresie wczesnorzymskim', Łódź 1962; Kostrzewski J., 'Ślady archeologiczne pobytu drużyn germańskich w Polsce w pierwszej połowie I stulecia naszej ery', Przegląd Zachodni 1951; Labuda G., 'Źródła skandynawskie i anglosaskie do dziejów Słowiańszczyzny', Warszawa 1961; Lehr-Spławiński T., 'Elementy obce w językach słowiańskich' 1946; Moravcsik G., 'Die byzantinischen Quellen der Geschicte der Turkvőlker', Berlin 1958; Oxenstierna E., 'Die Urheimat der Goten', Leipzig 1948; Schindler R., 'die Besiedlungsgeschichte der Goten und Gepiden in unteren Wiechselraum', Leipzig 1940 Taszycki W., 'Dotychczasowy stan badań nad

pobytem drużyn germańskich na ziemiach polskich w świetle toponomastyki', Przegląd Zachodni 1951; Vasillev A., 'The Goths in the Crimea', Cambridge, Mass. 1936.

2. L. Schmidt, 'Die Ostgermanen', p. 209-211.

3. K. Tymieniecki, 'Droga Gotów na południe', Archeologia 1952, p. 112-122, maintains that the Germans did not follow the Vistula-Dniester route to the Black Sea but the Elbe-Danube route, the idea not accepted by many historians.

4. J. Kostrzewski, W. Taszycki and others.

5. G. Labuda, 'Fragmenty dziejów Słowiańszczyzny zachodniej', Poznań 1974, p. 28.

6. The archaeological findings at Węsiory described J. Kmieciński in his book, 'Niektóre zagadnienia wędrówki Gotów w świetle dotychczasowych badań oraz w świetle wykopalisk w Węsiorach'.

7. J. Kostrzewski, 'Zagadnienie ciągłości zaludnienia ziem polskich w pradziejach', Poznań 1961, p. 40.

8. The Goths had good contacts with their former homeland Scandinavia. The information and help were shipped down the throughfare Baltic Sea-Vistula-Dniester-Black Sea. The best example is the runic inscription in Rok, Scandinavia, praising Theodoric the Great, king of Goths, who ruled in the 8th century (G. Labuda, 'Fragmenty dziejów Słowiańszczyzny zachodniej', p. 81).

9. Ammianni Marcellini, 'Rerum gestarum' lib. XXXI, ed. C.U. Clark, p. 562-563.

10. Jordanes, 'Gettica', p. 48.

11. Jordanes left no doubt that the Antes were of Slavic origin, when he wrote: 'ab una stirpe exorti, tria nomina ediderunt, id est Veneti, Antes, Sclaveni' (although they derive from one nation, now they are known under three names, the Veneti, Antes and Sclaveni). The Veneti were the West Slavs, the Antes the East Slavs and the Sclaveni, the South or Balkan Slavs.

12. According to J. Marquart, 'Osteuropaische and ostasiatische Streifzuge' p. 375, the word 'Vinithar' is by-name and means 'Vinita-harjis' — the conqueror of the Viniti (Veneti).

13. G. Labuda, 'Fragmenty dziejów Słowiańszczyzny zachodniej', p. 35.

14. J. Kuryłowicz, 'Związki słowiańsko-germańskie', p. 199; M. Rudnicki, 'Prasłowiańszczyzna', p. 76-77.

15. M. Rudnicki, op. cit., p. 81, maintains that the Goths loaned more words from Slavonic, like 'płat' — patch; 'hantag', 'hundags' — tidy; 'skattaz', 'skott' — cattle; and 'sile-bra' — silver.

CHAPTER XX

SLAVS AND HUNS

There is one short notice about the Slavic Hunnish relationship (1) recorded by Ammianus Marcelinus (2) and Jordanes(3). It happened at the beginning of the Hunnish expansion about Vinitharius and Booz described in the chapter: Slavs and Goths. Judging by this short notice there was a rather friendly relationship between the Slavic Antes and Huns.

Johannes Peisker, the German historian (4) arrived at a quite different conclusion. He took three Slavic words: 'twaróg' — curd; 'żupan' — high official; and 'smard' — peasant, and believing that all those words are of Hunnish origin, created the most ridiculous theory that the Slavs were slaves from time immemorial. They served the Germans as well as the Huns, who were 'żupans' — lords to them. The Hunnish lords called their Slavic serfs the 'smards' — stinking peasants, who were able to learn from the Huns how to make curd only. Hence the name Slav derives from the word 'slave' which indicates that the Slavic nations are good as slaves and nothing else.

Peisker's mad theory met with warm response in Germany. As a result, in a short time the Kaiser and Hitler, trying to make slaves of Slavs, plunged the world in two bloody wars.

As a matter of fact the Huns never subjugated the Slavs as they did with the German nations at the Black Sea.

The centers of the Hunnish Empire were between the Volga and the Dnieper Rivers and at the middle Danube, as the archaeological findings indicate (5). The Huns as Nomads and pastoral people preferred the steppe territories in the Ukraine and Hungary with their warmer climates and abundant grass and water. They found it difficult to live even in the border area between the steppe and wooded regions (6). The Slavs occupied the forested marshlands

126

impenetrable for the Huns. Only the Antes lived in the wooded-steppe region, hence they were in touch with the Hunnish Empire.

The Huns were not the only Turkish nation keeping close to the steppes of south-east Europe. So did their cousins: the Avars, Pechenges and Tartars. The Magyars, like the Huns, made many invasions deep into Germany, but they did not wish to settle there, but rather on the warm, grassy plains of Hungary.

It is possible that the Huns made some sporadic passes on a small scale into the Polish territories to capture slaves, especialy skilled ones like potters and iron specialists. Because of that the Igołomia tragedy occurred, but they never mastered all of Slavdom. After all, the Slavs were not a rich nation with big spoils.

Linguists present an interesting contradiction to Peisker's theory. Peisker's words supposedly loaned from the Hunnish language apeared to be Slavonic (7).

There are two words which might have been loaned by the Huns. Priskos (8) mentions that when he was in Pannonia (Hungary) the Huns entertained him with 'medos', an alcoholic beverage of the most prominent people and with 'kamon' an inferior drink, made from barley. There is no doubt that 'medos' is the favored Slavic 'miód' — alcoholic honey which the Huns learned to make from the Slavic Antes, or what is more probable, from the Goths, who in turn learned the recipe from the Slavs. The other drink 'kamon' must have been of local origin because its name derives from Illyric.

Jordanes (9) describing Attila's funeral mentions that the Huns made a big funeral repast on the grave of their great war leader which they call the 'strawa'. The word is Slavonic in sounding and meaning. It is questionable that the Huns loaned it of Slavonic with the funeral rite as well, or that Jordanes used it by mistake. If the first happening is possible, then the relationship between the Huns and Slavs must have been close and friendly, because one nation accepts the funeral rite from another when they are on very friendly terms only. It is possible that Jordanes, describing Attila's burial hundred years after it happened, could have mistaken the Hunnish word for funeral repast with the Slavic 'strawa' which he knew better.

Archaeology gives strong evidence how far the Hunnish influence went. According to J. Warner (10) the Hunnish relics are to be found from Tien-shan in Asia to the Rhone in Europe. These include graves richly endowed with the Hunnish silver and gold adornments and with deformed skulls.

The custom of skull deformation is historically confirmed as being practiced by the Huns. There are centers in Europe where those skulls appear: between the Volga, lower Don and Crimea; at the middle Danube; near Prague in Czechoslovakia; and at the upper Rhine. All those skulls belonged to the people who lived in the 5th century.

The first two centers pose no problems. They are on the territories settled by the Huns. The other two centers puzzle the scholars. There were no Hunnish settlements at Prague or the upper Rhine. The only explanation is that the Huns after subjugating the German Gepids and Burgunds at the Black Sea imposed upon them the custom of deforming skulls. Escaping from the Hunnish bondage those nations settled for the time being at the outskirts of Attila's Empire and perpetuated the custom learned from their oppressors (11).

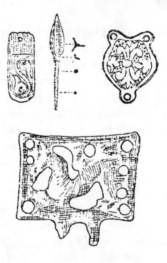

Fig. 32. The Hunnish objects from the 'princely grave' at Jakuszowice, after N. Aberg.

There are only two 'princely graves' with Hunnish adornments and one with deformed skulls on Polish territories. One is at Jakuszowice near Cracow and is known as a 'male' grave, the other, at Jędrzychowice in Lower Silesia is a 'female' grave. The grave with deformed skulls is at Przemęczany (12).

J. Werner (13) and H. Łowmiański (14) maintain the 'princely graves' with Hunnish and Gothic adornments belonged to the Hunnish war-leaders, perhaps of Gothic origin, who established the camps on the Polish territories to get captives.

G. Labuda (15) points out another possibility. Since one grave is situated on the route from Hungary through the Moravian Gate to the Baltic, and the second on another route from Hungary through the Carpathian passes to the Baltic, the Goths returning to Scandinavia from the south might have sold adornments they brought from the south to the Slavic leaders in Poland. When those leaders died, their relatives put the adornments into graves. After all, there are no Hunnish cemeteries in Poland, only three lonely graves.

NOTES TO CHAPTER XX

1. **Bibliography:** Alfoldli A., 'Funde aus Hunnerzeit und ihre etnische Sonderung', Archaeologia Hungarica 1932; Altheim F., 'Geschichte der Hunnen', Berlin 1962; Czekanowski J., 'Wstęp do historii Słowian', Poznań 1957; Dvornik F., 'The Making of Central and Eastern Europe', London 1949; Feist S., 'Etymologisches Wörterbuch der gotischen Sprache', Halle 1920; Kuzniecow W.A., 'Alanskie plemiena siewiernogo Kawkaza', Moskva 1962; Łowiański H., 'Zagadnienie roli Normanów w genezie państw słowiańskich', Warszawa 1957; Thompson E.A., 'A history of Attila and the Huns', Oxford 1948.
2. Ammiani Marcellini, 'Rerum gestarum', lib. XXXI, ed. C.U. Clark, p. 562-563.
3. Jordanes, 'Gettica', p. 121.
4. J. Peisker, 'Die älteren Beziehungen der Slawen zu Turkotataren und Germanen und ihre sozialgeschichtliche Bedeutung', Stuttgart 1905.
5. J. Werner, 'Beiträge zur Archaologie des Attila-Reiches', München 1956.
6. J. Kniezsa, 'Ungarns Völkerschaften in the XI Jahrhundert', 1938, p. 253.
7. The word 'żupan' — lord appears also in West Slavonic at the Elbe in Germany in territory which has never been invaded by the Huns or other Turkish nations. It means it was in use in Slavonic before the Great Migration and before the Huns made their spectacular appearance in Europe. Al. Bruckner in 'Kwartalnik Historyczny', 1908, p. 694-695, maintains that the word 'twaróg' — curd is of Slavic origin loaned by the Turks and not vice-versa.
8. M. Plezia, 'Greckie i łacińskie źródła', p. 53.
9. Jordanes, 'Gettica', p. 124, writes: postquam talibus lamentatis est defletus, stravam super tumulum eius quam appellant ipsi ingenti commessatione concelebrant".
10. J. Werner, op. cit., P. 4.
11. J. Werner, op. cit., p. 15-18.
12. J. Kostrzewski, 'Pradzieje Polski', p. 222.
13. J. Werner, op. cit., p. 88, 123.
14. H. Łowmiański, 'Ze studiów nad okresem wędrówki ludów', p. 25-26.
15. G. Labuda, 'Fragmenty dziejów Słowiańszczyzny zachodniej', p. 92-93.

CHAPTER XXI

SLAVS AND AVARS

Europe could hardly take a breath after the bloody Hunnish wars when new Turkish nomads appeared at her gates. They were the Avars (1). They crossed the steppes somewhere between the Black and Asov seas in 558 A.D.

Quite contrary to the stocky, small statured Huns the Avars were tall, strong and well built. Thus, in the language of the West Slavs they were called 'obrzyns' — giants (2). Perhaps it was because of their physical fitness that the Avars made themselves famous by their bravery among the Turkish invaders.

After arriving in Europe a small group of Avars started to subdue the other Turkish nations around the Caucasus who were making booty expeditions on the Byzantine Empire from the Black Sea zone.

The Avars sent their ambassadors to Constantinople promising to defend the Empire's border for tribute. Their offer was accepted (3).

Now the Avars turned against the Slavic Antes. Their leader Medzamir went to the Avars camp for negotiation. When he arrived with his aides the Avars killed him anticipating that the death of a leader would strike terror among his people. And they were right. The death of Medzamir was disastrous. The Avars attacked the Antes at the river Dnieper, where Siever is today, and organized their first state, called the khaganat (4).

In 562 the Avars attacked the German Gepids and took possession of their holdings at the river Tissa. Here they formed their second khaganat.

Since the shortest way from the first to the second khaganat was through Volhynia and Podolia, they invaded those regions (5), defeated the Slavic Dulebs and treated them harshly (6). Through the lands belonging to the Dulebs, the Ulitches and the East Croats the

Avars made their way from the eastern to the southern khaganat and used it from 567 to 670 A.D.

Invading Europe the Huns met Iranian nomads and German nations and they captured them. They did not need the help of the Slavs. Allied Huns and Germans became a large group and could undertake booty expeditions against the Roman Empire.

Avars found a different situation. When they arrived in Europe they met Gepids and Longobards only. They could not build any power with the help of these two nations. Thus, they reached for the Slavic resources.

The moment was a proper one. Slavic expansion to the west and south started about 50 years before the Avars invasion. The Serbs from Northern Poland moved to the river Elbe; Croats and Obodrits crossed the Carpathian and Sudetic Mountains; Sclavens and Antes had an epoch of struggle with the Byzantine Empire behind them.

As was the case with the other plundering nations, so too the Avars were lured by the riches of Byzantine cities, but they had no chance during the reign of Justinian I. The Empire had ended the Greek war and was strong, rich and mighty again.

Not having a chance the Avars directed their attention to the Gaulish-Frankish state of Merovings.

They had two routes to the West: the Hunnish one along the Danube and north of the Carpathians. They chose the second one because the German Gepids and Longobards had their habitats at the Danube. The Avars did not want to weaken themselves by fighting along the route.

Before his death the Frankish ruler Chlothar divided his state among four sons. Chorivert got Paris with the surrounding territories; Guntram, Orlean; Chilparic, Soissons; and Sigibert, Reims. According to the father's will the brothers should help each other. As it usually happens, this proved quite contrary.

When Sigibert moved against the Avars Chilparic attacked Reims and took the possessions of his brother.

Fortunately, Sigibert had friends among the Serbs at the river Warta. They informed him about the plans of the Avar invasion, and perhaps gave advice on fighting invaders.

All the Turkish nations used the same war tactics. They tried to penetrate the enemy's territory as deeply as possible, surprise them, confuse them and cause a panic. This manouvre the Tartars used with complete success against Kiev in 1238 and Poland 1241.

The Avars expected Sigibert to form his army somewhere near the eastern borders of his kingdom. They were mistaken. Sigibert used

Turkish tactics. He crossed the river Elbe with his army and rushed to the east. Thus, he surprised the Avars and defeated them in 562 (7).

The defeat did not discourage the Avars. Bayan, their khagan (ruler), under whom they suffered a setback headed the second booty expedition in 566-567.

The Serbs again warned Sigibert about the invasion. The Frankish king prepared his army for confrontation but the enemy was stronger in number. Sigibert suffered a defeat.

But he managed to negotiate peace with Bayan. After giving him some gifts, Bayan withdrew his Avars behind the Elbe.

The Avars settled at the Danube and began to make booty expeditions against the Byzantine Empire. In 628 they even sieged Constantinople.

The Avars had the same approach to the Slavic nations as the Huns had had to the German ones. They oppressed some of them and they led others in booty expeditions sharing the spoils with them.

Slavic units were not numerous. The Avars saved themselves by pushing the Slavs into the battles first. Probably, they did not trust the Slavs (8).

Historians noticed the large Slavic groups marching with the Avars who, after reaching new territories, started to build settlements. It means they looked for lands under cultivation more than for spoils.

The Avars marched twice through Southern Poland to meet the Franks. They left no trace of fights with the Slavs. Probably, hurrying west they avoided confrontation which might have weakened them and came to some kind of understanding with the Slavs.

That could explain a message of Simokattes (9) who in describing the times of the Byzantinian Emperor Maurice (582-602) writes: "Khagan of Avars sent his envoys as far as there (to Pomerania in Poland) to recruit men for his army, presenting splendid gifts to the tribal (Slavic) chiefs. They accepted gifts but refused to support him militarily saying they were afraid of the big distance to march (from Pomerania to Constantinople)".

Did Avars settle in Polish territories?

The Slavs called Avars 'Obry' or 'Obrzyni'. There are some rivers and places in Northern Poland whose name have the root 'obr'. Thus, there is a river 'Obra', 'Obrzyca', village 'Obrowo' and 'Obrzysko' etc. But these names are not derived from the Avars, but from Old Slavonic word 'obr' which means 'big', 'huge', 'great'. Hence the river Obra is a Big River and Obrowo is a Big Village (10).

Fig. 32. Avaric items found in West Slavs territories.

It is worth mentioning that the Slavic languages accepted the word 'żupan' which havve been of Avaric origin. It describes an administrator of a 'żupa' — district. Avaric żupans made history by unscrupulously exploiting the Slavic people.

The Avars were not in Northern Poiand. Their twofold passage through Southern Poland and Silesia to the west was short as archaeological findings indicate. Avaric remnants in Hungary total 77%, in Romania 21.7% and in Poland only 1.3%.

The Kesthelyan culture is connected with the Avars (11). It was developed by mixing a culture of nomadic Avars with the culture of Slavic people settled on the Hungarian Plains and in the Eastern Alps region. Its duration was from the second half of the 7th century to the beginning of the 9th century A.D. The name is derived from the cemetry discovered near Keszthely at Lake Balaton.

The Slavic elements in this culture consist of graves of cremation, ceramics, implements of agriculture and weaving and of women's adornments. The Avars elements include sketetal graves of horse raiders buried with horses, swords, arrows and sliver and bronze adornments.

NOTES TO CHAPTER XXI

1. **Bibliography:** Gregorii ep. Turon, 'Historia Francorum'; Hoffmann H., 'Untersuchungen zur Karolingischen Annalistik', Bonn 1958; Kollautz N.J., 'Die Awaren', Saeculum 1954; Klebel E., 'Longobarden, Bojuwaren, Slawen'. Wien 1939; Laszló G., 'Etudes archaologiques sur l'histoire de la societe des Avars', Budapest 1955; Merpert N.J., 'Avary v Vostocnoj Evrope', Moskwa 1958; Mikkola J.J., 'Samb und sein Reich', ASPhil. 1929; Nagy T. 'Studia Avarica', Budapest 1948; Pray G., 'Annales veteres Hunnorum, Avarorum at Hungarorum', Vindobona 1761; Szymański W., 'Zabytki awarskie na terenie Polski', PArch. 1950; Zasterova B., 'Avari a Slovane', VPSlov. 1958.
2. A Brückner, 'Słownik etymologiczny języka polskiego', p. 878.
3. H. Łowmiański, 'Początki Polski', Vol. II, p. 342-343.
4. Gy. Moravcsik, 'Byzantinoturcica', Berlin 1958, Vol. I, p. 72-76.
5. The existence of two khagants and the route between them from 567 to 670 A.D. is more strongly confirmed by archaeological findings than historical records, according to Gy. Laszló, 'Etudes archaologiques sur l'histoire de la societe des Avars', Budapest 1955, p. 252-256; and N. Fettich, 'Archaologische Studien zur Geschichte der spathunnischen Metallkunst', AHung. 1951, p. 109-117.
6. Nestor a Russian monk (10556-1114) in his 'Letopis' — chronicle writes about the Avars oppressing the Dulebs women as follows: "The same Obras (Avars) fought with Slavs and defeated the Dulebs who were Slavs and tortured Dulebs women. When an Avar wanted to ride he did not put a horse or ox to his cart but ordered three, four or five women to carry him". This oppression is confirmed by Fredegar, the Frankish chronicler, at the beginning of the 7th century A.D.: "Chuni (Avars) acmandum annis singulis in Esclavos veniebant, uxores Sclavorum et filias eorum strato sumebant".
7. H. Łowiański, op. cit., Vol. 11, p. 375-379.
8. Fredegar lib. IV, cap. 48: "Chuni (Avars) pro castra adunatum illorum stabant exercitum, Winidi (Slavs) vero pugnabant; si ad vincendum prevalebant, tunc Chuni predas capiendum adgrediebant".
9. 'Theophylacti Simocattae Historiae', p. 385-387.
10. H. Łowmiański, op. cit., Vol. II, p. 385-387.
11. D. Csallany, 'Archaologische Denkmäler der Awarenzeit in Mitteleuropa', Budapest 1956, p. 230-232.

CHAPTER XXII

HEROIC EPOCH

Hunnish wars destroyed a cordon of German nations camping at the northern border of the Roman Empire. Although at Nedao the Huns suffered a decisive defeat, the Germans paid their price, too. They came out considerably weakened.

The Moravian Gate in the west and the Iron Gate in the east with all the passes through the Carpathian Mountains stood open.

The Ancient Slavs took advantage. They started to migrate south (1).

As Jordanes recorded, a group of Slavs whom he called the Veneti, moved through the Moravian Gate, and the Sclaveni, also called Sclavini, went through the Iron Gate.

He did not notice an earlier group who migrated south through the Carpathian passes. They were the Dulebs. They must have been less numerous and played no significant role since the famous Byzantinian chronicler did not spot them.

Two large Slavic groups appeared at the Roman Empire borders in the east: Sclavens and Antes.

Antes were not Slavs at the beginning. It was a Caucasian nation, who after establishing a close relationship with the Slavs, became Slavicized but retained their old name (2).

Having crossed the Carpathian passes, the Sclavens occupied the territories in the Danube Delta to the rivers Dniester and Vistula in the north. The Antes placed themselves between the rivers Tissa and Dnieper (3). The Slavic front was rather wide at thee Byzantinian borders.

Why did the Sclavens and the Antes settle down? Why did they not march to the gates of Constantinople? After all, they were militarily trained by the experienced Goths.

Probably, the Slavic nature played some role, here. Slavs arrived to find the soil was better than they had had before, empty and with a milder climate. Being agriculturists they could not resist the temptation to settle down and to farm.

But the confrontation followed.

How could it happen?

Probably, the Byzantinians did not like the new settlers at the northern borders and started warfare to drive them away.

Dating from the turn of the 6th century A.D., is a military treatise written by an anonymous Byzantinian author. It is a kind of guide book for war leaders and describes how to plan easy attacks on Slavic settlements to capture spoils.

Here is an excerpt of it (4):

"Sclaveni and Antes have a big number of cattle and crops put in stacks and above all, millet and flax.

They live in woods surrounded by swamps, marshes and rivers and they have many exits from their habitats, helping them to take refuge if they are in trouble. All that they need they keep in secret places not trying to display it.

Since they have many princes quarrelling with each other, it is good to win the favor of some by persuasion or gifts, especialy those who sit near the borders and to make attacks on others, because to war with all of them might lead to unity and a ruler among them.

The Sclaveni and Antes settlements lie one behind another along the rivers and are connected, so there is no empty space between them and in the vicinity there are swamps, marshes and bulrush. It mostly happens that during invasions undertaken against them, all military units stop at the first setlements and grab what they want. The nearest neighbors seeing what's going on easily escape with their possessions into the forestts. Youth, on the other hand, take to arms and in the proper moment make surprising attacks on our soldiers. The result is that those who arrange invasions have no chance to give the enemy significant losses.

Thus, the attacks against them (Slavs) should be made suddenly from a side they least expect, but first establishing the order if banderias (a military unit with about 400 soldiers) or any other units, who should attack first who second, who third and so on and this way they could not mingle and make action difficult. Having crossed (the Danube) quietly it is necessary to find the proper spot to start the attack and to divide the soldiers into two columns. One of them should be led by the second in command. With no impediments or transport one column should move through the uninhabited area

136

about 15 or 20 miles deep and from the empty spaces start plundering the settlements in the direction where the first column under the commander lies in ambush. He should attack the settlement by surprise with his column from another side plundering and grabbing what is in his way until both columns meet together in the evening and arrange camping. Thanks to these tactics the whole booty expedition is safe and the enemy is routed before they have the chance to gather to attempt a defense.

Stock found in borderland (Slavic) is not to be used improperly (during the booty expedition) but it should be transported to the other side by beast of burden or boats. The local rivers discharging in the Danube (which was the border river of the Byzantine Empire in those times) are navigable''.

In the same way goes the advice given by the Emperor Maurice (539-602): "Since among them (Slavs) are many leaders who fight each other, it is not difficult to gain favor by promises or gifts to some of them and not the others. This is the only way to check them; otherwise their hatred against us, Byzantinians, might unite them into a powerful nation''.

From these two excerpts it is clear that: 1. Slavs occupied territories beyond the Byzantinian borders; 2. being industrious they were rich in agricultural crops; 3. they lived a quiet life; 4. there is no hint that they tried to make booty expeditions against the cities of the Byzantine Empire; 5. the Byzantinian booty expeditions against the Slavs organized by the Imperial army were numerous but with doubtful results that a special guide book and the Emperor's advice were needed to make them successful; 6. to survive attacks the Slavs were forced to undertake special precautions.

What could the Slavs do in this situation?

After the Huns, Europe was invaded by other Turkish nomads. They were the Bulgars. In 454-480 they coccupied the area between the rivers Dnieper, Volosha, Lower Danube and the Hungarian steppes. Here they met the Slavs and managed to develope some kind of cooperation (5).

Bulgars showed the Slavs how to fight in an open area. It was a novelty for them because the Slavs were used to fighting taking advantage of terrain screens. They attacked moving forward from forest to bushes to folds. Bulgars taught them to form columns and battle the enemy in the open.

The first positive information about Slavic attacks on Imperial domains concerned the Antes. They crossed the Danube in a big

137

number during the reign of the Emperor Justin (518-527) but as could be expected they suffered defeat.

Justinian (527-565), the successor of Justin, ordered the general Chilbudius to defend the borders at the Danube, and made him governor of the province Thracia. He stopped the Slavic attacks but he was killed in battle with the Sclavens.

Fig. 33. Slavic warriors in the 10th century.

A chain of painful Slavic attacks took place in 545-551.

In 545 a bigger column of Sclavens crossed the Danube, plundered the cities and took many prisoners. While returning home, they were ambushed by German Heruls and suffered defeat.

This misfortune did not discourage the Slavs. In 547-548 their column after crossing the Danube, ravaged the whole Iliria up to

Dyressi in Albania. They took many prisoners and even captured some fortresses. Byzantinian commanders in Iliria had no courage to face Slavic warriors in open fields.

In 549 the Sclavens invaded the Byzantinian domains again. They crossed the river Maritsa and defeated the Imperial units one after another. Then, they scattered, unpunished, over Thracia and Iliria capturing strongholds, taking prisoners and spoils.

A year later the Sclavens invaded again. They crossed the Danube in numbers greater than had been seen before and approached the city of Nish. But they resigned from the siege of the well fortified city of Thessalonica.

They spent the winter with no trouble in the Byzantinian domains. In the springtime they marched further south and delivered a painful blow to the Imperial army at Adrianople. Then, they stopped at the walls of Constaninople. After discussion they did not storm them, but returned home unmolested carrying enormous spoils.

Finally, in 551, the huge column of Sclavens invaded Iliria again with the same result as in the years before. The Byzantinian army could only use guerilla warfare, not daring to face the enemy in the open field.

After 551 the Slavic invasions stopped. The Byzantine Empire ended its Gothic wars and could afford to strengthen its borders at the Danube. Slavic invasions from the Iron Gate met resistance.

Slavs remained on occupied lands. They started to cultivate them and probably would have continued if there had not been the outbreak of the Byzantinian-Persian war in 572 (6).

Emperor Tiberius had to withdraw his troops stationed at the Danube to send them into Persia. Being afraid that Slavic units would march unmolested through ungarded borders to destroy Byzantinian possessions, the Emperor made an agreement with the khagan. He advised the Avars to attack the Sclavens (7).

In 578 the Avars crossed the river Sava and entered the Byzantinian domains. They had been directed to Dobruja and then, to the northern banks of the Danube. From this point the khagan attacked the Sclavens rear lines.

The khagan was a smart leader. He wanted to take advantage not only of the Slavs but the Byzantinians as well. He sent envoys to Daurentios, the leader of the Sclavens asking him to pay tribute.

The Slavic council rejected the khagan's demands and killed his envoys. The khagan promised to avenge them.

In 580 the khagan informed Constantinople that he intended to cross the Danube to subdue the Sclavens because they did not want to pay him tribute.

It was only an excuse. The khagan had something quite different in his mind. He attacked and captured the Byzantine city of Sirmium, a very significant, strategic post. The Slavs started to cooperate with him.

In the Slavic army the system of military democracy ruled. The 'wiec — gathering chose for a war leader one of the bravest warriors to lead the army in battle. His contribution to victory was mostly by gallantry rather than by using battle tactics. After the battle his role automatically ended. This is something unusual about the Slavic wars.

For after the battle the fighting sides negotiated a peace treaty. In the prepared documents the names of the leaders were mentioned. It was an important factor. Leaders of both sides guaranteed to keep the peace agreements.

When the Slavs warred with the Byzantine Empire the question arose in whose name the peace treaty should be made since the role of the war leader of the Slavs automaticaly ended when the battle was over. The only solution was to omit this part of the treaty where the name of the Slavic leader should appear. This fact led to a peculiar situation especially during the Avars wars with the Byzantine Empire. Sometimes the Slavic troops allied with the Avars were stronger and more numerous than the Avars but when the peace treaty was ready the names of the Avaric and the Byzantinian leaders were specified but not the Slavic (8).

Some scholars came to an erroneous conclusion trying to explain this phenomenon. They thought the Slavs were anarchists. They had no leaders and attacked the enemy like a horde (9).

The Slavs had their war leaders. Their names were not mentioned in peace treaties but were recorded by some chroniclers. According to this in 585 the Sclavens were led by the Ardagast (10). The name is typically Slavic.

Meanwhile the Byzantinians ended the Persian war. The Emperor sent his general Komentiolus with his army from Persia to the Balkans. He pushed Ardagast out at Adrianople.

A few years later another Byzantinian general, Priskos, attacked Ardagast, defeated him and in this way halted the Slavic invasion. Ardagast took to flight.

Musokios, the second war leader of the Sclavens, tried to save Ardagast but because of treason he fell into the hands of the

140

Byzantinians near the city of Bucharest of today.

The third leader of the Sclavens, Piragast, being informed of the defeats of his colleagues did not even try to meet the Emperor's army.

Invading the Balkans the Slavs did not forget to colonize the conquered lands. Thus in this period were established many Slavic settlements in the Byzantinian domains.

In 586 the khagan led the Avars and the Slavs against Thessalonica but he withdrew not being able to capture the well armed fortress (11).

Emperor Maurikios in 591 sent a large army who defeated the Avars and the Slavs in a few battles and secured the border at the Danube.

The situation changed in 602. The Byzantine Empire had been forced into a new war with Persia and then with the Arabs. The northern borders of the Empire stood open for the Slavs.

The Sclavens changed tactics. They gave up long marches. They carved small boats out of oak logs and on these dug canoes rushed down the Adriatic Sea to attack Tessalia and Cyclads. They settled on the shores of the Egean Sea to show the astonished Byzantinians that they could fight well on land as on the sea.

The third attack at Tessalonica was led by Chocian. The Sclavens arrived with their wives and children and all their possessions. They planned to capture the city and to settle in it (12).

The attack did not succeed. Chocian forced his way into the city, but he was stoned by the women defenders.

The Slavs asked the Avars for support (13).

When the Sclavens and the Antes were battling their way to colonize the Balkans (14) a second wave of migrating Slavs left the Polish territories and went to Pannonia (Hungary today) and Slovenia.

The Avars were pleased to see the newcomers. Weak in number because they had suffered losses in many battles, they badly needed new human resources. Thus, they cleared territories for the Slavs. The newcomers reached the Alps. As pagans they destroyed the Christian bishoprics at the Lower and Upper Drava (15).

In 593-595 Bavarians successfully attacked the Slavs at the Upper Drava. Alarmed Slavs asked the Avars for help. The united forces of Slavs and Avars defeated the invaders and kept the Bavarians quiet (16).

The third migrating wave of Slavs took the center road. Croats, Obodrits and Serbs (17) crossed the Carpathians through the Warecki Pass and occupied territories at the Tissa River. South of them the Avars had their habitat on the Hungarian Plain.

As a reminder of the Croats migration through the Carpathians there remain 18 names of places called 'Horvat' in Hungary today (18).

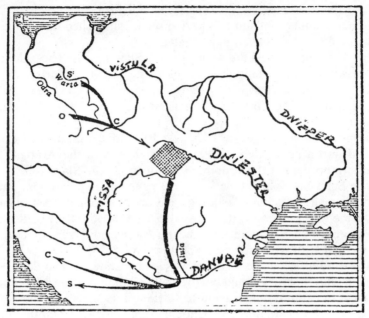

Map XIV Migration of the Croats, Obodrits and Serbs to the south in 570-630. C-Croats; O-Obodrits; S-Serbs, after H. Łowmianski.

The Obodrits must have lived next to the Croats at the Tissa River for some time. Two rivers received their names from them. They are: the Bodrog and the Bodra. The Obodrits settlements were destroyed by the Hungarians. The Serbs were a large group. They primarily migrated further to the south-west and because of that they left scanty traces in Hungary (19).

From the East Slavs the Severyans or ancient Antes arrived as a military group at the Balkans from the Dnieper and settled in Banat at the Thierna River.

The Dregovitches also took part in colonizing the Balkans, as the record of 620 A.D. mentions. One group of the Dregovitches settled at Salonica and the other at the river which got its name 'Dragovitsa' or 'Dragovec' from them. It is a tributary to the Maritsa River. There is also a small river in this region called 'Dragovistica'. The Dregovitches who settled here were called 'Drugovits'. As

142

archaeological findings indicate they lived at the Pripet River before they migrated to the Balkans.

In 591 the khagan sent gifts to the Baltic Slavs asking them to migrate to the Danube and take possession of the empty lands left by the German Gepids. Only a small number answered the call. They came to the Tissa River and after a short stay moved to Dalmatia (20).

The Avars suffered a double defeat; one in the battle at Constantinople in 626 and the other in the organization of the state by Samo. The defeat at Constantinople was caused by the rebellion of Slavic units who had had enough of the tyranny of the Avaric war lords (21).

Not all of the Slavic nations took part in the invasions of the Byzantine Empire. There were only two large groups: the Sclavens and the Antes.

It appears like 'the Slavs were not as blood-thirsty, vindictive and cruel as they are sometimes pictured. If they were, Procopius of Caesarea could never have written about his enemy as he did. Here is his account: "They (Slavs) are tall and unusually strong. Their way of life is hard and on the lowest level. And besides they are not cruel by nature or inclined to do malicious acts".

A similar opinion was expressed by the anonymous author of the treatise on how to plan invasion against the Slavs. He writes: "Sclavens and Antes are numerous, and persevering. They easily endure heat, cold and rain, lack of cloth and food. They are very friendly to their guests and they accompany them going from place to place and giving them all they want".

No matter how large an army the Ancient Slavs battled with, they preferred to fight in covered terrain which helped them to hide when the fortune of the battle became unfavorable. The Slavs employed this tactic in offensive as well as in defensive maneuvers.

Pseudo-Mauricius notes that the Slavs: "living on the spoils like to organize the booty expeditions on their enemy in forestal, narrow and craggy places. They prefer the ambush and sudden attack and the use of many tricks in the day as well as in the night".

The Slavs employed many ways of ambush. Sometimes they used tactics to provoke the enemy, for instance, escaping they threw away the spoils they seized. The party chasing them halted and got busy with the booty left on the road. At the proper moment the Slavs returned and by a sudden attack gained victory.

This tactic indicates that the Slavic warriors skillfully used every possibility to surprise the enemy. When the Slavs gained a partial success only, they broke off with the enemy and hiding in the vicinity, they attacked the small detachments that left the camp.

The Slavic battle tactics were so successful that they forced Pseudo-Mauricius to find counter-measures. According to his instruction, the Byzantinian army attacked the Slavs from many sides at the same time in plain, open terrains with no forests or bushes. When entering the Slavic lands, one part of the army plundered and collected the loot and another part secured the first part by dispersing the enemy. It was imperative to have a rear-guard. When the enemy invaded the Slavic lands, the Slavs made a booty expedition on his teritory to disrupt the invader's rear and to halt his further penetration.

The Slavs decided to attack in open fields only, when they sensed they could win. In this case they ran in big masses with a terrifying shout to terrorize the enemy. If they succeeded, they battled the opposed party, if they failed, they ran quickly for cover. It appears, they knew that their chances for a front attack of the well-trained and equipped Imperial army were not high, so they preferred the ambush tactics.

The Slavs must have used the 'Tabor' tactics in early times, too, which means they fought behind their wagons. The chronicler notes that in 587, when the Slavs were on their way home with huge amounts of spoils, Peter, the Roman general, debarred them from marching. Since it occured in an open space, the Slavs closed the circle with wagons and fought the attacker from behind them with some success. It is worth mentioning, that the Bohemian Hussites used the 'Tabor' tactics with good results in their religious wars in the 15th century.

The Slavs knew many ways of seizing the strongholds. They came in touch with siege machines when they stormed the walls of Constantinople in 626. But even in seizing the strongholds they preferred the ambush.

Procopius of Caesarea left the description of how the Slavs captured the fortified city of Toperos. First they hid a main force near the walls and let a small party attack the gates of the stronghold. Seeing the weak enemy, the defenders opened the gates and rushed to chase the marauders away. The escaping Slavs led these defenders to the place where the main force was hidden. Then at the proper moment, the hidden force divided into two groups. One, with terrifying shouts attacked the running defenders, while another ran to the open gates. In less than one hour the fortified city of Toperos was in Slavic hands.

NOTES TO CHAPTER XXII

1. **Bibliography:** Artamonov M.J., 'Istorija chazar', Leningrad 1962; Constantine Porphyrogenitus 'De administrando imperio'; Csallany D., 'Archaologische Denkmäler der Awarenzeit', Budapest 1961; Hauptmann L., 'Les rapports des Byzantins avec les Slaves et les Avares pendant la second moitie du VI-e siecle', Paris 1928; Kollautz A., 'Die Awaren', Saeculum 1954; Marquart J., 'Die chronologie der altturkischen Inschriften', Leipzig 1898; Preidel H., 'Awaren und Slawen', SOTor. 1952; Procopius, 'De bello Gothico'; Stein E., 'Histoire du Bas-Empire', Paris 1949; Szafarzyk P.J., 'Słowiańskie starożytności', Poznań 1844.

2. Jordanes, Getica V, 34, writes: "On the left side of the Carpathian toward the north and around the source of the Vistula river, a huge territory is inhabited by a rich nation called Venedi. Although they are divided into many tribes, each having a different name, they mainly call themselves Slavs or Antes. The Antes are very courageous and numerically stronger than Slavs, but both have the same physical structure". Procopius mentions: "Sclaveni and Antes speak the same language", and an anonymous author of the military treatise adds: "Nations of Sclaveni and Antes have the same way of life and doing things". Pomponius Mela, 'De chorographia' I, 13 and Pliny, 'Naturalis historia VI, 35, mention the Antes, but the name is not Slavic and the Slavs never used it (H. Łowiański, 'Początki Polski', Vol. I, p. 404-416). The name which probably the Goths turned over to Constantinople, disappeared in the 7th century A.D. Antes must have had a tribal state somewhere around the city of Kiev of today.

3. Jordanes, op. cit., 35: "Sclaveni a civitata Novietunese et laco qui appelatur Mursiano usque ad Danastrum et in boream Viscla commorantur".

4. S. Trawkowski, 'Jak powstawała Polska', p. 80-81.

5. H. Łowmiański, op. cit., Vol. 11, p. 262-269.

6. Johannis Abbatus Biclarensis, 'Chronica', AAnt. 1894, Vol. XI, p. 214, states that in the tenth year of the reign of Justin II (565-578): "Sclavini in Thracia multas urbes Romanorum pervadunt, quas depopulatas vacuas relinquare".

7. L. Hauptmann, 'Les rapports', Vol. IV, p. 156.

8. F. Dolger, 'Regesten der Kaiserurkunden des oströmischen Reiches von 565-1453', Berlin 1924.

9. A. Brückner, 'Słownik etymologiczny języka polskiego', p. 269.

10. Theophylacti Simocattae, 'Historiae', Lipsiae 1887, Lib. I, cap. 7.

11. S. Demetrii, 'Martyris Acta — Miracula' PCCompl. 1891, cap. XII, XIII, written shortly before 688 A.D.

12. S. Demetrii, op. cit., cap. I, mentions that the war leader of attacking Slavs was exarch 'Chacon'. J. Taszycki, 'Rozprawy i studia', Vol. I, p. 96, maintains the name of 'Chacon' could be of Slavic origin because it sounds like 'Chocian'. The name is familiar among the Slavs even today.

13. S. Demetrii, op. cit., points out that the Slavs took the initiative from the Avars to attack the Byzantine Empire.

14. S. Demetrii, op. cit., cap. 1, mentions that the Slavs arrived at Salonica with wives and all possessions, which means the purpose of their attack was not a booty expedition but the desire to settle in the city after capturing it.

15. L. Hauptman, op. cit., p. 166.

16. Paulis Diaconis, Historia Longobardorum IV', cap. 10: "Isdem ipsis diebus Baioarii usque ad duo milia virorum dum super Sclavos inruunt, superveniante cacano omnes interficiuntur".

17. The name Croats is intriguing. Linguists try to explain it using words from many languages. They think it is derived from the name of the Carpathian tribe called 'Carpi'; from the word 'hora' — mountain as the Croats (Horvats) originally came from the mountain region; from the Avars khan 'Kuvrate'; from 'hrvati se' — to defend; from Old Slavonic 'chrib' — the peak; from 'chrvat' — well armed; from the 'krvat' — short sword; from the Gothic word 'hrac'; from 'Choratkos' — the Avars war lord; from 'Chorovath' — a name of a family or tribe (H. Łowmiański, op. cit., Vol. I, p. 127-142). Croats lived in the western region of Southern Poland. Constantine Porphyrogenitus in 'De administrando imperio', cap. 30, 31, 32, mentions for the first time in history the existence of the Croats. The Emperor Heraclius asked them to come to Dalmatia settle down and to fight the Avars. Constantine's attention was centered on the Croats and Serbs who lived in Bohemia and Moravia, but he hinted there must have been Croats at the river Vistula in Southern Poland. According to one supposition, some of them went to Bohemia and Moravia, others went to the Elbe River, the third group migrated to the Dniester occupying empty areas left by the Sclavens. Thus, there were Eastern Western and Southern Croats.

18. V. Hornyansky, 'Geographisches Lexicon des Königreichs Ungarn und der serbischen Woiwodschaft mit dem temescher Banate', Pest 1858, p. 63.

19. H.H. Howorth, 'The Spread of the Slavs', part III: The Northern Serbs and Sorabians and the Obodriti', London 1880, Vol. IX, p. 207.

20. Constantine Porphyrogenitus, op. cit., cap. 30.

21. F. Barisić, 'Le siege de Constantinople par les Avars et les Slaves en 626', Byzantion 1954, Vol. XXIV, p. 371-395.

CHAPTER XXIII

STRONGHOLDS

Fig. 34. Reconstruction of a small stronghold.

In the period of Lusatian Culture the Ancient Slavs raised about two hundred (now discovered) fortified towns similar to Biskupin, described in Chapter VIII. No one knows exactly who was their enemy, but the strongholds lasted five centuries before they were out of use. New settlements in the places had an open character, which means the era of emergency was over.

Then the threat returned. Between 6th and 9th centuries new strongholds appeared, many of them in the same places as a thousand years ago. Biskupin is the best example. Since the Ancient Slavs returned to the same technique of building fortified towns as their forebearers did for ten centuries, the Kostrzewski's theory of the same ethnic group living there for over a thousand years without interruption gains validity.

Settlements of the West Slavs were mostly in the form of 'okolnica' — round village easy to defend. They appeared between the rivers Elbe and Bug. The East Slavs, on the other hand, built the 'ulicówka' — onestreet village along the rivers. Thus the West Slavs lived in more difficult conditions that their eastern cousins.(1)

When the threat was small the Western Slavs protected their settlement by fencing it with a palisade. Since fencing means 'grodzić' in Polish, the settlement fenced with a palisade was called a 'gród'.(2) Only one gate, closed at nights, allowed entrance to the stronghold.

Slavs built their strongholds either on a rise or lowest point of terrain. The first were visible from a distance for the enemy, but the defenders had better observation posts and better platforms to push down the attackers.(3)

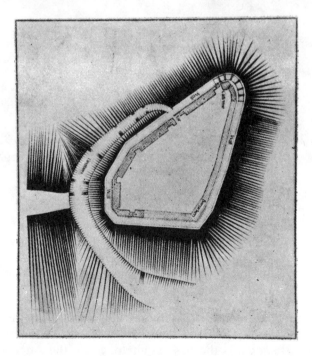

Fig. 35. Triangular form of Slavic stronghold in Kiestow, East Germany, after J. Kostrzewski.

The low situated strongholds, less visible for invaders, had been built on natural defensive points like the lake shores, river mouth islets, peninsulas, and on the heights of marshlands with difficult access.(4)

If the terrain was flat the Slavs raised the stronghold in the form of a circle (Kołuda Wielka, Poland) (5), sometimes even in an oval form (Lisew, Poland), but very rarely triangular (Kiestow, East Germany) or rectangular. On the other hand, when the terrain offered natural protection like high and steep shores, or sharp cliffs, the stronghold took a form of a horseshoe (Lubin, Poland), being fenced from the weak side only.

Fig. 36. Reconstruction of the stronghold Nowotroickoje in Ukraine, after L. Leciejewicz.

Analyzing strongholds, the scholars are amazed at seeing how good the old Slavic builders were in selecting the best possible points in terrain for their fortified towns.

When palisades became of little protection (the first stronghold of Santok in Poland), the Slavs did what their forebearers for over a thousand years had done, building Biskupin. They fenced their settlements with bulwarks.

The bulwark, in genuine form, was nothing but an enbankment (Kleniec, Poland). To strengthen their defense the Slavs dug a ditch outside the palisade and the removed earth was used to make a dike which, with fosse, constituted the first defense line. It was not much. To raise a bulwark of promising height it had to be wide at the bottom and coniform in shape, and it didn't give much protection. The earth slid under its own weight and atmospheric activity.

The Slavs found here a good solution. They strengthened the bulwarks with layers of wood, using oaks for this purpose. On the layer of logs was a layer of earth mixed with clay, and another layer of logs. Clay bound the logs and protected them against fire. Using this technique the Slavs built higher bulwarks with steep walls, and armed them with a palisade on the top (Daleszyn, Poland).

The construction of bulwarks improved when the builders started to stack log layers lengthwise and broadwise and to cover it with earth. This system, known as scaffolding, took the upper half of the bulwark, the lower being made of earth only (Popęszyce, Poland).

The outside logs, laid lengthwise, sometimes slid down. To keep them together, a hook construction had been invented. The builders laid first the logs broadwise, with some logs having strong branches cut short to serve as hooks (Gniezno, Poland) to keep together the upper layers of logs put lenghtwise in a distance of 5-7 feet.

The earth-wooden bulwarks of scaffolding construction had proven not to be the best ones. They needed too many logs for construction. A new system had to be invented.

It was the box structure.

Fig. 37. Reconstruction of the bulwark in Gniezno, Poland, after J. Kostrzewski

The Slavs made boxes from the logs in size 10 by 8 ft. which they filled with earth (Kleck in Poland) or stones (Ujście, Poland).

Improvements of bulwark construction are visible in towns which built bulwarks on the same places many times down the centuries. A good example is Santok in northern Poland. Its bulwarks had been raised twelve times on the same spot, between the 8th and 15th centuries, with the earliest of very rude form and the latest highly sophisticated structures.

Fig. 38. The remnants of the stone-wooden bulwark in Poznań, after J. Kostrzewski.

Bulwarks built in later epochs had mixed construction. The bottom enbankment was of earth, the middle part was scaffolding with layers of oak logs, and the upper part the box construction with palisades on the top.

There had been different sizes of bulwarks, depending on how important the stronghold was. In Poznań, the capital of the first Polish rulers, the bulwark was 60 ft. wide, in Opole and Wolin — 45 ft.; and in Popęszyce 10 ft.

The bulwark was not stcep but conoidal, wider at the bottom and narrower at the top. Its height varied between 15 and 35 ft.

The gate, the only entrance to the stronghold, was 8-5 ft. wide and had a 'samborz' — tower upon it for warriors to defend the entrance.

Strongholds differed in size, from 80 ft. (Popęszyce, Poland) to 800 ft. (Gdańsk, Poland) in diameter. The big strongholds had many huts inside, built along the streets. Some settlements like Tibusz (Poland) had been encompassed with three bulwarks, being of special importance to the settlers.

Around important strontholds the artisans, merchants, warriors and servants had their dwellings. These suburbs had been circled with bulwarks too, (Ociąż in Poland) giving start to cities.

Fig. 39. Reconstruction of the bulwark in Poznań, after J. Kostrzewski

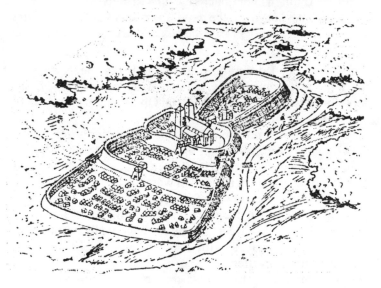

Fig. 40. Reconstruction of the stronghold of Gniezno with its suburbs, after L. Leciejewicz.

Strongholds were scattered all over the West and East Slavs territories. It seems that every 'opole' — territorial unit, composed of several settlements, had its own stronghold, placed usually in the center, where the 'żupan' — headmaster and elite dwelt. Several neighboring 'opoles' formed the territory of the 'plemię' — tribe, with the 'włodyka' — tribal chief. The Bavarian Geographer tells that in the 9th century even small Polish tribes, like the 'Ślężanie', 'Opolanie', 'Dziadoszanie' had 15-20 strongholds, meaning 15-20 'opoles'. The Slavs in Germany were wealthier. The Obodrits had 53 and Vyelets 95 strongholds. The more strongholds the tribe had the more powerful it was.

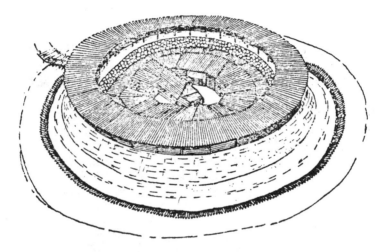

Fig. 41. Reconstruction of the stronghold in Tornow, East Germany, after L. Leciejewicz.

The East Slavs had so many strongholds that the Varengians called their territories 'Gardarike' — the land of strongholds.(6)

Why did the Slavs build so many strongholds?

Since the fortified places were not concentrated at the borders, but scattered all around the country it is obvious they were not raised against the enemy outside the Slavdom, but from inside. This was a stormy period of forming Slavic states. Tribal chiefs tried to increase their domains by subjugating neighboring tribes. They kept large and costly troops. Since the system of taxation was poorly established the firm source of income became spoils and tributes. So, the princes "worked" for the wages of their warriors by robbing the neighboring tribes. They did not expect the attacked neighbors to stand still and suffer humiliation in silence. The urge of revenge was strong. To secure their own people against the counterattacks, the princes had to build strongholds at the most strategic points. The archaeological findings indicate that they did excellent work in this matter.

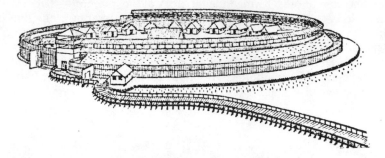

Fig. 42. Reconstruction of the stronghold in Behren-Lubchin in East Germany, after L. Leciejewicz.

The raising of earth-wooden strongholds became a common practice among the Slavs until the 15th century, when the stone wall replaced the bulwark.

The question arises, why did the Ancient Slavs instead of building stone walls cling to their earth-wooden bulwark? It is impossible to believe that they knew nothing about stone walls invented some thousand years ago at the Mediterranean Sea. After all, the Slavs stormed the walls of Constantinople in the 7th century.

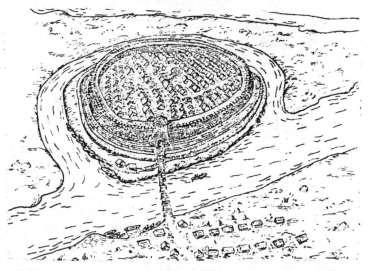

Fig. 43. Reconstruction of the stronghold of Opole in Poland, after L. Leciejewicz.

There are two reasons for this. First, the Slavs settled on fertile lowlands where stones happened to be a rarity. Their construction material at hand was earth and wood. They used it, not only in building huts and strongholds, but in crafts as well.

The second reason is that the earth-wooden bulwark was a better defense line than the stone wall. The battering ram could not crush it because the bulwark was wide and massive. Fire could not destroy it because the logs supporting the bulwark had been covered with clay and earth. Even the enemy, with flaming arrows, burnt down huts inside the stronghold, the defenders still had their bulwark to protect them. Since the Slavs were known as fierce defenders of their homes, the attackers could count only to seize the stronghold by hunger. After three weeks of siege of the stronghold Niemcza in Silesia, the German Emperor Henry II with shame had to withdraw his huge army, not being able to capture the city in 1017, as the German chronicler Thietmar records.

Fig. 44. The remnants of the stronghold in Grodzisko Mazowieckie in Poland, after L. Leciejewicz.

155

NOTES TO CHAPTER XXIII

1. Bibliography: Dynaczewska H., Hołowińska Z., 'Z dziejów Santoka i kasztelanii santockiej', Poznań 1961; Dylik J., 'Analiza geograficznego położenia grodzisk', Poznań 1936; Hellmich M., 'Die Besiedlung Schlesiens in vor-und Fruhgeschichtlicher Zeit, Breslau 1923; Jażdżewski K., 'Kształtowanie się wczesnośredniowiecznej kultury miejskiej w Polsce w świetle badań w latach 1945-1954', Warszawa 1957; Kowalenko W., 'Grody i osadnictwo grodowe'; Kurnatowski. W., Nalepa J., 'Z przeszłości Międzyrzecza', Poznań 1961; Ludat H., 'Die Anfänge des polnischen staates', Kraków 1942; Łowmiański H., 'Zagadnienie Normanów w genezie państw słowiańskich', Warszawa 1951; Rajewski Z., '10,000 lat Biskupina i jego okolicy', Warszawa 1958; Radig W., 'Der Burgberg Meissen', Augsburg 1929; Tymieniecki K. 'Zagadnienie początków miast w Polsce', Warszawa 1919; Uhtenwoldt H., 'Die Burgverfassung in der Vorgeschichte und Geschichte Schlesiens', Breslau 1938; Zakrzewski S., 'Opis grodów i terytoriów z północnej strony Dunaju', Lwów 1917; Żurowski K., 'Konstrukcje obronne wczesnośredniowiecznego Gniezna', Arch. Pol. Vol. I.

2. Many localities in Poland have names ending 'gród', like: Wyszogród, Nowogród etc. which means they had been strongholds in the past. The same situation is in Russia. Since the 'gród' is called 'goród' in Russian, there is Novgorod in Russia. Czechs pronounce the 'gród' as 'hrad', so there is Velehrad in Czechoslovakia, and the Balkan Slavs called their fenced settlement 'grad', so there is Belgrad. The oldest form of this word was 'gard' which appears as the ending of the names of much cities like Starogard or Białogard common on the Elbe-Slavic territories. The ending must be of Indo-European origin because it points to 'garden' a fenced and defended area.

3. Archaeologists found 211 remnants of such strongholds in northern Poland.

4. There are 307 remnants of low situation strongholds in northern Poland.

5. In brackets the names of strongholds discovered lately, after J. Kolstrzewski, 'Kultura prapolska.'

6. H. Łowmiański, 'Zagadnienie Normanów w genezie państw słowiańskich,' Warszawa 1957, p. 15 — 34.

CHAPTER XXIV

CULTURE

Arabic and German travellers were amazed at seeing Slavs storytelling singing and dancing long hours without being tired. It appears that the fondness for liberal arts is deeply rooted in the Slavic soul and had manifested itself in the remote past, but recorded when Christianity came.

It is evident in literature. Since the Slavs developed no alphabet of their own, all literary production perpetuated in oral form. (1)

Then appeared two brothers, Cyril and Methodius. Their alphabets in Glagolitic and Cirillic forms made an impact upon the Slavs.

Expelled from Great Moravia, the disciples of the Slav Apostles founded in Bulgaria two literary centers, called sometimes the schools of Slavic literature.

One in Okhrid, with Clement and Naum at the top, followed strickly the Cyrillo-Methodian tradition and used Glagolitic in writing, only; another in Preslav, with Naum in the beginning and then with Constatine, took a different position and used Cirillic from the start.

Both centers in a short time reached fine results in quantity as well as quality, especially during the reign of tsar Simeon, called the golden era of Old Bulgarian literature. No wonder, for the tsar himself was among the writers.

The literature started with translations of religious texts from Greek into Old Slavonic, which was the continuation of Cyril and Methodius writing in Moravia. The copyists strictly followed the manuscripts, but even in the earliest times there appeared attempts of genuine production. The best examples were the 'Proglas' — introduction in rhyme to the Gospel, and 'Szestodniew' — six days of world creation.

Next to religious production of the copyists reached for civil codex and following the example of Byzantine historians, they started to write the 'istorija' — history or a 'latopisiec' — chronicle of the Bulgarian nation. A special position was given the 'zborniki' (or 'izborniki') — encyclopedic collections of different stories to enlighten, moralize and entertain the reader.

The Bulgarian literature gained impetus when the sect of Bogomils appeared. Since they relied on written material, the pamphlets and books praising and denouncing new and old religion flooded the land. Trying to reach the grassroots, the writers used the old Bulgarian vocabulary. In this way, next to the Old Church Slavonic, the first Slavonic literary language, which was a dialect of the Slavs in the region of Salonica, Greece, there started to develop the genuine Old Bulgarian language.

The blooming Bulgarian literature was halted when the Byzantinians destroyed the first Bulgarian state in 1018.

In the critical years of the Bulgarian state another Slavic country embraced Christianity. Vladimir the Great, the prince of Kiev, became baptized with his Russian subjects in 988 by the missionaries from Constantinople, on the condition that the liturgy of the new religion be entirely in Slavonic. The clergy had no other choice but to transplant the richly developed Bulgarian literature in Old Church Slavonic into Russian. So, while the literary production barely existed in subjugated Bulgaria, it flourished in Kiev.

The cathedral of St. Sophia in Kiev was the main center of writing during the reign of the prince Yaroslav the Wise. After his death in 1054, the famous monastery known as Lavra of Pechersky, near Kiew, headed the literary production.

Similar to Bulgarian writers, the Russian authors had not limited their talents to copying the works of the Byzantinian and Bulgarian masters. They tried their own strength, with imposing results. The 'letopis' — chronicle, became very popular with the Nestor's 'Povest vremenykh let' — Tale of Past Times, at the top. A high position was given the 'Putchenie' — Instruction of Vladimir Monomakh (1113-1125), but the top was reached by the 'Lay of Campaign', narrating the expedition of a prince of Novgorod against the Polovtsians in 1185 or 1186, which is acknowleged as the best epic poem of the world in those times.

Again, as in Bulgaria, the Old Church Slavonic literature helped to develop the national literary language, which is the Old Russian language. The invasion of the Tartars in 1240 halted the bloom of Old Russian literature.

Old Church Slavonic helped to develop the national literature in another Slavic country. In Serbia, during the times of the Nemanija dynasty, the literary production followed the same patteren as in Bulgaria and Russia, giving the Old Serbian a chance to get started.

Two other countries had the opportunity to develop a national language and literature in connection with the Old Church Slavonic: Moravia and Bohemia. They both destroyed their chances by expelling the Cyrillo-Methodian rite from their territories.

Perhaps Poland belongs to these two countries, too. She expelled the Slavonic monks, also, but there is no evidence of literary production in Old Church Slavonic on Polish soil.

Bohemia, Moravia and Poland relied on Latin, thus their national literature was more than two centuries behind the others Slavic nations.

Settled on the fertile loess soil and periphery of the forest, Ancient Slavs showed no special inclination to use stones in construction and art. They left no monumental buildings and very few statues. The material they used in construction and art was mostly wood, clay and earth, of little duration, hence there are not many artistic achievements from this epoch.

Archaeologists have not yet found the remnants of the Slavic pagan temple which had been raised, according to German and Danish chroniclers, who saw and described it.(2) The small number of statues, serving probably in some religious cult, are carved either in stone or wood.

The stone statues are either in the form of a prism with reliefs, as famous Światowit (3), or a round pillar with a human head at the top, like idols from Great Novgorod in Russia, or a bigger rock with relief like, the rock with three heads found near Zagreb in Yugoslavia.

Among the wooden statues which escaped being thrown into the lakes by the Christian missionaries, most known is the head from Janków in northern Poland.

Nestor mentions that in Kiev there stood a wooden statue of 'Perun'-god of thunderbolts, with silver head and golden moustaches. And Herbord left a description of and idol in Wolin, Poland, made of pure gold or covered with a sheet of gold. The fate of those statues is unknown.

Ancient Slavs achieved full artistic expression in goldsmithery, less in articles made of horn and ceramics. The goldsmithery included not only articles made of gold, but of silver and bronze, also. Best know are the 'kabłączki skroniowe' — little moons in silver, bronze and sometimes in gold; earings, necklaces, chainlets, pendants (called 'lunulae' because of half moon form), bracelets, rings and buckles. Since the production was oriented to satisfy the women, one cannot help note that Slavic girls and ladies in those times were very sensitive in elegance.(4)

Fig. 45. 'Kabłączki skroniowe'. A Reconstruction of a head with a little moon attached to the ribbon; B- 'kabłączki skroniowe' — little moons.

With Christianity, the new art came to the Slavs from Rome and Constantinople. Although it was of a strict religious character, recipients did the best to transform foreign models to their own taste. Even in the earlier churches one can find a Slavic touch more or less evident.

The Slavic pre-Christian art, concentrated mostly on geometric ornaments, received a tremendous boost in painting, sculpture and stone construction. It appears that the artistic ability of the Ancient Slavs waited for this favorable moment. In a short time they expressed themselves in every way. No matter which Church they belonged — Eastern or Western — their sacral art is impressive.

Artistic creativity depended upon the distance from Rome and Constatinople. Those Slavic nations that were near the ancient centers of civilization developed their art earlier than their cousins occupying the regions farther north. Bulgaria and Poland were examples. Nonetheless, even the northerners managed to develop standards to express themselves.

160

Ancient Slavs had many things to cure illness. The common medicines were herbs, especially bitter and stingy, applied with magic cantations. Some of these cures are doubtful in results, but some are effective.

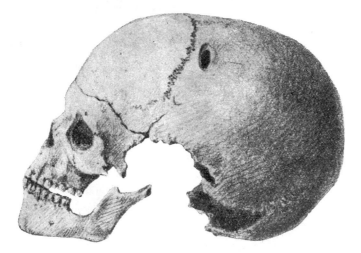

Fig. 46. The trephined skull from Pruszcza in Poland, after J. Kostrzewski, 'Kultura prapolska'. p. 368

It was surprising to find in graves from the early Middle Ages, in Pruszcz, Poland, a skull with the oval hole. Someone had trephined it for medical reasons, and he did it well because the wound was healed and cicatrized.

Ancient Slavs were fond of music and dancing. They used 'gęśle' — violine; 'piszczałki' — pipes; 'dudy' — shawn; 'trąby' — trumpets and 'będny' — drums. Playing instruments and singing, they danced hours during the many festivities. Goths were so impressed by the Slavic 'pląsy' — dancing, that they introduced the word 'plinsjan' to their vocabulary.(5)

NOTES TO CHAPTER XXIV

1. **Bibliography:** Ałpatow M.W. 'Historia sztuki', Warszawa 1968; Brückner A., Lehr-Spławiński T., 'Zarys dziejów literatur i języków słowiańskich', Lwów 1929; Friedberg M., 'Kultura polska', Poznań 1946; Georgiev E., 'Razcwetatna Balgarska literatura w IX-X v.', Sofija 1962; Grabar A., 'L'art du moyen age en Europe orientale', Paris 1968; Grabar I., 'Istorija russkogo iskustwa, Moskva 1917; Hołubowicz W., 'Badania na Ostrówku w Opolu w roku 1955'; Jakimowicz R., 'Okres

wczesnohistoryczny', Kraków 1939; Jeremin P., 'Literatura drewniej Rusi', Moskva 1966; Knorr H., 'Die slawische Keramik zwischen Elbe und Oder', Leipzig 1937; Lichacew D.S., 'Kultura russkogo naroda', Moskva 1961; Mawrodinow M. 'Starobalgarskoto izkustwo', Sofija 1959; Mole W., 'Sztuka Słowian południowych', Wrocław 1962; Patersen E., 'Der Ostelbische Raum', Leipzig 1939; Silnicki T., 'Historia Śląska', Kraków 1939; Strzygowski J., 'Staroharvatska umjetnost', Zagreb 1927; Vlasto A.P. 'The Entry of the Slavs into Christendom', Cambridge 1970.

2. German chroniclers: Theotmar, Adam of Bremen, Harbord, Helmold; the Danish chronicler: Saxo Grammaticus.

3. Światowit, angular pillar with four faces and relief on three sides found in the river Zbrucz in Ukraine in 1846, ascertained by the scholars to be a genuine one is now in Museum of Archaeology in Cracow, Poland. It fits description of the idol called 'Świętowit' in Arcona on the Rugen Island in East Germany, hence its name.

4. A. Bruckner, 'Encyklopedia staropolska' p. 130; A. Blum, 'Historie du costume en France', p. 22.

5. J. Kostrzewski, 'Kultura prapolska', p. 408.

CHAPTER XXV

CYRIL AND METHODIUS

Cyril and Methodius are two saints deeply revered by all Slavs. The question is only, where does their greatness lie — in religious or national life. If it were not for them, the Poles and Czechs would be the only Slavs today. The Russians, Bulgarians, Serbs, Croats and Slovenians would live in scanty memory like Slavic Polabs in Germany. The two Greek brothers saved four-fifths of Slavs from national death (1).

Cyril and Methodius derived from a rich family of Salonica, perhaps of Slavic origin, but Grecized in those times. Methodius (815-885) received a higher post in Macedonia administration before he became a monk. His younger brother, Constantine, known better as Cyril (836-869), was the friend of Photius, the patriarch of Constantinople and was called "the philosopher".

Michael III, the emperor of Byzantium knew how good Christianization was in Grecizing people of foreign ethnic origin. For over two hundred years the imperial army could not subjugate the Slavs who colonized the whole Peloponesus, but the Christian missionaries did the work quickly and with astonishing results. They not only subordinated Slavs to Constantinople but Grecized them as well. Michael III decided to use religion in his ambitious political plans. He sent Cyril to the Khazars at the Black Sea to convert them, but the mission failed and Cyril returned to Constantinople. He went with his brother, Methodius, to Bulgaria and they both managed to convert prince Boris I to Christianity in 861.

Newly baptized Boris I knew also what effect Christianity made on the Slavs in Peloponesus, so he tried to save his Bulgarians from denationalization and becoming Greeks. He sent a request to

163

Constantinople in 863 for missionaries to convert the whole Bulgaria, establish an archbishop, and thus an autocephalic head for the Church of Bulgaria with, to follow, a crown for himself. He met rejection. So he submitted the same request to the pope and King Louis of Germany (2), but he had got no luck. Not having much choice, Boris I accepted Christianity from Constantinople for Bulgaria in 865.

At the same time another Slavic prince had similar apprehension. Rostislav I, the ruler of the Great Moravia state, was Christian since his predecessor, Mojmir I, had been baptized in 831 by Bavarian missionaries. Dependent upon the German emperor, Rostislav I tried to save this country from Germanization by replacing the Bavarian clergy with priests of other nationalities. He sent a request to Constantinople.

It is not known who got the idea of Slavic clergy — the prince of Great Moravia or the emperor of Byzantium. Michael III accepted the request and sent Cyril and Methodius to Rostislav I.

The brothers started eagerly to work spreading Christianity in Slavonic known now as the Old Church Slavonic, used in those times in Salonica and vicinity. Although there is a distance between Macedonia and Moravia, the linguistic differences were of no significance. The Christianity in Slavonic spread rapidly in Moravia. Cyril and Methodius founded the seminary and introduced the Slavonic to liturgy. In this way a new rite had been established, called the Roman-Slavonic Rite.

In the Roman-Slavonic rite the liturgy is Roman in its ceremonies and Slavonic in its language. Therefore it belongs to the Western, Roman liturgy, from which it differs only in language. On the other hand, it differs from the Byzantino-Slavonic liturgy in its ceremonies (3). The oldest documents of this rite, the 'Folia Kioviensa' (4), preserved in copy of the 10th century belong to the Roman liturgy and are translated (directly or indirectly) from Latin into Slavonic.

In those times an opinion prevailed that Latin, Greek or Hebrew were the only languages worthy for use in liturgy. Using 'barbaric' languages, like Slavonic, meant a desecration in religion. The Bavarian prelates, shocked by the progress made by Cyril and Methodius, accused the brothers of heresy. Unfortunately Rostislav I, their protector, had been defeated by Germans. Cyril and Methodius had no other recourse but challenge the German prelates in Rome.

Travelling to Rome, the brothers stayed as guests of the Slavic prince Kocelj at Balaton Lake in Hungary. He became a great enthusiast of the Roman-Slavonic rite.

Cyril and Methodius arrived in 867 in Rome. They were greeted by Pope Hadrian II who, after listening to their argument, solemnly approved the Roman-Slavonic rite in the same year. Having had trouble with Constantinople, the Pope was afraid of another force in his Church, of German bishops who, as fierce nationalists, could establish the third Church with the blessing of the German emperor. The Roman-Slavonic rite helped him to check the German influences inside the Church. What is more, it could be a good instrument to free the Slavonic nations from the influence of Constantinople. Following great politics Hadrian II not only acknowledged the Roman-Slavonic rite, but elevated Methodius to archbishop. During the stay in Rome Cyril died. The Pope accepted the request of prince Kocelj, and established the first archbishopric of Roman-Slavonic rite in Sirmium (Metrovica Srjemska in Yugoslavia, today).

The Bavarian bishops were furious. They exploited the death of Hadrian II to bring Methodius to Germany, and to accuse him of heresy, because Methodius was the pupil and friend of patriarch Photius of Constantinople. After a mock trial they threw him into jail in 876. The sharp intervention of a new Pope, John VIII, released him from prison in 878. Following a request of Svatopluk, the prince of Great Moravia, the Pope created a new archbishopric for Methodius, presumably in Velehrad, where the Apostle of Slavs died in 885.

But the Vatican was not consistent in its action. The German prelates gained influence in the Church, and in 880 and Pope nominated the German priest of Latin rite as a suffragan to Methodius with the seat in Nitra. He was to be a watchdog, not letting Methodius do anything which might have been 'schismatic'. In fact, the suffragan did all he could to topple his archbishop.

Cyril invented a Slavonic alphabet in 855, six or seven years before he went to Moravia. He translated a Gospellectionary, perhaps the Psalter and the chief service-books into a Slavonic dialect, and it seems that Methodius translated the Epistle, some parts of the Old Testament, a manual of cannon law and other liturgical matters.

Mention must be made of Bruckner's theory (5) that Cyril made Cyrillic first, but degraded into Glagolitic to hide its Greek origin from the Latin clergy, the whole object of his mission being hostile to Rome.

The Glagolitic (6) is a genuine alphabet based on alphabets of the eastern languages. It is in two forms: in the 'spectacled' form of which

165

certain very early Old Slavonic documents were written, and the 'square' or 'Croatic' form which survived as a liturgical script in Dalmatia.

The Cyrillic is the Greek Liturgical Uncial of the 9th century, enriched with special signs for Slavonic letters. It is used by all Orthodox Slavs.

When Methodius died, Wiching, his suffragan bishop, in fierce opposition to the metropolitan and his rite, went so far as forging a papal letter in which he stated that the Pope made him successor and forbade the Slavonic rite. Prince Svatopluk, making Methodius' life difficult, too, arrested the archbishop's followers and banished them from Moravia.

Expelled from Moravia, the adherents of the Roman-Slavonic rite found welcomed refuge in Dalmatian monasteries and in Bulgaria. Boris I accepted the refugees with open arms. They came right in time. He let them convert Bulgarians to the Roman-Slavonic rite. Clement, the oldest disciple of Methodius, did the same in Preslav, the capital of Bulgaria in those days. Based on two centers, Simeon, who succeeded to the throne after Boris I and proclaimed himself tsar of all Bulgars and Greeks, made Bulgarian patriarchat independent form Constantinople. In this way he saved Bulgarians from loosing their national identity. The church in Preslav spread the use of Cyrillic in writing.

The Wiching forgery came to light. Pope John IX sent his legates to Moravia and they consecrated a new archbishop and three bishops of the Roman-Slavonic rite in 898. The German prelates protested in a letter sent to Rome in 900.

The fight between the Pope and the German bishops about the Roman-Slavonic rite in Moravia ended in 907 when the Hungarians invaded Moravia and destroyed it once and for all. Many notable Moravians, among them the prelates, sought refuge in neighboring countries. In Bohemia they founded a famous monastery in Sazava.

Lanckorońska maintains (7) that during the Hungarians invasion Gorazd was the archbishop of Moravia. He fled to southern Poland, which belonged to Moravia in those days, and settled in the city of Wiślica, where he was safe, because the Hungarians did not pass the Carpathians. Wiślica became the seat of the Roman-Slavonic rite. After the death of Gorazd the metropolitan moved to Cracow which was the capital of Poland.

Introduced by prince Mieszko I, the Latin rite in Poland in 966 became a rite of the elite. In time a struggle began between the two rites, which caused the expulsion of the monks of Slavonic rite from Poland in 1022 by the King Boleslas the Great. During the reign of his son, Mieszko II, bi-ritualism led to civil war. The Slavonic rite started to loose ground and was completely liquidated by Boleslas III (1085-1135) with the help of the French clergy (8).

The Slavonic rite met a similiar fate in Bohemia. It had been purged by Prince Bretislav II in 1095.

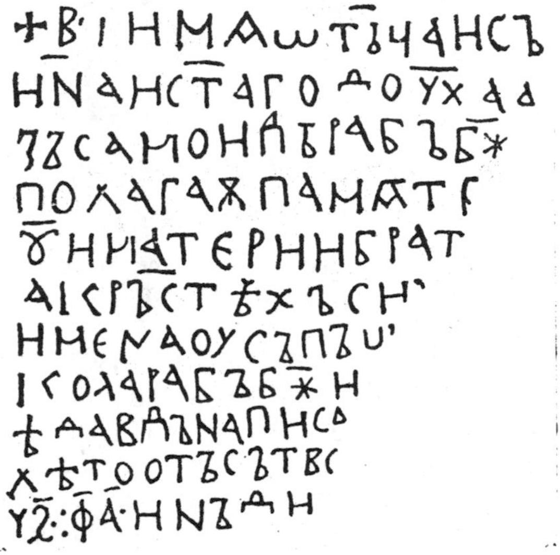

Fig. 47. Earliest know inscription in Cyrillic on a tombstone in Macedonia.

Pope Gregory VII officially condemned the Slavonic rite as supposedly being linked with the Aryans. Croatian kings, Kresimir IV and Zvonimir I did all they could to remove the Slavonic rite, but they failed. The monasteries on the archipelago Kvarner, especially the isle of Krk in the Adriatic Sea, withstood the pressure. Not having much choice the Vatican acknowledged the rite. In this way the Slavonic rite in the Roman Church survived to our times in Dalmatia only, where in dioceses of Veglia, Spalato, Zara and Sobenico and in Montenegro the Glagolitic in 'square' form is still in liturgical script.

The Slavonic rite became so popular among the Slavs that when Vladimir the Great, the prince of Kiev Russia, asked the patriarch of Constantinople to send him missionaries he pointed out that they had to speak Slavonic and that all liturgy must be in Slavonic as it was in

Fig. 48 Earliest known writing in Glagolitic

Bulgaria. The clergy in Kiev were Greek using Slavonic, but the situation changed when Prince Jaroslav the Wise nominated the Russian monk, Illarion, archbishop of Kiev, independent of Constantinople, in 1051.

The Greek brothers, Cyril and Methodius, contributed tremendously to the national feeling of the Slavic nations. They gave impetus to national literature. Armed with religion and writings of their own, the Balkan Slavs withstood the Turkish pressure for over four centuries and Russians the Tartars pressure for over the same time. Poland and Bohemia, better nationally developed, could fight off with positive results the German pressure in the Roman Church without the help of the Slavonic rite.

Shortly after their death Cyril and Methodius became saints in the Eastern Church. Condemned by the Western Church as 'heretics' the Greek brothers had been elevated to the Roman Catholic altars by Pope Leo XIII who in 1881 declared them saints. It took over 1100 years for the Roman Church to acknowledge by the II Vatican Council in 1964 the idea of national liturgy introduced by Cyril and Methodius.

NOTES TO CHAPTER XXV

1. **Bibliography:** Balcer O., 'Genealogia Piastów', Kraków 1895; Dvornik F., 'Les Slaves, Byzance et Rome', Paris 1926; Grivec F., 'De versionibus Palaeoslavicarum Vitorum Constantini et Methodii', Velehrad 1937; Gumplowicz M., 'Zur Geschichte Polens in Mittelalter', Innsbruck 1898; Havranek B., 'Otazke existence cirkevni

slovanstiny w Polsku', SL 1956; Kętrzyński S., 'O zaginionej metropolii czasów Bolesława Chrobrego', Warszawa 1947; Klich E., 'Polska terminologia chrześcijańska', Poznań 1927; Labuda G., 'Studia nad początkami państwa polskiego', Poznań 1947; Lanckorońska K., Studies on the Roman-Slavoic Rite in Poland', Roma 1962; Lapotre A., 'L'Europe et le S. Siege a l'epoque carolingienne', Paris 1895; Lehr-Spławiński T., 'Czy sa ślady istnienia liturgii Cyryło-Metodiańskiej w dawnej Polsce?', SL 1956, Vol. XXIX; Naegele A., 'Kirchengeschichte Bohmens, Wien 1918; Runciman S., 'The Eastern Schism', Oxford 1956; Sakac S., 'L'Origine del rito Romano-Slavo e SS. Cirillo e Metodo', Roma 1948; Smrzik S., 'The Glagolitic or Roman-Slavonic Liturgy', Cleveland-Roma 1959; Widajewicz J., 'Państwo Wiślan', Kraków 1947.

2. K. Lackorońska, 'Studies on the Roman-Slavonic Rite in Poland', p. 28.

3. S. Smrzik, 'The Glagolitic or Roman-Slavonic Liturgy', Cleveland 1959, p. 15.

4. G. Mohlberg, 'Ill Messale Glagolitico di Kiev', Roma 1928.

5. Encyclopedia Britannica 1911, Vol. XXV, p. 232.

6. The name "Glagolitic" derives from the Old Slavonic "glagol" — word.

7. K. Lanckorońska, op. cit., p. 1.

8. K. Lanckorońska, op. cit. p. 150-155.

CHAPTER XXVI

SLAVS AND SLAVES

The Royal Castle in Cracow, where the Polish kings resided for over 500 years, stands on the rocky hill 'Wawel' in which is a den, called the 'Dragons Cave'. Wincenty Kadłubek, one of the earlier Polish chroniclers (1) recorded a fairy tale concerning the cave. Once upon a time there lived a horrible dragon. The people in the vicinity had to deliver him hundreds of beautiful girls and handsome boys every year, which the beast devoured. It lasted a long time, but one day a man called 'Krak' killed the dreadful dragon and became a national hero. He also built the city of Cracow named after him.

The fairy tale tempted the scholars, who tried to find "a grain of truth" in the story, because it contains some element of mystery. Why did the beast want the beautiful girls and handsome boys for his meal? Why did he not prefer the fat calves, cows and sheep? Is there not, in this fairy tale, an element of slavery camouflaged?

Another chronicler recorded that in the 880's the slave market in Venice was jammed with blond slaves. In those years Svatopluk, the prince of Great Moravia, conquered southern Poland of which Cracow might have been the capital. There is another chronicler who mentions that a man called 'Skok' was one of the prince's lieutenants. There is a big temptation to connect those loosely given facts with the fairy tale, and to accept that, after conquering southern Poland, Svatopluk installed Skok as his governor in Cracow to collect tribute in hundreds of the best youngsters every year, who were sold as slaves in Venice. Hating the horrible governor, the people changed his name from 'Skok' to 'Smok' — dragon, but no serious historian would build a theory upon a highly hypothetical supposition, although slavery played quite a role in the history of Slavdom.

"The word 'slave' and its cognates in most European languages (2) date from the time when the Germans supplied the slave-markets of Europe with Slavonic captives" — states the Encyclopedia Britannica (3).

How could it have happened?
Slavery is a phenomenom practiced almost all over the world on certain stages of economy. In the hunting period the savage warrior does not enslave his vanquished enemy, but slays him. The women of a conquered tribe he may, however, carry off and appropriate as his wifes or servants, for in his period domestic labor falls almost altogether on their sex. In the pastoral stage slaves will be captured only to be sold, with the exemption of a few who may be required for the care of flocks or a small amount of cultivation which is then undertaken. It is in proportion where sedentary life prevails and agricultural exploitation is practiced on a large scale while warlike habits continue to exist, that the labor of slaves is increasingly introduced to provide food for the master and at the same time save him from irksome toil. Of this stage in the social movement slavery seem to have been a universal and inevitable accompaniment.

Slavery was common in ancient Egypt, Babylon and Greece, but it was at Rome that the institution was more than anywhere else extended in its operation and methodized in its details.
For almost five centuries of our era the warring German tribes had been held at the borders of the Roman Empire with more or less success by the Roman legions. They did many odd things, ambushing the Roman posts and units, coalescing against the other tribes, paying and taking tributes, trading all the merchandize they could. Among them were slaves, very valuable trade objects in those times.
German expeditions to capture Slavs became an everyday occurence. The captives were sold to the slave markets in Rome and other cities.

Since the German cordon along the northern Roman borders lasted a long time they could have sold quite a number of Slavs. But it seems their reputation as Slav traders is rather overdone. Slavs had been captured in masses in later times, when they started to colonized the Balkans and their suitor was the Byzantine army.
Why did enslaving the Slavs become so enormous in size that their national identity became a synonym of slaves (4)?
Three factors could play a role here: either the Slavs were big in number, or easy to capture, or valuable as slaves.

It appears that all three factors played a role.

No doubt that Slavs in the 5th and 6th century were numerous if they occupied the whole Balkan peninsula, driving away the Byzantine army and storming the walls of Constantinople. As captives they must have flooded all the slave markets of the Mediterranean.

The Byzantine writers were surprised at seeing crowds of men, women and children marching south to seek a new land to settle down. In many cases no army was clearing their path. They drudged defenseless, an easy prey for armed slave traders.

Slavs were skillfull farmers and fond of agriculture, and because of that were valuable slaves. Besides, they must have been mild and easier to handle, since historians did not record Slavic rebellions, although the number of slaves of Slavic origin was quite big. Hence the Roman patrician at the slave market asked for the 'Sclavus' and not for 'servus', because he was sure to get a proper labor force in his vast latifundia.

There are no statistics giving the number of Slavic slaves working in the Roman empires. It would not be a surprise if some scholars, after painstaking research, came to the conclusion that those states survived and flourished down the centuries because of the slave labor done by the Slavs. After all, there had been many warriors, writers, politicians and churchmen in Constatinople of Slavic origin who made careers starting from the bottom of society. Not long ago historians maintained that the Emperor Justinian the Great (527-565) and Emperor Basily I (867-886) were Slavs.

Next to Romans the Arabs got the lion share of Slavic slaves. They got in touch with the Slavs during the Arabic-Byzantinian wars in Asia Minor.

Some Slavs had been forcibly transferred by the Byzantinians from the Balkans to Asia Minor, some served as soldiers in the Imperial army. When it came to wars with the Arabs, the Slavs defected. In 663 many soldiers of Slavic origin joined the ranks of the enemy, and in 690 the number of defectors headed by the prince Nebulos was enormous. The Arabs settled them near Antioch in Syria (5).

The Arabs found Slavs in Sicily, also, when they started to conquer the island in 827. They met Slavs who were transferred here and forcibly settled by the Byzantinians.

Many 'dirhems' — Arabic coins of this time, found in Slavic territories indicated that Slavs had good commercial relationship with the Arabs. The East Slavs traded with the Arabs in Asia, the West

Slavs with the Arabs in Spain and Africa. The objects might have been furs and slaves against Arabic silk, glass, ivory and ornaments.

The Arabs did not trade directly with the Slavs. They used middlemen like Bulgars at the river Kama in trade with the East Slavs, Scandinavians, Italians and Jews in trading with the West Slavs.

According to Byzantine records there were no slaves among the Slavs in the 6th century A.D., meaning they were not warlike people. They did not need help in farming. The situation changed when the wars started. Someone had to replace the men fighting the wars. They were the captives. When the tribal chiefs noticed how valuable the prisoners of war were to enlarging richness and power, they introduced slavery in all its kind.

The first were the Russians. Having had relations with the Byzantine Empire, the state of Kiev established the slavery system in the 8th century. Following it, every Slav country had its own sources of income, drawing from the slave labor and slave markets.

The captives were divided into two groups: the 'czeladź' — domestic servants and the 'chłopi' — farm workers. They had no right to possess anything or to follow their own wish. Since their status was the same as the boys, the youngster got the same name (6).

The rulers founded special villages for the captives to farm and to pay tributes to their masters in crops, sometimes in handicrafts and special services. These settlements were named after the nationality of the captives: 'Pomorzany' — Pomeranians; 'Prusy' — Prussians; 'Czechy' — Czechs; 'Lachowice' — Poles; 'Niemce' — Germans etc., or after the special services they rendered: 'Kowale' — the smithes; 'Mydlniki' — the soap makers; 'Szczytniki' — the warrior shield makers, etc.

Next to men captured in the war, the number of slaves was enlarged when parents started selling their children, people voluntarily selling themselves, and the debtors who could not pay their debts becoming slaves, too.

The system of slavery developed in all the Slavic countries. It would be no surprise to find that all the strongholds built by the Slavs in this epoch served, not against an alien enemy, but against other Slavic tribes trying to capture as many as possible of their cousins and to sell them to the Arabs. It could be the only reason why Svatopluk, the prince of Great Moravia, invaded southern Poland, as mentioned at the beginning of this chapter.

During this time the big international slave market developed in Kiev, Prague and Venice, with the slaves captured or brought from all nations including the Germans, Romans and Greeks. No doubt the Slavs dominated among them.

Ibn Hauqala, the Arabic writer of the second half of the 10th century mentions that Slavs had been brought to Spain by four routes: 1) by land through Franconia (France); 2) by sea to Spanish Galicia; 3) from Venice by sea, and 4) from Calabria in Italy also by sea. They came from the West and Balkan Slavs. The Arabic sources mention Slavic slaves already in 762.

The Slavs played an important role in Arabic Spain at the end of the 9th century until the half of the 11th century. They had been high ranking officers in the army. Some of the former slaves got rich, bought land and lived in palaces. At the end of the caliphate in Cordoba there appeared some Arabic writers of Slavic origin. When the caliphate distintegrated, the Slavs became princes of some principalities in the first half of the 11th century.

From Spain and Italy the slaves of Slavic origin had been brought to Northern Africa, also, mostly to Maghreb and Egypt. They served in the army and as palace guards in Maghreb. Here some of them made a splendid career. General Djauhar, the conqueror of Egypt and founder of the city of Cairo; al Mu'izza, governor of the eastern part of the state of Fatimids; and Qajsar as-Saqlabi, the governor of the western part of this state; all were of Slavic origin.

The exporting of Slavic slaves to Northern Africa ended in the 10th century.

The Jews, who in the 8th century reached the Slavic nations from Byzantium, had their communes in Prague, Przemyśl, Wrocław, Kiev, Nitra and Vladmir. Called the Radanits, they became the main middlemen in trade between the Slavs and Arabs, exporting furs and slaves to Spain (7). Competing with them, the Christian merchants pressed princes to edict prohibition. The first banning of the slave trade by the Jews was introduced in the 9th century. The slave markets ceased to exist in the 13th century, but in Mechlin (Mecklenburg, Germany) to the end of the 12th century anyone could buy or sell a slave with the city approval.

About Slavs as slaves many words have been written (8), some of them sympathetic (9).

NOTES TO CHAPTER XXVI

1. Bibliography: Hitti Ph. K., 'History of Arabs', London 1960; Laufer S., 'Die Sklawerei in der griechisch-romischen Welt', Uppsala 1960; Symonyi D., 'Die Kontinuitatsfrage und das Erscheinen der Slawen in Pannonien', Budapest 1955; Vittinghoff F., 'Die Theorie der historischen Materialismư über den antiken Sklavenhalterstaat', Saeculum 1960, Vol. II, also 'Bedeuntung der Sklawen fur den Ubergang ins Abendländische Mittelalter', 1961; Westermann W.L. 'Sklaverei', Stuttgart 1935, also, 'The Slave Systems of Greek and Roman Antiquity', Philadelphia 1955.

2. The 'slave' in English, der 'Sklawe' in German, le 'slave' in French, il 'slavo' in Italian.

3. Encyclopedia Britannica 1911, Vol. XXV, p. 229.

4. Romans called the Slavs 'Sclaveni' or 'Sclavini' and the slaves 'sclavi'.

5. L. Leciejewicz, 'Mały słownik kultury dawnych Słowian', p. 23.

6. In Polish the 'chłop' — peasant, the 'chłopiec' — boy. In Russian captive was called the 'chołop' or 'otrok' — boy.

7. It appears that Ibrahim ibn Jacob, a Jew in the service of Spanish Arabs, made his journey to Slavic countries in 962 to explore the possibility of slave trade. The report he wrote is a priceless source of history of the early Slavs.

8. Some German 'scholars', especially in Hitler's era, tried to convince 'scientifically' that Slavs are good as slaves only, as the name indicates.

9. There are some books picturing the horrible fate of Slavic slaves, but it would be hard to find out who have been better treated: slaves in ancient times or migrant workers of today. Besides, we are not qualified to blame the Greeks, Romans or Germans for what they did to captives in antiquity since in our eyes Hitler and Stalin destroyed millions in concentration and slave labor camps.

175

PART THREE:
EARLY SLAVIC STATES

Two events mark the new epoch in the history of the Ancient Slavs: the ending of the great migration and the establishing of the Great Moravian kingdom of Samo in 624 A.D.

After two centuries of fighting and colonizing new territories, the Slavs were tired. They tried to hold firm their domains. Besides, the new reality forced them to make profound changes in their political, economic and social life. The loose federation of the tribes called the kingdom of Samo could not work for a longer period. A new political organization of a stronger bond must have been invented. This led to the establishment of states, which after many mishaps down the centuries, exist today.

There were many attempts among the Ancient Slavs to form a state in early stages of their history. With the help of archaeology we can accept the supposition that there must have been a strong society which raised the stronghold at Biskupin, some 500 B.C. The archaeological findings point out that at least 12 political centers might have been in the Polish territories and 3 in South West Russia in the third century A.D. During the Avaric epoch there was a strong political organization at Wapno in Northern Poland, and in Cracow in Southern Poland. Since there are no records dealing with these centers no one knows the names of the rulers or their deeds.

The first Slavic chief recorded by chroniclers was Booz, the leader of the Antes. He had been defeated in 362 A.D. and crucified with his "primates" — leutenants by Vinithar, the king of the Ostrogoths.

Two hundred years later during the Avaric invasion the names of Slavic leaders appeared more often in chronicles. There is Medzamir (in the same region where Booz was), Ardagast, Daurentios (Dauritas), Musokios, Pirogast, Samo and Dervan. They were leaders of very loose federations of Slavic tribes.

The new epoch produces more stable political organizations and more information about the activities of Slavic leaders.

177

CHAPTER XXVII
STATEHOOD

Some (1) historians maintain (2) that the Ancient Slavs were unable to form political organizations called states. Where the Slavic state appears in early times it is either a result of subjugation of the Slavic nation by some foregin force which imposed upon it the state organization, or by taking over the model of the foreign statehood by the Slavs. History disavows these suppositions. Foreign forces contributed to the organization of some Slavic states by imposing their rules, and some Slavic nations followed foreign models, but they followed their own path to statehood, also, as Poland indicates.

No trace of state organization could be found in the period when the clan constituted the base of the social system. All members of the big family worked according to their ability. The 'starosta' — head (3) of the clan, presided in meetings, but with no power to rule.

There is no doubt that clans made some sort of federation from time to time when they saw some advantages, but they were very loose and shortlived political organizations. Hochholzer (4) maintains that the clan federations must have existed when the Proto-Slavs marched west from the Eurasiatic steppe, because the groups of 50-60 people were helpless and lost if they tried independently to occupy land already taken by another group. If it is true, the loosely formed federation of clans did not represent statehood at all.

Although clans were the basic organizations of the social system, the big 'kurhany' — barrows, richly furnished, appeared in an early epoch (5). Since poor families could not have afford to raise big mounds for their deceased, it means that some personalities respected or feared by more than one clan must have existed. Archaeologists gave those barrows the name 'the princely graves', assuming the buried dead were some sort of prince or war leader or archpriest. Here could be observed the first hint of formation of state authority. One could accept the idea of some German scholars (6) that here we have another step in developing statehood, after the clannish system which was the first.

The second hint of some sort of state organization is the fortified towns built in areas of Lusatian culture (7). One clan could not have raised a stronghold like Biskupin. Eleven long houses indicate they could have been occupied by eleven clans. Since the number of occupants was 1000 to 1200, to keep law and order in such a big group concentrated in such small place, some sort of authority must have been used rather effectively.

When the clan gave way to the 'opole' — territory composed of several settlements closely tied with the region, the urge of political authority must have been strong. All free men of 'opole' were entitled to participate in opole-gathering, the highest authority, with the 'żupan' (8) presiding.

Several 'opoles' in the vicinity of the same ethnic background instinctively formed the larger social organization, the 'plemię' — tribe, with gathering headed by what might have been called 'włodyka' — ruler (9). The religious beliefs and observances were strong factors cementing the unity of the tribe. It is possible that all vital decisions were made during festivities in which tribal meetings took place.

In time of war the tribe selected a 'wojewoda' — war leader.(10)

Then appeared a new title, this time of foreign origin, the 'książę'-prince (11), which puzzled many scholars, especially because the 'książę' displaced the native 'włodyka'. The reason is not known. Perhaps the new leader was more powerful because he led a troop on horses, which was new to Slavs, or he was more successful in executing bounty raids. Nonetheless, the new title put deep roots in the social and political system.

When the country was in danger the tribes would form a short-lived federation to defend themselves.

Even in this stage of social development one can hardly see a statehood structure, because the organization was lacking a stable source of income, which means the tax system.(12)

But some historians see in this stage of political development a transition form of statehood, because authority was being shaped. They call this political organization a tribal multitribal state.(13) It had more or less a powerful and stabile heád named the 'włodyka or 'kneź' in Slavonic and 'dux' or 'rex' in Latin. The 'żupans' — heads of 'opoles' called in Greek records 'archontes' and in Latin 'primores', 'principes' or 'optimates', constituted not only the council of the prince to solve lesser problems, but his best military unit, the heavy troops on horses. The elite became the nucleus of future magnates. Neither the prince nor his council had full power. Important decisions were still made by the 'wiece' — gathering of all free men, mostly under arms. The principality was not hereditary. The prince was elected for some definite period at the beginning, for time of emergency only, then he stayed for life in that office.

Such Slavic 'states' appeared early on the political arena. Jordanes records that about 380 A.D. the Slavic prince Booz had been defeated by the Gothic prince Vinithar and crucified with his 70 'primates'. Records also mention Mezamir, Dobręta and Mężyk — three princes of the Balkan Slavs in the 6th century, then Dervan, prince of the Lusatians, Samo in Czechs and Walduch in Carinthia in the 7th century.

The income of those 'states' must have been drawn from the spoils, contributions and the prince's estate.

It is worth mentioning that the warrior in those times was the 'raciądz' (14). If he brought home the 'wici' — spoils, they called him 'wiciądz'.(15)

The state as a political organization had chances to develop when in the farming economy the animal traction was introduced. The farmer could produce more than he needed. The surplus of his production allowed him to feed the people who were not engaged in farming, like artisans and warriors.

Flint miners in the Holy Cross Mountains must have been the first handicraftsmen in the Polish territories. Since flint axes were found far from the place where they had been manufactured, trading was a common feature. But those two groups did not make a state.

Surplus in farming achieved by some families, clans and tribes generated the temptation to steal for those who for some reason could not produce it. The war for spoils started, and another group emerged — the warriors.

Since the farmer could produce more than he consumed, slave labor appeared. Tribes warred among themselves, not only to rob each other, but to take prisoners of war, too, who could work for the victors. Spoils and slaves contributed heavily to develop the tax system. So the surplus in farming gave start to far reaching consequences.

Fiscus, which gave base in forming states, started among the Slavs, as the sources indicate, in the 7th century. The 'danina' — tribute, was the first tax, paid voluntarily to the ruler by his people for defending their country. In the course of time this duty, made occasionally, had been transformed to the 'narok'-yearly tribute in form of the 'narzaz'-animals, first pigs, then cattle and sheep, and the 'sep'-cereals. (16) The 'żupan'-head of the territorial unit 'opole, was the tax collector.

Since in the early times no one could read or write the 'narzaz'-an ingeneous system of tax recording developed. They made parallel incisions on two sticks or small boards. The tax payer received the one, the tax-collector kept another. Since the incision was named 'narzaz' the word also meant tax at the beginning.

A special form of tax was doing public service. People had obligations to build and repair strongholds, bridges and roads; to guard the settlements and strongholds; to feed and house the prince and his troop if he made a stay in some places, and to deliver horses and carts for transporting things belonging to the prince.

In addition to taxes the treasury made income by the 'winy' or 'grzywny'-fines; the 'myto'-toll paid at bridges and city gates and 'targowe'-toll paid by merchants.

Taxes paid in goods and services in time were transformed into regular money payments. When it happened the state in full power appeared.

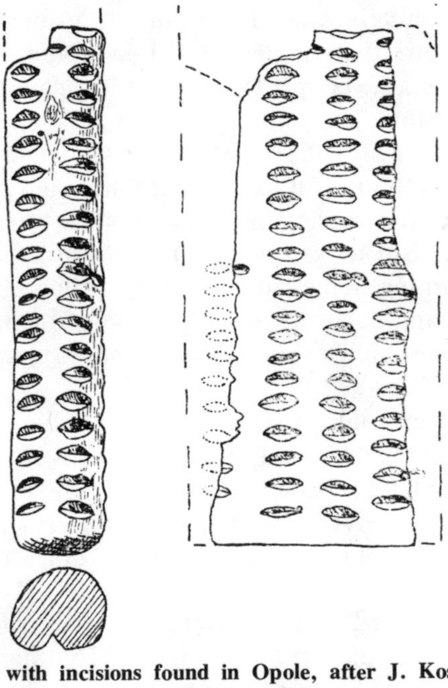

Fig. 49. The stick with incisions found in Opole, after J. Kostrzewski, 'Kultura prapolska', p. 435.

Ibrahim ibn Jacob (17) wrote about Mieszko I (died in 992) the first Polish ruler historically ascertained: "He collects taxes in money which he uses to support his warrios, and every month he pays some sum to every warrior". This statement indicates that the first prince of Poland had not only a tax system, but the modern monthly payroll as well.

The cities played a big role in the development of statehood. Biskupin was a fortified town and trading post, too. Merchants and artisans felt safer under the guard of armed men than being alone in an open field. Therefore they concentrated their activity around the strongholds.

There were many points of such concentration in Slavic territories in early times. The best example are: Vogastiburg in Bohemia, Rerik in Polabian country and Old Ladoga in Russia. In Latin sources the settlements serving as fortified towns and trading posts are called 'civitates'.

Next to merchants and artisans, the heads of powerful tribes sought here a place to stay. They had their residences in the country, but they looked for a special income in the cities. Here they built second residences, (sometimes even with chapels) in which they supervized artisans working for them. Some of these magnates became merchants.

The fortified town was too small to embrace the increasing number of merchants, artisans and magnates, so they had to place their quarters outside the city walls. Thus around the strongholds developed the 'podgrodzie' — settlement close to the fortified town. They were open in the beginning, but they got their own bulwark in time.

The earliest cities of this type appeared in Moravia at the Morava River (Czechoslovakia, today), at the crossroads of Carolingian, Byzantinian and Slavic influences. The archaeological excavations at Stare Mesto, Mikulcice and Nitra revealed extremely well developed city centers in the 9th century.

Cities connected by water and land routes played an enormous role in the consolidation of states. Having had good relations with each other, they focused on the evolution of national identity.

In some Slavic countries the growth of cities went even farther. They became independent republics, like the Slavic ports at the Baltic (18): Lubeck, Rostock, Wolin, Kołobrzeg and Szczecin, or Novgorod and Ladoga in Russia. These cities were sometimes so powerful that the new prince had to make special agreements with them to secure their cooperation, nullified if the prince did not live up to his obligations.

Since the Frankish merchant Samo organized the first Slavic political body 'kingdom', the Varangian Ruriks giving shape to the Russian state and the Bulgars khan to Bulgarian state, some scholars (19), mostly German arrived at the wrong conclusion that all states were the creation of foreign rulers, and that invasions and subjugation by aliens caused the formation of Slavic states because the Slavs were unable to create states of their own.

The idea applies to some Slavic nations, but not to the Poles. Poland emerged at the end of the 10th century as a fully developed state. Trying to explain the anomaly, scholars accepted the possibility that the Polish state had been created by the Scandinavian Vikings. The "proofs" on which they based their speculations are so poor that they are ridiculous (20).

Having had a peripherial situation off the crossroads in those times, Poland enjoyed a tranquility which helped her to develop political institutions in her own way. She appeared late on the political arena, but so well matured as a powerful kingdom that she could repel attacks from all sides down the centuries.

There is no doubt that all Slavic nations could have developed their statehood in the same way, but the process had been hastened by foreign interventions, because those nations found themselves earlier in the orbit of the big powers struggle.

NOTES TO CHAPTER XXVII

1. **Bibliography:** Brunner O, 'Land und Herrschaft', Brunn 1943; Czernak W., 'Ilustrowane dzieje Polski', Wiedeń 1905; Jellinek J., 'Ogólna nauka o państwie Warszawa 1926; Kadiec J., 'O prawie prywatnym zachodnich Słowian przed X wiekiem', PAU, Vol. IV; Kelsen H., 'General Theory of Law and State', Cambridge, Mass. 1945, also: 'Hauptprobleme der Staatslehre entwickelt aus der Lehre vom Rechtsatze', Tubingen 1923; Kocka W., 'Zagadnienie etnogenezy ludów Europy', Wrocław 1958; Kostrzewski J., 'Czy państwo polskie zawdzięcza powstanie Gotom? 'PArch. Vol. IX; Ludat H., 'Vorstufen und Entstehung des Stadtwesens in Osteuropa', Koln 1955; Łowmiański H., 'Podstawy gospodarcze formowania się państw słowiańskich', Warszawa 1953, also: 'Zagadnienie roli Normanów w genezie państw słowiańskich', Warszawa 1957; Maleczyński K., 'Najstarsze targi w Polsce', Lwów 1926; Meughin O, 'Grundlinen einer Methodik der urgeschichtlichen Stammeskunde', Heidelberg 1936; Tymieniecki K., 'Podgrodzie w północno-zachodniej słowiańszczyźnie i pierwsze lokacje miast polskich na prawie niemieckim', SA 1922, Vol. II, also: 'Społeczeństwo Słowian lechickich', Lwów 1928, also: 'Narocznicy w gospodarstwie feudalnym', Toruń 1955; Thurnwald R., 'Werden, Wandel und Gestaltung von Staat und Kultur im Lichte der Völkerforschung', Berlin

1935; Widajewicz K., 'Kilka słów o narzazie', Sl. Ant. Vol. VI; S. Weymann, 'Cła i drogi handlowe w Polsce piastowskiej', Poznań 1938.

2. M. Hellmann, 'Grundfragen slawischer Verfassungsgeschichte des frühen Mittelalters', IGOst. 1954, p. 387-404.

3. J. Kostrzewski, 'Kultura prapolska', p. 421, mentions the word 'starosta' as a title of the head of the 'ród' — clan. The title was very popular among the Slavs, especially Poles. The 'starosta' was the master of ceremonies at peasant weddings and the head of the country district in Poland until 1951.

4. H. Hochholzer, 'Typologie und Dynamik der Völkerwanderung', DWGesch. 1957, Vol. XIX, p. 139.

5. J. Kostrzewski in his books, 'Od mezolitu', p. 141, and in 'Pradzieje', p. 39, as well as K. Jażdżewski, 'Olbrzymi grób kujawski w pow. kolskim', ZOW. 1936, Vol. XI, p. 121-129, give a description of these barrows. They were of megalithic size, 350 do 380 ft long, richly furnished.

6. E. Meyer, 'Geschichte des Altertums', Stuttgart 1907, p. 10; H. Mittels, 'Staatliche Konzentrationsbewegungen im grossgermanischen Raum', Weimar 1941, p. 53-86; O. Brunner, 'Land und Herschaft', Brunn 1943.

7. See Chapter Biskupin.

8. It looks like the 'żupa' — territorial organization known to the Balkan Slavs down the centuries had been created in Polish territories before the Ancient Slavs started to migrate. Some Slavic nations changed its name to 'opole', 'okolina' and 'vierw', but the trace of original organization survived in the title 'żupan' — head of the 'żupa', which in course of time had been shortened to 'pan', which means 'mister' in Polish today, but meant the head of a district or fortified city in Poland until the 16th century.

9. A. Brückner, 'Dzieje kultury polskiej', Vol. I, p. 82, maintains, the word 'włodyka' derives from the 'włody' which in Old Slavonic meant authority. It was a genuine title of the Slavic prince. The word 'włodyka' in Polish had been transformed into the władca — ruler, souvereign, monarch.

10. The term 'wojewoda' had the same sounding and meaning in all Slavic languages. It meant a man who led the warriors. In Polish the word survived in the name of 'województwo' — administrative district composed of several counties.

11. A. Brückner, 'Dzieje kultury polskiej', Vol. I, p. 18, thinks the word 'książę' derives supposedly from the Gothic term 'kuning' — tribal chief. The Ancient Slavs picked it up and transformed it to 'knęg', in Polish 'kniądz', 'ksiądz' and 'książe'. In other Slavic languages the kunning became the 'kniaź' or 'kneź'.

12. H. Łowmiański, 'Początki Polski', Vol. I, p. 18.

13. L. Leciejewicz, 'Mały słownik kultury dawnych Słowian', p. 562.

14. The word 'raciądz', which survived in Polish in name of places like Raciąż, only, derives from the word 'rać' — battle, war. But there is another word in Polish vocabulary, the 'racice' — hoofs. It is possible that warriors had been armed with spears with hoofs as heads, hence from the 'racice' was 'rać' and 'raciądz'.

15. J. Kostrzewski, 'Kultura prapolska', p. 429.

16. The term 'sep' derives from the word 'sypać' — to pour, strew.

17. Ibrahim ibn Jacob, a Jewish traveller from Arabic Spain.

18. It is possible that those Slavic port-republics at the Baltic Sea gave the idea to introduce the city government when they were subjugated by the Germans.

19. R. Holzmann, 'Böhmen und Polen in 10 Jahrhundert' VGS 1918; A. Brackmann, 'Die Anfange des polnischen Staates', Berlin 1934; H. Janichen, 'Die Wikingen im Weichsel — und Odergebiet', Leipzig 1938.

20. A. Brückner, 'Dzieje kultury polskiej', K. Potkański, 'Drużyna Mieszka a Wikingi z Jomsborga', Kraków 1906; Z. Wojciechowski, 'Polska nad Wisłą i Odrą w X w.', Katowice 1939 ; H. Łowmiański, 'Imię chrzestne Mieszka I', Sl. Occ. Vol. XI; H. Laudat, 'Die Anfange des polnischen Staates', Krakau 1942. It is worth mentioning that the first Polish chronicler Gallus Anonymous, in the beginning of his chronicle, states very clearly: "Poland, many times attacked by the enemics in the past, never had been subjugated".

185

CHAPTER XXVIII
THE BALKAN SLAVS

The Southern Slavdom was formed as a result of Slav migration and settlement on the Balkan Peninsula in the 6th and 7th centuries. The northern border to the new Slavic homeland ran up the lower and middle Danube and the Save with its tributaries.

Beginning of Slavic expansion (1) to the south was reached by the 5th century, especially its second half, if we exclude the possibility that some small groups could migrate a little earlier(2). The epoch prior to expansion in this area of Europe was the most turbulent. The great migrations and regrouping of many different nations, like the Germans, Sarmatians and Huns took place, but there were no Slavs among them. It was not until the short lived Hunnish empire fell in 455 that the situation became ripe for Slavic expansion to the south.

The first stage of Slavic migration was the middle and lower Danube. In the middle of the 6th century colonization ended. The written sources acknowledge the existence of Slavs called the 'Sclavini' to the north of the lower Danube as far as the Dniester, and behind them another Slavic group called the 'Antes'. Slavs in this time were also present at the middle Danube on territory which was Moravian and Bohemian in later times.

From the moment of strengthening, Slavs at the Danube began their second stage of expansion toward the south, which lasted the whole 6th century. The proper action of colonization sometimes followed after the destructive attack made by the Sclavini and Antes.

More and more groups of Slavs made their permanent settlement on the territory of the Byzantine Empire to the south of the Danube. There are many archaeological findings of this colonization, especially in the places of the ancient crossing of the Danube, like 'Durostorum' (Silistra, today) and 'Bononia' (Widin, today).

Map XV. The Balkan Slavic nations, after L. Leciejewicz.

The end of the 6th century brought the serious weakness of the Byzantine Empire on the Balkan Peninsula. The Slavs in bigger groups crossed the Danube, reaching Peloponesus.

At the same time the Slavs started colonization of the Eastern Alps. Historical sources mention it at the end of the 6th century, but the action had to be started much earlier, perhaps at the beginning of that century, because at the end of it the regions of the upper Save, Drave and Mur were in the hands of the Slavic settlers.

Slavic colonization of the Balkan Peninsula had the insular appearance at the beginning. Groups settled among the remnants of natives. In the colonization not only the Slav nations of the Danube took part, but, also from the east, north and west.

At the end of the 7th century the colonization of the Balkan Peninsula closed. The eastern part of the Peninsula was densely populated by the Slavs, excluding the area of Constantinople and Thessalonica, which despite many Slavic attemps, remained in possession of the Byzantine Empire.

187

The region from the Danube down to the Peninsula, sometimes called by the Byzantinian sources as 'Sclavinia', was occupied by the Slavic nations, from which one was known as the tribe of 'Seven Clans', another the 'Severyans' which points out on their East Slav origin. West of Seven Clans lived the 'Timotchans', their name being derived from the river 'Timok', and the Obodrits.

There are numerous names of the Slavic tribes in Macedonia, particularly near Thessalonica. At the middle of the lower Mesta settled the 'Smolentsi'; to the east of Thessalonica, on the coast of the Aegean Sea, the 'Rintchins'; to the north-west of that city, the 'Sagudatsi'; in their vicinity at the Bistrica River — the 'Drugovitsi'; to the north at the Struma River — 'Strumintsi'; deep in Macedonia — the 'Brsatsi'.

Slavic colonization also reached the Greek territories down to the end of the Peloponesus Peninsula (3), which at the beginning of the 8th century was called the 'Sclavonia Terra' — Land of Slavs. Slavic

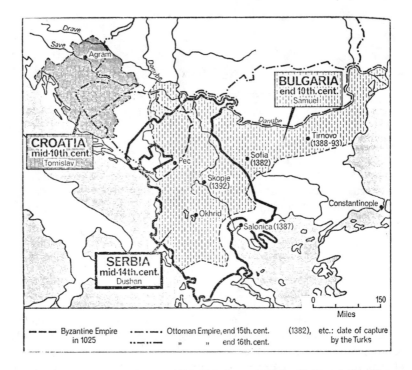

Map XVI. Slavic Balkan States, 10th-15th Centuries, after R. Portal, The Slavs.

188

population enjoyed full freedom in Greece (4), and at the end of the 8th century the Byzantine Empire started to subordinate the Slavic settlers.

Some Slavic nation lasted longer than others on Peloponesus, being subdued not earlier than in the 10th century (5). The written sources mention the 'Vajunitsi', settled in Epirus, and the 'Velegesitsi', who were in Thessalia. The southern outskirts of Peloponesus were in possession of the 'Millings' and the 'Yesvertsi'.

Judging by the name of many localities in Greece, there could have been some Serbian and Croatian settlements in Greece.

There was also Slavic colonization in Asia Minor, mentioned in the sources in the 6th century. The capacity of this settlement was quite different from the Balkan colonization. The settlers were the Slavs in military service of the Byzantine Empire, or Slavic prisoners of war forcibly settled in Asia Minor by the emperors of Constantinople. Their largest settlement, founded by the Emperor Justinian II at the end of the 7th century, was in the territory called 'Opsikon', where the Slavs managed to survive until the 10th century.

The Balkan Slavs organized more or less powerful political bodies in the course of time. The most known are: Bulgaria, Croatia and Serbia.

BULGARIA

First to start was Bulgaria. In 679 the Bulgars (6), under their khan Asparukh (or Isperikh), crossed the Danube and, after subjugating the Slavic population of Moesia, advanced to the gates of Constantinople and Thessalonica. The East Roman emperors were compelled to cede to him the province of Moesia and to pay him an annual tribute. The invading horde was not numerous, and during the next two centuries it became gradually merged with the Slavic population. Like the Franks in Gaul, the Bulgars gave their name and a political organization to the civilized race which they conquered, but adopted its language, customs and local institutions.

The history of the early Bulgarian dynasties is little else than a record of continuous conflicts with the Byzantine emperors. The tribute first imposed on the Greeks by Asparukh was again exacted by Kardam (701-797) and Krum (802-815). Under his rule the Bulgarian realm extended from the Carpathians to the neighborhood of Adrianople.

The reign of Boris I (852-884) is memorable for the introduction of Christianity into Bulgaria.

Fig. 50. Church of St. Sophia in Okhrid, Bulgaria.

The national power reached its zenith under Simeon (893-927), son of Boris, a monarch distinguished in arts of war and peace. His dominions extended from the Black Sea to the Adriatic, and from the borders of Thessaly to the Save and the Carpathians. Having become the most powerful monarch in Eastern Europe, Simeon assumed a title of 'tsar' — emperor of all the Bulgars and Greeks (7), the title which was recognized by pope Formosus. During the later years of his reign, which were spent in peace, his people made great progress in civilization. Literature flourished, and Preslav (Komonczija, today) their capital, according to contemporary chroniclers, rivalled Constantinople in magnificence.

After the death of Simeon the Bulgarian power declined due to internal dissensions. The land distracted by the 'Bogomil heresy' (8) and a seperate or Western Empire, including Albania and Macedonia, was founded at Okhrid by Shishman, a boyar from Trnovo.

A notable event took place in 967, when the Russians under Sviatoslav, made their appearance in Bulgaria. The Bulgarian tsar Boris II with the aid of Emperor Jon Zimisces, expelled the invaders, but the Greeks took advantage of their victory to dethrone Boris II, and the Bulgarian Empire came to an end and after existence of three centuries.

In general insurrection of Bulgars under the brothers Ivan and Peter Asen of Trnovo, who claimed descent from the dynasty of Shismanovitsi, the nation recovered its independence in 1186, and

190

Ivan Asen assumed title of 'Tsar of the Bulgars and Greeks'. The seat of the second empire was Trnovo.

Koloyan, the third of the Asen monarchs, extended his dominions to Belgrade, Nish and Skopie. He' acknowledged the spiritual supremacy of the pope and received the royal crown from a papal legate.

The greatest of all Bulgarian rulers was Ivan Asen II (1218-1241), man of humane and enlightened character. After a series of victorious campaigns he established his rule over Albania, Epirus, Macedonia and Thrace and ruled his wide dominions with justice, wisdom and moderation. In his time the nation attained a prosperity hitherto unknown.

At the end of the 14th century Bulgaria was subjugated by the Turks and suffered their yoke until 1878, when in a Treaty in Berlin, the Bulgarians regained their independence.

CROATIA

To the north west of Bulgaria in Dalmatia the second Slavic state began to form on the Balkan Peninsula, called Croatia (9).

The Croats, a Slavonic nation from the Western Carpathians, entered Croatia of today between 634 and 638, encouraged by the Emperor Heraclius to attack the Avars. They brought with them their tribal institution based partly on military democracy and the patriachal system.

In 877 Croats were temporarily subdued by the Byzantine emperor, but after succissive insurrections which helped to centralize their loosely knit tribal organization and to place all power in the hands of a military chief, they regained their independence and founded a national kingdom about 910. It is probable that Tomislav or Timislav who led their armies to victory, assumed the title of king in that year. Some historians maintain that Drzislav (978-1000) was the first king properly so called. Many Croats regard this period as the golden age of their country.

Among the kings who gained a lasting fame by their success in war and diplomacy were: Kresimir I (940-946) his successor Miroslav, and especially Kresimir II, surnamed the Great (1000-1035), who conquered a large part of Dalmatia, including some Italian cities. The Croats built a fleet, which they used first for piracy and after for trade. Their skill in maritime affairs was remarkable.

191

Zvonimir was crowned by the legate of the pope Gregory VII, in 1076, as the king of Croatia.

After the death of Stephen II in 1089, Helena, his widow, appealed for aid to her brother, Ladislaus I, king of Hungary. Ladislaus took possession of the country in 1091. Through a personal union Croatia became a part of Hungary. She regained its independence in 1918, and now it is one of the republics of Yugoslav federation.

To the north-west of Croatia the Slavic expansion began in the middle of the 6th century. It met with rivalry from German colonization, especially Bavarian, in the 8th century. In spite of it, most of Austria of today was called 'Slavinia' in written sources. The Slavs equally with the Bavarians, participated in developing the social and economic life of Austria.

SLOVENIA

Below Austria the Slavs colonized the right bank of the Danube and the basins of the rivers Save, Drave and Mur, which means the territory of Slovenia of today. They were subordinated by the Avars at the beginning, but in the 7th century they managed to organize a tribal federation under the prince Walluk, who joined with his federation the Slavic empire of Samo.

After the death of Samo the Slavs in this area acted independently. The most important was the principality of Carinthia (10) which had to defend herself against the Longobards and Bavarians from the west, and the Avars in the east. Carinthia acknowledged the sovereignty first of Bavaria then of Franconia in the 8th century (11).

Also Kraina to the south of the Drave, subdued by the Avars, came under the Frankish influence.

When Charlemagne defeated the Avars at the beginning of the 9th century, Slavic colonization comprised the lower Pannonia. There was a principality ruled by the princes Pribina and Kocelj, respectively, in some dependence upon Franconia.

The Slovenes of Carinthia and Kraina supported the uprising of the prince Ljudevit of Passau. The Franks suppressed the rebellion, chased the Slavic princes, and put both countries under the rule of Frankish counts.

At the end of the 10th century the German emperor organized Great Carinthia against the attacks of the Hungarians. It was comprised of all Slovenes territories without lower Pannonia, which was conquered by Bulgaria.

From the beginning of the 10th century the German colonization in Slovenia started supported by the state and church, but the Slovenian language managed to survive among the peasants and nobility.

Slovenia joined Yugoslavia in 1918 and now is a republic of this federal country.

SERBIA

According to the Greek emperor Constantine Porphyrogenitus, the emperor Heraclius (610-640) invited also the Serbs to come over from Poland and to settle down in the devastated nort-eastern provinces of the Byzantine Empire, and to defend it against the incursions of the Avars. Their history as a Balkan nation begins toward the middle of the 7th century.

In their new settlements the Serbs did not form a united political organization at the beginning. The tribes, more or less related to each other, occupied a certain territory, which as a geographical and political unit was called 'Zhupa' or 'Zhupanija' — county, with the political and military chief called the 'Zhupan'.

The country was divided into many such 'Zhupas', which originally were independent of each other. The history of the Serbs during the first five centuries after their arrival was a struggle between the attempts of making a union of the 'Zhupas' with strong central authority and resistance to such union. It led to many civil wars, revolutions and political assassinations.

Another cause of turbulance was found in the struggle between the ancient Slavonic order of inheritance, according to which a 'Zhupan' ought to be succeeded by the oldest member of the family and not necessarily by his son, and the natural desire of every ruler to put his son upon the throne after his death.

The internal political process was complicated by the struggle between the Greek Church and Greek emperors on one side and the Roman Church and Roman Catholic powers like Venice or Hungary on the other, for the possession of exclusive ecclesiastic and political influence. The danger increased when the Bulgarians came, towards the end of the 7th century, and formed a powerful kingdom on the south-eastern borders of Serbia. Practicaly from the 8th to the 12th century the bulk of Serbian lands was under either Bulgarian or Greek sovereignty, while the Serbo-Croat provinces of Dalmatia acknowledged either Venetian or Hungarian supremacy.

The first Serbian princes who worked with more or less success in uniting some 'Zhupas' were the Visheslav dynasty. Zhupan Visheslav lived in the beginning of the 9th century. His son Radoslav, grandson Prisegoy, and great-grandson Vlastimir, continued his work.

Vlastimir successfully defended the western provinces of Serbia against the Bulgarians with the help of the Greek emperor Basil the Macedonian. One of the consequences of this event was the Serbian vassalship to the Byzantinians and embracing Christianity, between 871-875. Then, the Bulgarian tsar Simeon conquered Serbia again in 924.

Towards the end of the 9th century the political center of the Serbs was transferred to 'Zetta' (Montenegro, today) and the 'Primorye' — the coasts of the Adriatic. About 1042 prince Voislav of Travuniye (Trebinje, today) started a successful insurrection against the Greeks, and united under his rule Travuniye, Zahumlye and Zetta. His son Michael annexed the important Zhupaniya of Rashka, and in 1077 proclaimed himself king, receiving the crown from pope Gregory VII.

Serbia gained her zenith under the rule of Bodin, the son of king Michael (1081-1101). He united all Serbian territories and created a powerful empire. In his time the Latin Church and Latin culture flourished in Serbia.

After the death of Bodin the importance of Serbia diminished, but at the end of the 12th century Stephan Nemanya, the grand zhupan of Rashka (1169-1196) then founded the Nemanya dynasty which ruled Serbia until her fall in 1389.

The further history of Serbia ran with seesaw fortunes. The country flourished under king Stephen Dushan, who in 1346 proclaimed himself "Tsar of all Serbs and Greeks". Trvtko, his successor in the battle at Kossovo in 1389 suffered a painful defeat from the Turks, and Serbia became a Turkish vassalage.

After a series of bloody uprisings the Turkish sultan agreed to form a miniature but autonomous principality of Serbia in 1830. Serbia regained her independence in 1878 and became a kingdom in 1882. In 1918 she constituted the backbone of Yugoslavia.

NOTES TO CHAPTER XXVIII

1. **Bibliography:** Andrew M., Angelow D., 'Istorija Balgarskała daržava i prawo', Sofija 1959; Arnandow M., 'Oczerki po bulgarskija folkor', Sofija 1934; Buschan G., 'Die Bulgaren', Stuttgart 1907; Cankova-Petkova G., 'Za agrarnite otnoszenija w srednowekowana Balgarija', Sofija 1964; Corovic V., 'Bosna i Hercegovina', Belgrad 1925; Crnja z., 'Cultural History of Croatia', Zagreb 1962; Dellin L.A., 'Bulgaria',

New York 1957· Dinić Đ., 'Za istoriju rudarstwa u Slovencev', Ljubljana 1944; Doflein F., 'Mazedonien', Jena 1921; Dopsch A., 'Die alteste Sozial — und Wirtschaftsverfassung der Alpenslawen', Weimar 1903; Dujcev I., 'Medioevo bizantino-slavo', Roma 1971; Eterovich F.H., Spalatin G., 'Croatia' 1946; Grafemauer B., 'Le Development national des Slovenes de Carinthie' 1946; Guidescu S., 'History of Medieval Croatia', 1964; Helpern J., 'A Serbian village', New York 1958; Haussig H.W., Historia kultury bizantyńskiej', Warszawa 1970; Ilic L., 'Narodni slavonski oblicaji', Zagreb 1846; Ischirkoff A., 'Bulgarien Land and Leute', Leipzig 1917; 'Istorija Crne Gore', Titograd 1967; 'Istorija naroda Jugoslavije', Beograd 1960; 'Istorija Srba', Beograd 1952; 'Istorija na Balgarija', Sofija 1961; Klacic N., 'Historija hrvatskogo naroda', Zagreb 1970; Lipkowski A.L., 'Chorwaty', Petersburg 1860; Lozar R., 'Narodopisje Slovencev', Lubljana 1944; Melik A., 'Slovenija' 1960; Pinto V., 'Bulgarian Prose and Verse' 1957; Pundoff M.V. 'Bulgaria', Washington 1965; Runciman S., 'History of the First Bulgarian Empire', London 1962; Stawski F., 'Bułgaria — dzieje piśmiennictwa w zarysie', Kraków 1947; Temperly H.W. 'History of Serbia' 1917; Vakarelski Ch., 'Etnografia Bułgarii', Wrocław 1965; Wasilewski T., 'Historia Bułgarii', Wrocław 1970; Zlatarski N., 'Geschichte der Bulgaren' 1918.

2. The Slavic penetration as mercenaries started earlier as the 'Schola Barbarorum' founded for them in Constantinople as Lech Leciejewicz in 'Mały słownik kultury dawnych Słowian' p. 35, indicates.

3. According to the chronicles of the city Monenvasia on Peloponesus, written probably in the second half of the 10th century, the Slavic rule in Peloponesus lasted 218 years, from about 588 to 805.

4. How big the Slavic influence was is indicated by the rebellion in 820-823 led by Thomas the Slav. It embraced the whole empire, and Thomas proclaimed himself Emperor Constantine. After the siege of Constantinople which lasted a whole year, the Emperor Michael II managed to crush the rebel forces with the military assistance of Bulgarian khan Omurtag (Lech Leciejewicz, 'Słownik kultury dawnych Słowian', p. 385).

5. According to F. Grabler, 'Europe in XV Jahrhundert von Byzantinern gesehen', Graz-Wien-Koln 1954, Vol. II, p. 103-105, the Byzantinian traveller Laskaris Kananos visited in 1438-1439 northern Europe. He states in his report that the Baltic port of Lubeck (East Germany) was in the country called 'Slavonia' and its inhabitants used the Slavic language similar to the Slavic language spoken by the Zigots in Peloponesus. It appears that Slavonic vivid and in use in southern Greece in the 15th century.

6. The Bulgars a Turanian race akin to the Tatars, Huns, Avars, Petchenges and Finns made their appearance on the banks of the Pruth in the latter part of the 7th century. They were a horde of wild horsemen, fierce and barbarous, practising polygamy, and governed despotically by their 'khans' — chiefs, and 'boyars'-nobles. Their original abode was the tract between the Ural Mountains and the Volga, where the kingdom of Great Bulgaria existed until the 13th century.

7. 'Tsar' was the highest title of the ruler of the Balkan and East Slavs, borrowed from the Byzantium title 'katsar'-the emperor. Simeon, the ruler of Bulgaria was the first Slavic ruler who proclaimed himself tsar in 914 to point out his independence from Constantinople. The title vanished with the loss of independence of Bulgaria in the 11th century. It was revived in Serbia when Stephen Dushan proclaimed himself tsar of all Serbs in 1346. In the 16th century the rulers of Russia accepted the title.

8. 'Bogomils' was a Slavic sect formed by mixing the Christian beliefs with agnostic dualistic beliefs which the Slavic settlers in Asia Minor brought to Europe. According to tradition, a priest called 'Bogomil' was the founder of the sect, hence its name. The Bogomils rapidly expanded in Bulgaria, Serbia and Dalmatia in the 11th century. They spread in Western Europe under the name of 'Bugri', 'Cathars', 'Albigensi'. They were destroyed by the crusades and bloody persecutions in the 14th century (R. Portal, The Slavs, p. 93-94).

9. The Croats, as a Slavic nation, are mentioned in written sources in the 10th century in three different places: in Bohemia, among the East Slavs and in the Balkan

peninsula. From the 11th century they are spotted in the Balkan only. According to Constantine Porphyrogenitus the Croats migrated to their country of today from White Croatia which some scholars place in southern Poland.

10. 'Carinthia', 'Carantana', 'Chorutania' was settled by the nation called 'Carni' in antiquity, hence, probably the name of the land. The 'Carni' were not the Slavs.

11. There were two rulers of Slavic Carinthia: Boruta and Cacacius. Boruta, the war leader (about 743-749), fighting Avars, asked the Bavarians for help which he received, but he had to accept Bavarian sovereignty. His son Cacacius (749-751) baptized by Bavarians, became a vassal of the Franks (L. Leciejewicz', Mały słowinik', p. 42, 161).

CHAPTER XXIX
RUS AND RUSSIA

"Our country is large and rich but lacks order. Come and be our prince", so said the Novgorodians to the Viking leader Rurik in 862 (probably in 856) according to Nestor (1).

In this time the East Slavs were firmly rooted at the river Dnieper and its tributaries. After all, some tribes stayed there for over six centuries. They managed not only to colonize the land but to Slavicize the remnants of the native population and came over from the primitive organization on a patriarchal basis to autonomous communities with fortified towns, surrounded by palisades, as centers of local power with its own prince in command. There were more than 30 of those fortified towns, but Kiev, Smolensk and Novgorod were the most important among them.

Placed at rivers, the fortified towns had convenient communication between the Baltic and the Black Sea. Although they were independent they developed some kind of relationship to further the trade.

The waterways along the Dnieper lured another nation. They were Scandinavians-Norsemen interested more with Byzantium than with Slavic fortified towns. But to open the route called "the way of the Varangians to the Greeks" they had to solve the problem of those towns blocking their way. The Norsemen, known here as Varangians, (2) were composed of military units well organized and drilled, but too small to wipe out the Slavic fortified towns. So they raised their own posts along the route and they had to pay some dues to the towns when passing them.

There is no doubt that the coexistence between the agricultural Slavs and the seafaring Vikings was difficult and led to open hostility.

About 859 the Slavs expelled the Norsemen, but finding that they quarrelled among themselves, they asked them to return. This is what Nestor says and which was quoted at the beginning of this chapter. Three brothers called Rurik, Sivens and Truvor accepted the invitation and founded the dynasty.

Information given by Nestor (3) should be accepted with some caution.

The Russian monk wrote a panegyric glorifying the Scandinavian-descended sovereigns of Kiev. In his perspective everything they did was splendid. Perhaps the truth was not as laudable as the chronicler writes. It is possible that the Slavs expelled the Varangians to organize their own expedition against Constantinople but lacking experience, they came to the conclusion that for their own good it would be better if they let the Varangians lead them. Therefore they proclaimed Rurik their prince and war leader.

The new rulers of Novgorod at the Lake Ilmen did not confine their attention to the tribes who had invited them. They at once began to conquer surrounding countries in all directions, and before two centuries elapsed they had firmly established themselves at Kiev on the Dnieper, invaded Byzantine territories, threatened Constantinople with a fleet of small craft, and learned to hold in check the nomadic hordes of the steppe. In short, they became a considerable power in eastern Europe.

It is possible that the Varangians gave power not only to the Slavic nations, but to the name as well. The first Russian state was called 'Rus' (4) or the state of Kiev.

Accepted as the prince, Rurik ruled in Novgorod with the help of his Varangians, against the wish of the inhabitants. The disillusioned Novgorodians, led by Wadin, rebelled. Rurik crushed the uprising and punished the rebels severely.

Rurik died in 844. Oleg, his successor, was a custodian of Igor, infant son of Rurik. Oleg captured Smolensk, the main stronghold of the Slavic tribe, the Krivitches, then Kiev, the capital of the other Slavs, the Polans.

He subjugated other eastern Slavic nations, among them the Derevlans, Slavienians and Radymitches.

In 907 Oleg led the expeditionary force against Constantinople. He concluded a profitable treaty with the Byzantinian emperor (5). In this way Oleg got possesion of all the trading routes between the Baltic and the Black Seas.

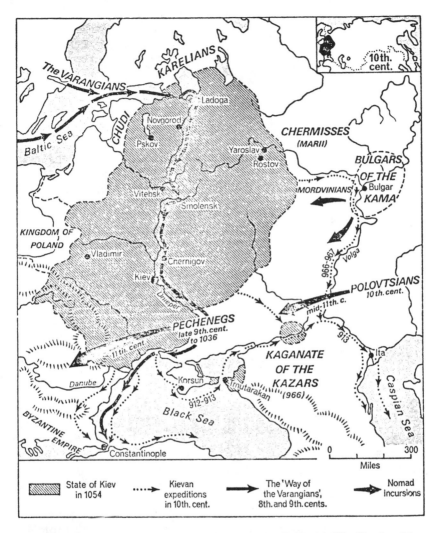

Map XVII. The State of Kiev in the Tenth Century, after R. Portal, 'The Slavs', p. 36.

His successor was Igor, the son of Rurik. As the prince of Kiev, he dispersed the invasion of the Pechengs in 915 and led two expeditions against Constantinople. The first ended with Igor's defeat, the second with the treaty of 944, but less profitable than the treaty of 911. Ivor was killed by the Derevlans when he collected taxed from them.

After Igor's death princess Olga, his widow, came into power as princess-regent of the infant son, the prince Sviatoslav. She severly avenged herself for the death of her husband. As an administrator

199

Fig. 51. Reconstruction of the Golden Gate in Kiev.

Olga rendered good service to Rus, establishing 'pogost' (6) civil service and taxes.

Olga accepted Christianity, and in 955 or 957 travelled to Constantinople. The cold reception she met there induced her to seek friends with the Germans.

Olga died in 969. The succession went to her son, the prince Sviatoslav, known for his many wars with neighboring Slavic states, as well as with the Khazars and Pechengs. He even, with the blessing of the Byzantine emperor, subdued the Bulgars at the Danube and established his seat at Pereyeslav, their capital, for a short time. Ambushed by the Pechengs, Sviatoslav was killed in 972.

His son, Vladimir the Great, battled several years with his brother Yaropelk, until he took the throne in Kiev in 977. He raised many fortified towns against the Pechengs and made expeditions against the Bulgars.

Vladimir the Great embraced Christianity from Constantinople in Slavonic and married the sister of the Byzantinian emperor, Princess, Anna, in 988 or 989. The time of his reign belongs to the best in the history of the state of Kiev. He died in 1015.

Yaroslav the Wise (978-1054), his son and successor, continued the action of his father. He founded new fortified towns and enlarged the city of Kiev, endowing her with magnificent churches like St. Sophia and other edifices.

Yaroslav nominated the Russian monk, Ilarion, metropolitan of the whole Russian Church in 1051, stressing the religious independence from the patriarch of Constantinople (7). He wiped out the Pechengs and warred successfully with his neighbors. Through his wife, a Scandinavian princess, Yaroslav the Wise developed a good relationship with the north as well as with France, when his daughter, Princess Anna married the king of France. Rus reached her peak. Her territory included Novgorod, Byeloozero, Tchernigov, Murom, Pereyeslav, Riazan, Suzdal, Viatcheslav, Smolensk and Volhynia.

Yaroslav the Wise is probably the author of the 'Russkaya Pravda', a first legal code, or sponsor of it. He was the last grand prince who upheld vigorously the political system. After his death in 1504 the process of disintegration of the state went on apace.

Fig. 52 Sarcophagus of Yaroslav the Wise.

In theory, the whole Russian land was a gigantic family estate belonging to the Rurik dynasty, and each member of that great family considered himself entitled to a share of it. It had to be divided therefore, into a number of independent principalities, but it continued to be loosely held together by the senior member of the family, called the grand duke, who ruled in Kiev. What added to the practical difficulties of this arrangement was that the post of grand duke was not an hereditary dignity in the sense of descending from

201

father to son, but always to be held by the senior member of the dynasty. Hence family quarrels became multiplied at an alarming rate. During the next 170 years (1054-1224) no less than 64 principalities had a more or less ephemeral existence, 293 princes put forward succession claims, and their disputes led to 83 civil wars.

When the Mongols in 1240 put Rus to an end, the first Russian state, Kiev, "mother of Russian cities" was already littered with ruins and its population decimated (8).

The East Slavs did not cease to exist. Subjugated in the south, they managed to hold some independence in the north, first with the center at Novgorod, then at Moscow. In this way the second Russian state came into power under the name of Muscovy (9), until the 18th century, when the name Russia appeared.

NOTES TO CHAPTER XXIX

1. **Bibliography:** Abu'l-Raiham Muhammed ibn Ahmed al-Bimni (973-1043), 'The Treatise of the Chronology of the East Nation'; al-Idrisi Kitab Rudżdżar (1100-1166), 'The Book of Roger'; Carr E.H. 'History of Soviet Russia', London 1950; Giterman V., 'Geschichte Russlands', Zurich 1949; Grekov B.D., 'La Culture de la Russie de Kiev', Moskva 1947; Gudzii N.K., 'History of Early Russian Literature', New York 1949; Hruszewskyj M., 'Istorija Ukrajiny-Rusi', Lwiw 1905; Lyashchenko P., 'History of the National Economy of Russia to the 1917 Revolution', New York 1949; Nasonow A.N., 'Istorija kultury Driewniej Rusi', Moskva 1951; Nestor, 'Povest vremenykh let'; 'Oczerki istorii SSSR', Moskva 1953; Pares B., 'History of Russia', New York 1947; Portal R., 'The Slavs', New York 1969; Smith R.E., 'The Origin of Farming Russia', Paris 1949; Solowjow S.M., 'Istorija Rossii', Moskva 1956; Tichomirov M. N., 'Driewnierusskije goroda', Moskva 1959; Vernadsky G., 'A History of Russia', New Haven 1959.
2. The Varangians were the Scandinavian mercenaries serving Russian princes and Byzantinian emperors. The name probably derives from the word 'var' — oath. Varangians were also traders and administrators. They easily assimilated.
3. Nestor, a monk, is probably the author of the 'Povest vremenykh let' (The Tale of Past Times) written in 1377 and covering three centuries of history, from the 9th to the 12 century.
4. The name 'Rus' is of non-Slavic origin. The discussion about its derivation started in the last century and is still vivid. According to Nestor the Varangians gave the country this name. The Scandinavian scholars acknowledge it. They point out that this part ot the Varangians was called the ''Rossmen', 'Rosskarlar' — the seafarers, hence the Finnish name of the Swedes — 'Ruotsi'. They did not form a tribal unit, but a sort of military-trading fraternity. When they settled after 862 among the Slavs, the name

202

'Rus' applied to the military unit composed of the soldiers of many nationalities, Slavic including, under the Varangian command. Then Oleg conquered Kiev and the name was spread on state Kiev, and all tribes in its borders. The Scandinavian theory is rejected by the Russian scholars. They maintain the name 'Rus derives from the river 'Ros'. In the 6th and 7th century at the middle Dnieper existed a federation of the Slavic tribes with the center at the river Ros, hence the name Rus. When the Varangians had been accepted by the Slavs, they only picked up the Slavic name and transferred it to the state of Kiev. This theory is based rather on national pride than on facts. Not only Nestor, but Byzantinian and Arabic writers point out a Scandinavian origin of the word 'Rus.' The latter until the 12th century under 'Rus' acknowledge the Scandinavian military unit. At the beginning of the 12th century the name 'Rus was applied to all territories occupied by the East Slavs.

5. The treaties which Rus concluded with Byzantium were translated from Greek into Slavonic in the 13th century and included into the Nestor's chronicle. They became a priceless source for the history of Rus and for development of Slavic laws. The treaties are of 907,944 and 971.

6. 'Pogost' was a territorial administrative unit composed of dozens of villages centered around the biggest one, where the seat of the prince's tax collector was.

7. The Bishop of Kiev was under the jurisdiction of the patriarch in Comstantinople since the introduction of Christianity by Vladmirir the Great.

8. R. Portal, The Slavs, p. 37.

9. The distinction between three branches of the East Slavs came into life in the 14th century. These brances were: the 'Byelorussians' (White Russians) between the river Pripet and the western reaches of the river Duna; the 'Great Russians' of Novgorod and Vladimir-Suzdal, and in the south the 'Little Russians' or 'Ukrainians'. The name 'Ukraine' (Okraina) was first mentioned in the document of 1187 which was included in the Ignatiev Chronicle. But in folk literature it goes well into the pre-Christian era. In the literature of Western Europe the name 'Ukraine' was introduced in the 17th century by the French author and traveler, G. le Vasseur Beauplan in a volume titled 'Desription de l'Ukraine', Rouen 1650. Before Beauplan the Ukrainians were usually referred to as 'Cossacks.'

CHAPTER XXX
SLAVS AT THE DANUBE

The territory of Czechoslovakia of today was occupied in the earliest historical period by the Boii, a Celtic tribe, whose capital was called Boiohemum. Thus the name of the land — Bohemia. The Boii were subdued by the Teutonic tribe of Marcomanni about 13 B.C., to be expelled by the other Teutonic tribes. Then, Bohemia was occupied by the Slavic tribes (1), of whom the Czechs were the most important.

The date of arrival of the Slavs in Bohemia is uncertain. Recent archaeological research has proven the existence of Slavic inhabitants as far back as the beginning of the Christian era.

They came from Silesia and southwest Poland as the Patronymic names of localities ending on 'ice' indicate. They are characteristic for south west Poland and Silesia, like 'Myślenice', 'Mysłowice' etc (2). In Czechs' territories 24.5 percent of the names of places end with 'ice' such as 'Pardubice', 'Lidice', 'Mikulcice'. Moreover, those names are scattered evenly over the whole country.(3)

At the foot of the 'Kusne Hory' — Ore Mountains, in the valley of the Bilina River, were the settlements of the 'Lemuzi' and the 'Detchans' at the Sudeten Mountains. The 'Litomierzitse' occupied the valley of the upper Elbe and next to them the 'Pshovians' with their main stronghold of Mielnik. All those tribes, culturally belonging to the Serbs, settled on the other side of the Ore Mountains.

The 'Lutchans' at the middle of the Ohrza River, with their main stronghold of 'Zatec', and the 'Siedlitchans at the upper of this river, differed in culture from the others.

The Czechs occupied the big loess regions at the lower Veltava River. Their main stronghold was 'Levy Hradec', but at the end of the 9th century Prague took the first place. The 'Dulebs', who maintained their archaic culture, settled at the upper Veltava. The 'Zlitchans' placed themselvs to the East of the Czechs on both banks of the Elbe River with their main center of 'Stara Kourim', until 10th century when 'Libice', the stronghold of the Slavniks, became more important. The Croats settled at the foot of the Sudeten Mountains.

The first Slavic political organization in this area was the kingdom of Samo. A Frankish chronicler (4) of the 7th century A.D. writes about it: "In 624 a man named Samo, originally from the Frankish Kingdom, from the Semonagus district, gathered many merchants and went for trading purposes to the Slavs called 'Vinidi'. Those Slavs just started to rebel against the Avars called Huns and their king, khagan. The 'Vinidi' were the servants of Huns for a long time.

When the 'Vinidi' marched against the Huns, the merchant Samo joined their army. He showed so many fighting abilities that he was generally admired. A large number of Huns were killed by the 'Vinidi' swords. Seeing the usefulness of Samo, the 'Vinidi' elected him king and he ruled them happily for 35 years. Under his command the 'Vinidi' won many other battles against the Huns. Samo had 12 'Vinidi' wives who bore him 22 sons and 15 daughters".

This kingdom of Samo, established by uniting the Moravian Slavs who fought the Avars (5) existed from 625 to 660 A.D. About the further acts of Samo the chronicler writes: "In 632 or 663 Slavs called 'Vinidi' killed and robbed many Frankish merchants in the Samo kingdom. It was the beginning of the quarrel between Dagobert and Samo, king of the Slavs".

How could it happed that a Frankish merchant led the Slavs to victory over the Avars?

Samo as a leader of the merchants traded with many nations. Thus, he was acquainted with the South and the West Slavs. As mentioned before, the Avars greatly oppressed the South Slavs. Seeing that the rebellion was near, Samo rushed to help the Moravians with his advice. Probably, thanks to his counsel, the united Slavic nations accepted the new fighting tactics shown by the Frankish merchant, who seeing many lands had learned quite a lot about all walks of life. His experiences appeared to be invaluable and won him the hearts of Slavic tribal chiefs. They chose him their king.

Probably a certain Slavic tribe must have adopted Samo because according to the Slavic customs a foreigner could participate in Slavic gatherings only after adoption. Then, he could even become their leader.

It is a possibility that Samo was a Christian, but when he had been adopted by Slavs he turned Pagan to share the Slavic religion. Thus, he could have 12 Slavic wives, which was not possible for a Christian ruler, as the chronicler mentions.(6)

It could be that at the adoption he received a Slavic name. 'Samo' is the name frequently found among the Slavs and Old Prussians. It describes a man who has the ability to unite people. Accepting the Frankish merchant as one of their men the Slavs called him 'Samo' because they valued the ability to unite and hold the nation together. Although the chronicler mentions that Samo came from the Frankish district 'Semonagus" and some historians maintain this district gave him his name, it seems that the name was Slavic rather then Frankich (7).

Tribal alliances among the Slavs lasted for a short time. They were made only in time of war and were dissolved as soon as the fighting ended. Allied forces chose leaders but their authority was greatly limited by tribal chiefs and assembly of all warriors.

After the victory over the Avars the alliance of Slavic nations created by Samo achieved its goal. It should have been dissolved.

The chronicler writes that 9 years after the Avars defeat Samo went into trouble with Dagobert, king of the Franks, because in the Great Moravian kingdom of Samo the Frankish merchants were robbed and killed. Did by any chance Samo put to death his previous collegues on purpose to keep the tribal alliance working?

Further events rather confirm such a supposition. Since the Avaric enemy ceased to exist a new enemy should be created. Thus, Samo led the Slavic warriors against Frankish Thuringia and other domains. The war with Dagobert was unavoidable.

Here Samo's leadership in fighting shone again. The Frankish king suffered a defeat at Wagastiburg in 631.

This victory made Samo famous in the whole of Slavdom. As the Huns had maintained Attila was a wizzard so did the Slavs with their Frankish leader.

Dervan, the prince of the Lusatian Serbs took advantage of Dagobert's defeat. He cast off the Frankish bondage and joined the Great Moravian kingdom ruled by Samo.

Samo died in 658. His kingdom was not a state in proper perspectives.(8) It represented a very loose alliance of Slavic nations which lasted as long as Samo lived. His experience and ability kept it alive. (9) After his death not one of his many sons was able to carry on the political organization. Besides, they quarreled about the inheritance left by their father.

The center of the first Great Moravian kingdom was Moravia. Thus, its name. The seize of this kingdom is object of discussion. Probably, in its sphere of influence were Southern Polabians, Slovakia, Czechs, and the lands of the Vislans in Southern Poland. Samo showed the Slavs how they could organize a powerful state by uniting themselves. The idea was not forgotten. The Slavs were at the level of development where the creation of political organization became a necessity. Thus, dating from Samo's epoch in the area occupied by the Slavs a number of more or less stable states began to rise.

The next rulers of the Slavic tribes in this area appeared in the 9th century, like 'Lecho' or 'Becho', who fought with the army of Charlemagne in 805. The tribe of the Czechs started to unite the country in the second half of the 9th century. Their name applied to all tribes excluding the Moravians who constituted an independent political body until the 11th century. The origin of the name 'Czech' known already in the 10th century, is obscure.

The first Bohemian dynasty was of the 'Przemyslids'. Their founder was supposed to be 'Przemysł' a legendary hero. (10) The first historic prince of the house of Przemyślids was Borzyvoj. (11) Profiting by the warring of the Germans with the Moravians, he liberated the Czech tribes from the dependence of Great Moravia and started to build an independent state with Prague as its capital.

Under influence of neighboring Moravia, the Czech princes accepted Christianity. (12) The consolidation of their country took place after the fall of Great Moravia in the beginning of the 10th century.

In the years to follow Bohemia found herself under enormous German pressure. Henry I, the king of Germany, invaded Bohemia and seized Prague in 929. Otto I, the German emperor, forced the Czechs to pay him tribute in 950.

Brzetyslav I, the prince of Bohemia, incorporated Moravia permanently (13) to his country in 1031. After his death his sons divided the state. The oldest took Bohemia and his younger brothers shared Moravia.

The kingdom of Bohemia had it golden age until it fell in the battle at the White Mountain in 1620. Under the rule of Hapsburgs the Czechs suffered repressions and forced Germanization. After almost 300 years of hardship Bohemia regained her independence in 1918 and the Czechs with the Slovaks created the state of Czechoslovakia.

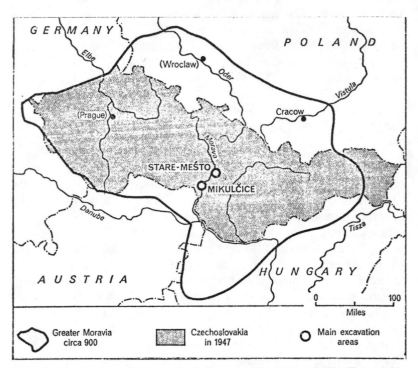

Map XVII. Great Moravia in the Tenth Century, after R. Portal, The Slavs, p. 22.

In the valleys of the Morava River and its tributaries settled the Slavs called Moravians. They arrived from the north, probably from the Polish territories in the 5th century, and took the empty spaces after the Teutonic Quadi and Vandals migrated to the west. Shortly after their arrival the Moravians were subdued by the Avars. The Moravian territory became a backbone of the first Slavic state organized by Samo in the 7th century.

After the wars of Charlemagne Moravia found herself in zone of Frankish dominance at the beginning of the 9th century. In this time the political organization appeared under the name of 'Moravia' or 'Great Moravia.'

The fact that the Moravians came out as one united nation at the very beginning, while the neighboring Bohemia represented a chessboard of small tribal territories, must have been a

208

result of a higher social development and political integrity which allowed them to create a powerful state of Moravia in that early time. The Moravians were first among the Western Slavs to establish a multitribal state organization of an early stage of the feudal system. Historic sources do not mention their internal divisions. Judging by the archaeological findings, especially in ceramics and the characteristic of settlements, three tribes at least constituted the state. One of them included the settlers at the upper Morava River at the city of Olomouc. The second was at the middle Morava, where the main center of Great Moravia was built in the 9th century, known now from archaeological findings like Stare Mesto, Mikulcice and others. The third tribe occupied the basin of the rivers Svatka and Sazavar near the cities of Znojma and Rajhrad. Characteristic for Moravia were the big fortified towns, some of them in the course of time being transformed into cities.

Being near former Roman provinces, the Moravians accepted from them many useful accomodations.

Fig. 53 Reconstruction of basilica in Mikulcice

Mojmir I, who died about 846, was the first historic ruler of Moravia and perhaps the founder of the dynasty which after his name was called the Mojmirovits. The sources mention his name for the first time in 833 when he expelled the prince Pribina out of Nitra. Mojmir I accepted Christianity in 831, which caused dependence of his state on the diocese in Passau. Also politically Moravia was dependent upon the rulers of East Franconia and paid them tributes. The Moravian rulers one by one tried to free the country from the German oppression, with rather poor results because their action made the emperors' interventions more frequent.

After the death of Mojmir I the emperor, Louis the German, placed prince Rostislav upon the throne of Moravia in 846. He was the nephew of Mojmir I, and appeared to be friendly with the Germans, but when in power he started a war with his masters for independence of his realm. Rostislav managed to repell the Louis invasion in 855.

To weaken the influence of the German clergy in his country, Rostislav brought Cyril and Methodius from Constantinople to teach the Gospel in Slavonic.

A plot of the Moravian leaders, headed by prince Svatopluk, the nephew of Rostislav, put Rostislav into prison in 870. The German emperor Louis ordered them to blind the prisoner and kill him.

The emperor then placed Svatopluk I upon the throne of Moravia, who pledged allegiance to Germany, but at the same time sought ways to free his country. One of them was to get rid of the German Church organization. He was successful. As a result of his action the independent Moravian archbishopric was founded in 873, with Methodius as the first archbishop.

Svatopluk I expelled two German invasions in 872 and 873, but in the end he made peace with Germany, accepting the emperor's sovereignty.

Under the rule of Svatopluk I Great Moravia developed as a powerful state to subordinate the neighboring Slav countries of Bohemia, Silesia, Pannonia and probably Southern Poland.

After the death of Svatopluk I in 894, Mojmir II, his son, took over. A year later he lost his supremacy over Bohemia. His brother, Svatopluk II started a civil war trying to gain the throne, which lasted from 897 till 900. The further fate of Mojmir II and Svatopluk II is unkown.

The final blow to Great Moravia was made by the Magyars. The Hungarians defeated the Moravians and destroyed their state in 907.

When Great Moravia ceased to exist as a political body, on her territory appeared a small tribal principality under Hungarian rule. In the second half of the 10th century Moravia became a territory of rivalry between Bohemia, Poland and Hungary. Boleslas the Great incorporated Moravia to Poland in 1003, but his son Mieszko II lost it permanently in 1033 to Bohemia.

After the death of Brzetyslav I in 1055, ruled by junior Czech princes, Moravia became a center of opposition against Bohemia.

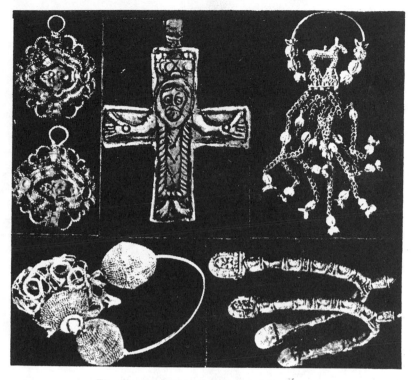

Fig. 54. Archaeological findings in Mikulčice.

The separateness of Moravia strengthened the erection of an independent bishopric in Olmouc in 1063.

In the second half of the 11th century Moravia was divided into principalities with the seats in Olmouc, Brno, Znajom and Braclav. The last attempts to make Moravia independent from Bohemia were under taken in the 12th century, when the Moravians accepted the German sovereignty. Przemyśl Otakar (1220-1270), king of Bohemia, permanently liquidated the separateness of Moravia. Since then Moravia is an integral part of Bohemia.

Great Moravia was the first Slavic state with a highly developed economy and far advanced social standing. The ruling dynasty, with the strong prerogatives to the throne, organized efficient system of administration dividing the country into districts around the fortified towns. Archaeological research in the last two decades has revealed, on the territory of Great Moravia, the spectacular remnants of the past.(14)

Territories of Slovakia of today were occupied by Celtic tribes in antiquity. Then, Teutonic Quadi appeared in this region. During the wars of the Marcomanni, Roman Emperor Marc Aurelius held a part of Slovakia for a short period. Slavs settled the area in the 5th and 6th centuries. Their tribal state under Pribina with the capital in Nitra was established in the 9th century.

Prince Pribina ruled, dependent upon Great Moravia. Expelled by Moravian prince Mojmir I in 833, Pribina went to Ratbod, the margrave of East Mark, and accepted Christianity. The Germans gave him the marshlands of lower Pannonia.

Pribina was very active in colonizing and Christianizing his new territory. He built his capital in Mosaburg (Zalavar, today) and was killed by the Moravians during their struggle with Emperor Louis the German in 860.

His son Kocelj cooperated at the beginning with the archbishop of Salzburg in spreading Christianity, but in 866 he became ar ardent supporter of the Slavic rite introduced by SS. Cyril and Methodius. Thanks to his efforts, the Slavic archbishopric was founded in Sirmium, with Methodius as an archbishop in 869. Svatopluk I, the prince of great Moravia, expelled Kocelj and seized his domains in 874. Since then they became a part of Great Moravia.

After the fall of Great Moravia Bohemia, Poland and Hungary rivaled in getting Slovakia, which was incorporated into Hungary in the 11 century, for a long time.

Slovakia gained independence in 1918 by joining Bohemia in establishing a common state with the Czechs under the name of Czechoslovakia.

In the vicinity of Slovakia was another Slavic state in Transilvania in the 7th century. The Slavs raised their capital upon the ruins of Apulum, the capital of ancient Roman province of Dacia, and called it Belgrad (Alba Julia in Romania, today). Their state dissappeared, being incorporated into Hungaria in the 10th century. Nevertheless, inhabitants kept their Slavic identity until the 13th century.

NOTES TO CHAPTER XXX

1. **Bibliography:** Bednarik R., 'Slovaci w Juhoslavii', Bratislava 1964; and 'Slovakische Volkskultur', Bratislava 1943; Bobek W., 'Lud słowacki', Kraków 1937; Busek V., 'Czechoslavakia', New York 1957; Chalupecky V., 'Stare Slovensko', Bratislava 1923; Cosmas of Prague, 'Chronica Boemorum'; Havlik L., 'Velka Morava a stredevropsti Slovane', Praha 1964; Husa V., 'Dejiny Ceskoslovanska', Praha 1961; Labuda G., 'Pierwsze państwo słowiańskie', Poznań 1949; Mikkola I.I., 'Samo und

sein Reich', ASP. 1929 Novotny V., 'Ceske Dejiny, Praha 1912; and 'Slovenske dejiny, Bratislava 1951; Schranil J., 'Die Vorgeschichte Böhmens und Mährens', Berlin 1928; Seton-Watson R.W., 'A History of the Czechs and Slovaks', London 1965; Thompson S.H., 'Czechoslovakia in European History', Princeton 1953; Vernandsky G., The Beginnings of the Czechs State', Byzantion 1944.

2. F. Bujak, 'Studia nad osadnictwem Małopolski', RAHist. 1095, p. 285, states that among 3175 names of localities in south west Poland mentioned by Jan Długosz in his 'Liber Beneficiorum' in 1470, 710, which is 22.2%, had patronymic names. A Podkowiński 'Polska', Warszawa 1886, maintains that the most of the patronymic names (23.3%) were in the district of Cracow. H. Łowmiański, 'Początki Polski', Vol. II, p. 328, accepts 20.6% patronymic names for settlements in Silesia.

3. H. Łowiański, pp. cit., p. 328, writes: "Taking under consideration the fact that groups settling on new territory used old names for the new settlements, as the English did in the United States, Canada, Australia and Africa, we can accept the supposition that migration to Czechs' territories started from the district of Cracow and Silesia".

4. Fredegar, lib. IV, cap. 48.

5. The kingdom of Samo is recorded many times by Frankish chroniclers but there were no traces in records of the Constantinople chroniclers who were eager to record even small details of the past, when Slavic warriors stormed the Byzantine Empire. The puzzle is understandable. The Slavs led by Samo attacked the Frankish kingdom and coexisted peacefully with the Byzantinians, so the Constantinople writers were less interested in Samo and his deeds.

6. S. Trawkowski, 'Jak powstała Polska', p. 109-111.

7. A. Bruckner, 'Słownik etymologiczny języka polskiego', p. 480.

8. G. Labuda, 'Pierwsze państwo słowiańskie', 332.

9. Fredegar, op. cit.: "Suo (Samo) consillo et utilitate Winidi semper Chunus superant".

10. Hence the dynasty of Przemyslids who ruled in Bohemia until 1306.

11. Borzyvoj died about 891. Although he has the reputation of being the first historical ruler of Bohemia, it was Spytigniev (died in 905) who started the unbroken succession of Bohemian princes and kings.

12. According to the chronicle there were 14 Bohemian princes baptized in Regensburg in 845, but tradition maintains that Borzivoj I accepted Christianity in Slavic rite from St. Methodius in 884.

13. Some historians think that Great Moravia of the 9th century is nothing else than the continuation of the state of Samo. Hence they call it the Second Great Moravia. The First Great Moravia probably had been divided by many sons of Samo after his death. Perhaps they fought each other, but not being endangered from outside, they played no role in the international political arena. Thus, over 200 years from Samo to Mojmir I, nothing is heard about Moravia. The Frankish invasions of Charlemagne forced many Moravian principalities to unite to fight the enemy. Having the great deeds of Samo in mind, the Moravians in a short time organized an efficient state under Mojmir I, who might have been a descendant of Samo.

14. Archaeological research centered around the fortified towns like Stare Mesto, Velehrad, Mikulcice and Pohansko. The most spectacular findings were at Mikulcice near Hodomin on the right bank of the Morava River, which probably was the capital of Great Moravia.

CHAPTER XXXI
SLAVS AT THE ELBE

The area between the rivers Odra and Elbe, the Baltic Sea and the Sudeten Mountains (1), which mostly constitutes the territory of East Germany of today, was colonized by Slavs in the 5th and 6th centuries. They are known under a common name of 'Polabianie', 'Polabians' or 'Polabs' (2). They migrated either from Bohemia down the Elbe to the Baltic as the Serbs, or from Silesia as the 'Obodrzyce' (Obotritae) — Obodrits, the Lusatians and the Milchans, or from the region of the middle Odra as the 'Vieleci' — Vyelets.

The Polabs used to form the tribal settlements occupying the regions of 100 to 300 square miles, divided each from another by dense forests, quaggy marshlands and raise of terrain. The center of their colony became in the 9th and 10th century a 'gród' — fortified town of the Feldberg type (3), hence its name 'civitas' in the West European sources (4). It was a territorial organization known in Poland as an 'opole'. Tribal chiefs usualy dwelled in the fortified town.

The political organization of these clannish settlements was based on so called military democracy in which the highest authority enjoyed the 'wiece' — gathering of all free men of the tribe under arms, among which the tribal chiefs played a decisive role. Some of its authorities, especially of administrative nature, the gathering assigned to the chiefs, war leaders or priests.

The exact distribution of Polabian tribes is not known, but we can form a fragmentary picture of their existence from annalistic records.

The farthest territories to the north and west (5) were occupied by Slav tribes known under a combined name of the 'Obodrzyce' — Obodrits, called by some chroniclers as 'Bodrici' or 'Obotritae'. They were divided into three groups: the 'Wagrowie' — Vagri, settled at the Baltic shores in Holenstein, with the main stronghold in

'Starogard' (Oldenburg, today); the 'Połabianie' — Polabs, in the region between the rivers Travna and Elbe, with the main stronghold 'Racibórz' (Ratzenburg, today) and the duly 'Obodrzyce' — Obodrits between the Wismar Bay and the 'Swarzyńskie Jezioro' (Schweriner See, today), with their main stronghold 'Mechlin' (Mecklenburg, today). To the union of the Obodrits belonged also the 'Warnowie' — Varnians at the upper Warnowa River (Warnau, today) and the 'Glinianie' — Glinyans or Linyans, at the Elbe with their main stronghold either 'Łączyn' (Lenzen, today) or 'Pothlustin' (Putlitz, today). In this region the Franconian Annales mention in the 9th century the 'Smolincy' — Smolintsi, the tribe later unknown. In the vicinity of Hamburg the 'Drzewianie' — Dshevians. placed themselves. Dwelling in the deep forests they managed to maintain their ethnic identity until the second half of the 18th century (6).

Further to the north, up to the Odra River, the territories were occupied by the tribe of the 'Wieleci' — Vyelets, called also the 'Lutycy' — Lutits, at the end of the 8th century. Among them from the west to the east were: the 'Chyżanie' — Hysans, at the middle and the lower Warnau, with their stronghold 'Chyżyn' (Kessin, today); the 'Czrezpienianie' — Tcherezpienians, between the rivers 'Reknica' (Reknitz, today) and 'Piana' (Peene, today); the 'Dołężanie' — Dolenzans, at the middle and the lower 'Dołęża' (Tollensee, today) and the 'Redarowie' — Redars, with their well known center of Slavic Pagan cult, 'Radogoszcz' (not identified today). At the lower 'Wkra' River (Ucker, toady) and the city of Szczecin in Poland today dwelt the 'Wkrzanie' — Vkshans.

A more homogeneous unit was the 'Ranowie' — Ranas, who settled on the Isle of Rugen. Their main center of the Pagan cult was Arcona. The Ranas had many common features with the Vyelets of the mainland.

To the west of the Vylelets settled tribes considered in the 9th and 10th centuries as the Vyelets: the 'Morzyce' — Moshits, at the 'Jezioro Morzyckie', the 'Doszanie' — Doshans between the rivers Elbe and Havel at the 'Dosza' River (Dosse, today); the 'Rzeczanie' — Retchans, at the upper Havel; the 'Nieletycy' — Nyeletits, called the 'Brzeżanie' — Breshans in the 12th century with their main stronghold Havelberg; opposite to them on the left bank of the Elbe the 'Lipianie' — Lipyans; the 'Morzyczanie' — Moshitchans, near Magdeburg today, with their main stronghold 'Malechów' (Malchow, today). At the middle Havel dwelt the 'Stodoranie' — Stodorans, called also 'Hawelanie' — Havelans, with their main stronghold 'Brenna' (Brandenburg, today). To the west of the Stodorans settled

Map XVIII. West Slavs, after L. Leciejewicz

a small tribe of the 'Płonianie' — Plonyans, and to the east, the 'Sprewianie' — Sprevyans at the Spreva River, with their main stronghold 'Kopnik' or 'Kopanica' (Kopenick, today, a suburb of Berlin).

The settlers between the 'Solawa' River (Saale, today) and the Lusatian Nysa River, termed jointly as the 'Serbo-Łużyczanie' — Serbo-Lusatians, were not homogeneous in their origin and inner structure. In the basin of the Saale and the Elbe dwelt the Serbs, known under this name in the 7th century, who never created a more important political body. Between the Saale and the Mulde were the small groups, composed rather of neighborhood communities: the 'Żytycy' — Shitits; the 'Żyrmunty' — Zirmoonts; the 'Kolednicy' — Kolendnits- the 'Nudzicy' — Noodits; the 'Susłowie' — Sooslovs; and the 'Nieletycy' — Nyeletits.

Farther to the south at the foot of the Ore Mountains, the

216

'Chudzicy' — Hoodits had their settlements, and from this point they penetrated in small groups the regions to the west of the Saale and the upper Men and the Naba, as the linguistic data indicates. At the middle Elbe dwelt the 'Nizicy' — Nisits; the 'Scytycy' — Scitits and the 'Głomacze' — Glomatches or the 'Dalemińcy' — Dalemints, as the Germans called them, with their main stronghold 'Gana' and the 'Niżanie' — Nizans, near Drezno (Dresden, today). The 'Łużyczanie' — Lusatians, settled at the middle Spreva having 'Lubusza' as their main stronghold and the 'Milczanie' — Milchans, at the headspring of the Spreva, near the city of Budziszyn' (Bautzen, today). The 'Lebuszanie' — Lebooshans, with their main stronghold 'Lubus' (Lebus, today) placed themselves on the left bank of the Odra.

The region between the Odra and Vistula at the Baltic was colonized by the Polish tribes, among which the 'Pomorzanie' — Pomeranians, composed the most seperate group. On this territory dwelt the 'Pyrzyczanie' — Pishitchans, around the city of 'Pyrzyce' and the 'Wolinianie' — Volynians, on the Isle of Wolin. The seperate groups settled at the lower Odra with their main stronghold 'Szczecin' and in the basin of the Ina River, around the city of 'Stargard'.

There were three periods in the history of the Polabs: the period of tribal states; the period of tribal alliances and; the period of crusades.

a) Period of tribal states

When the Slavs started to colonize the western territories the Franks played an important role in Europe. The Polabs maintained rather friendly relations with them. They warned the Franks when the Avars made preparation to invade West Europe, and helped to fight the Saxons and Thuringians. In return the Franks allowed the Polabs to occupy the lands of the Saxons and Thuringians after they were defeated. It is possible that the Slav settlers were in some sort of dependence on the Franks. Perhaps they paid them tributes, because when Samo, the Slav leader defeated Dagobert I, the king of the Franks at Wagastiburg in 631, Dervan of the Polabian Serbs repudiated the Frankish dependency and joined Samo.

Charlemagne found alies among the Obodrits. They supported him in battling the Saxons in 780. In return Charlemagne expelled the Saxons from the Danish borderland and the region near Hamburg he gave to the Obodrits. He also helped them to battle the Vyelets and the Polabian Serbs.

Charlemagne built many strongholds in the territories occupied by the Polabs, among them Magdeburg, and created the Mark, a political organization in which all the administrative and military power rested in the hands of the margrave. Created by him, Mark was destined to defend the Frankish state against the Vyelets, but in reality it helped the Franks to subdue the Polabs.

Next to the Franks the Polabs were in touch with the Danes. The Danish prince Godfred resettled the Slav merchants from the town of 'Rerik' to 'Hedeby' (Haithabum, today) in the Jutland Peninsula.

When the Charlemagne Empire became extinct and the German state formed with the Saxon dynasty as its head, the situation in the Polabian territories deteriorated considerably. Henry I (876-936) organized in the Polabian territories the administrative units called 'Burgwards' (7) and battled the Slavs, applying terror and mass executions. His son, Otto I the Great (912-973) formed the East Mark and placed over it the margrave Gero. He subdued almost all the Polabs and became a menace to the emperor. Therefore, when Gero died, Otto I, dreading that a new margrave might reach for the crown, divided the huge East Mark into six small Marks, among them the North Mark, the Lustian Mark and the Meissen Mark.

Otto I was well aware that the Church was a good instrument for his German politics. Thus, he started to organize the bishoprics in the Slav territories. The first was erected in Havelberg and Brenna in 948. Then followed the bishoprics in Meissen, Merseburg and Oldenburg in 968 and in Mechlin and Racibórz a little later. All these bishprics were German and under the jurisdiction of the German archbishopric in Magdegurg, founded in 948.

Otto I was right. Next to the margraves the bishops became excellent tools of oppression. Their tithe and arrogant attitude forced the Slav nations to rebellion. The Vyelets had risen first. They made a successful uprising in 983. The Obodrits and Stodorans were next. The rebellious Polabs stormed the bishops seats, expelled or killed the clergy and returned to their Pagan gods. Slavs gained independence for one and a half century.

b) Period of tribal alliances

Now, the Polabs understood that their small principalities could not defend themselves against the huge German aggression. Therefore, they started to unite.

The German oppression forced the Obodrits, Vyelets, Stodorans, Ranas and Pomeranians to create the multitribal states.

The return to Slavic gods was not evoked by religious factors, but by political and economic ones. The Polabs were traditionally followers of military democracy, in which the gathering of all free men under arms had attribution of highest authority in legislation, administration and jurisdiction of society. German principalities, on the contrary, derived their strength from the feudal system which started to bloom in West Europe. Its main feature was the powerful prince. Since the Church became a staunch supporter of the feudal system the Polabs saw in the clergy the enemy of their traditional system of military democracy. They prefer their Pagan priests, who enjoyed much less political influence than the Christian ones.

On the other hand, where the prince came into more significance in the Slav nation he supported Christianity, being aware that in the feudal system he and his dynasty had more chance to survive and prosper.

There are no details of the history of Stodoranian and Pomeranian states. The state of the Obodrits tried to catch the feudal system. The Vyelets organized a Union of Vyelets Nations based on republican principles with the gathering as the main political institution. On the other hand, on the Isle of Rugen crystalized the state ruled by the Pagan priests headed by the archpriest residing in Arcona.

c) Period of crusades

The third period in the history of the Polabs began when Albrecht the Baer, since 1134 the margrave of North Mark, subdued the Bsheshans and Vkshans. With Henry the Lion, who was the prince of Bavaria and Saxony, he raised the question at the Diet of the Reich in 1147, to organize a Christian crusade against the Pagan Polabs in a time when the knights of England, France and Germany made preparation for the second crusade to the Holy Land. Albrecht and Henry got the blessing of the Pope Eugene III and the support of Valdemar I, the prince of Denmark; Mieszko III, the prince of Poland; and the Bohemians.

The crusade started in the same year. The Polabs were attacked from all sides, but in spite of it they managed to defeat the crusaders.

Knights had to make as many as 21 crusades to break down the Polabian resistance, compared to the 8 crusades to the Holy Land.

Henry the Lion conquered the territory of the Obodrits, and out of part of it he formed principality of Mecklenburg, giving the rest to some German dukes.

219

In the same time Albrecht the Baer, who got the North Mark from the German emperor, subdued the Vyelets. His next conquests and his son, Otto, gave them Brenna and the principality of Kopanik.

Meanwhile, Valdemar I, the prince of Denmark, conquered the Isle of Rugen and destroyed Arcona.

In the 12th century four feudal states were established in Polabian territories: one with the capital in Brenna; second the former state of the Obodrits which was called the Principality of Mecklenburg; the third on the Isle of Rugen after the fall of Arcona in 1168; and the fourth of West Pomerania.

New settlements started to appear in the conquered territories, with Germans as settlers. The process of Germanization caught the Polabian elite first, then the grassroots.

There is only fragmentary information concerning the Polabian princes and their states. Based on it, the history of the state of Obodrits appears as follows:

"Dražko', the prince of the Obrodrits and successor of 'Wilczan' murdered in 795, was an ally of the Franks. He battled with the Vyelets, Saxons and Danes. He defeated the Saxons at 'Święciany' in 798, but was forced to leave the country when the Danes, Saxons and Vyelets invaded his land in 808. A year later he returned and was murdered in 'Rerik', the commercial center of the Obodrits.

'Nakon', who died in 966, was one of the four powerful Slavic princes in his time. There is little known about his life and death. Together with his brother 'Stoigniew' he fought with the armies of Otto I and Gero at the Reknitz River. The Slavs suffered defeat and Stoigniew fell.

After a successful uprising in 983, 'Przybigniew', the prince of the Obodrits, began to unite the Obodrites tribes around the main stronghold of Mechlin. His son 'Gotszalk' (1010-1066) finished his work. All Obodrits between the lower Elbe and the Baltic, as well as Saxon and Vyelets territories found place in his state. After the civil war Gotszalk in 1057 had under his rule the Tchrezpienians and Hyzans. He kept good relations with the Saxons and Danes, and promoted Christianity, seeing in the feudal system a solid base for his dynasty. It destroyed him. The uprising flamed in 1055, connected with the Pagan reaction. Gotszalk escaped to Łączyn, where he was killed.

After Gotszalk's death 'Krut' came into power, being elected by the people on gathering in 1066. The period of his ruling was the best in the history of the Obodrits. First he fought Gotszalk's sons, who were trying to regain power after their father. Then he defeated the Saxons at Nordalgringen and forced them to pay him tributes. Krut was murdered by Henry, the son of Gotszalk, who then became the ruler.

Henry (died in 1127), the youngest son of Gotszalk, managed to gain power with the help of the Saxons. The Obrodrits made an uprising against him, but were defeated. As the Saxonian vassal, Henry enlarged the territories of his state from the Elbe to the Peene and in the south the Glinians and Stodorans owed him allegiance for a short time. Like his father, Henry supported Christianity and the feudal system. He was murdered, too.

After the death of 'Świętopełk', the last son of Henry, 'Niklot' became the prince of the Obodrits in 1131. He offered a successful resistance against the crusade in 1147. In 1160 he expelled the Saxo-Danish invasion. Niklot fell defending the stronghold 'Orle' (Werle, today). Three years later Orle became a main point of resistance for Niklot's sons.

Henry the Lion conquered Mechlin, the chief stronghold of the Obodrits, changed its name to Mecklenburg and reestablished the bishopric.

Among Niklot's sons 'Przybysław' came to power. He was the proper founder of the dynasty of Mecklenburg princes. Przybysław fought with the Saxons and Danes with variable luck in 1160. In 1168 he made alliance with Henry the Lion, and in 1172 he took part in a crusade to the Holy Land.

The Stodorans, called also Havelans, dwelt at the Havel River. Their main stronghold was Brenna. It is possible that 'Drogovit', attacked by the Franks in 789, was their prince. The Stodorans were defeated by the Germans under Henry I and incorporated into the diocese of Brenna in 948. They managed to shake off the yoke by successful uprising in 983, and kept their independence until the second half of the 12th century.

'Przybysław Henryk' was the last prince of the Stodorans. He took over from the prince Meinfried.

Przybyslaw Henryk minted his own coins with the mark the 'kneź-prince, and wanted to be crowned as a king. He consolidated Christianity in his country and maintained good relations with the Poles, Bohemians and Germans.

After his death, Albrecht the Baer seized Brenna in 1150. Jaxa of Kopanik, the prince of the Sprevans and only known ruler of this nation, with the help of the Polish troops pushed out the Germans from Brenna in 1154, but was forced to abandon the stronghold in 1157.

Albrecht the Baer retook Brenna, changed its name to Brandenburg and the state of the Stodorans was transformed into Mark of Brandenburg.

The Vyelets, called since the 10th century as Lutits, regained their independence after successful uprising in 983. With the Tchrezpienians, Dolezans, Hyzans and Redars they formed the Union of Vyeletian Nation based on republican principles.

The Redars played a dominant role in the Union. Their stronghold Radogoszcz (8) was the known center of the Polabian Pagan cult. There was rivalry between the Redars and Tchrezpienians, which led to the civil war in 1057. The Tchrezpienians won, with the help of the Saxons and Danes. The Union of Vyeletian Nations ceased to exist. Next the Tchrezpieians were subdued in the west by the Obodrits and by the Pomeranians in the east. Their fate was shared by the Hyzans and Dolenzans.

A different Slav state developed on the Isle of Rugen. It was based on a theocratic system, with the priests as rulers. The city of Arcona became its capital. There stood the temple of 'Świętowit', the highest sanctuary of the Polabs when Radogoszcz of the Redars lost its meaning. There resided the archpriest, the highest religious and political authority of the Isle of Rugen.

The country of the Ranas, as the Isle of Rugen was called, had been attacked by the crusaders of Valdemar I, the prince of Denmark in 1157. 'Ciesław', the war leader defended the Isle. After heavy fighting he made peace with Valdemar I in 1160, being a dependant of the invader. He tried to get rid of the yoke by resisting in the stronghold of 'Gardziec' (Garz, today), but when Arcona fell he accepted the Danish sovereignty, in 1168.

After Ciesław his brother, 'Jaromir', came into power on the Isle of Rugen, as Danish vassal. Canute IV, king of Denmark, gave him the regency of Pomerania. Jaromir contributed to the consolidation of Christianity in his country and supported the German and Danish colonization of the Isle of Rugen.

The territories between the rivers Vistula and Odra and the Baltic Sea, called West Pomerania, were under the Polish influence. 'Boleslas I' king of Poland, founded the bishopric in 'Kołobrzeg' in 1000, which existed for a short time.

The attacks of the Pomerians forced 'Boleslas III', the prince of Poland, to undertake the invasion against them in 1113. The fighting lasted 10 years. Boleslas III captured the stronghold of Szczecin in 1121 and then he conquered West Pomerania to the river Odra. 'Warcisław', the prince of Pomerania and the founder of the dynasty which ruled this country until 1637, accepted the Polish sovereignty. Boleslas III undertook Christianity of Pomerania on a large scale. He organized a mission with Otto, bishop of Bamberg, at the head, to reach this goal.

The Polish sovereignty was heavy for the Pomeranian elite. Prince Warcisław tried to get free from it by accepting the sovereignty of Lothar, the German emperor. Then the prince of Poland made his second expedition against Pomerania in 1129 with the help of the Danes. The Pomeranians suffered defeat and promised to cooperate with the Poles.

NOTE TO CHAPTER XXXI

1. **Bibliography:** Adam of Bremen, 'Gesta Hammaburgensis Ecclesiae Pontificum'; Alfred the Great, 'The History of the World'; Arnold of Lubeck, 'Chronica Slavorum'; Bavarian Geographer, 'Descriptio civitatum et regionum ad septentrionalem plagem Danubii'; Bogusławski W., 'Dzieje Słowiańszczyzny północno-zachodniej aż do wynarodowienia Słowian zaodrzańskich', Poznań 1900; Brankack J. 'Studien zur Wirtschaft- und Sozialstruktur der Westslawen zwischen Elbe- Saale und Oder aus der Zeit vom 9 bis zum 12 Jahrhundert', Bautzen 1964; Bryl-Serbin J., 'Serbski Dom w Budysinje', Bautzen 1924; Diels P., 'Die Slawen', Berlin 1920; Harbord, 'The Life of St. Otto of Bamberg'; Hermann J., 'Siedlung, Wirtschaft und gesellschäftliche Verhältnisse der Slawischen Stämme zwischen Oder, Neisse und Elbe', Berlin 1968; Ibrahim ibn Jacob — al-Bekri, 'The Book of Roads and Kingdoms'; Leciejewicz L. 'Miasta Słowian północnopołabskich', Wrocław 1968; Pata J., 'Łużica', Bautzen 1920; Pniewski W., 'Łużyce', Poznań 1924; Schneeweis E., 'Feste und Volksbrauche der Lausitzen Wenden', Berlin 1931; Schulenburg W., 'Wendisches Volkstum im Sage, Brauch und Sitte', Leipzig 1934; Sermijaga M.I. 'Łużiczanie', Moskva 1955; 'Siedlung und Verfassung der Slawen zwischen Elbe, Saale und Oder', Giessen 1960; 'Slaven in Deutschland', Berlin 1970; Strzelczyk J., 'Po tamtej stronie Odry, Dzieje i upadek 'Slowian połabskich', Warszawa 1968; Slaski K., 'Słowianie zachodni na Bałtyku w IX-XIII w.', Gdańsk 1969; Tymieniecki K., 'Społeczeństwo Słowian lechickich', Lwów 1928; Trautmann R., 'Baltisch-Slawisches Worterbuch', Getingen 1923; Wachowski K., 'Słowiańszczyzna zachodnia', Poznań 1950; Widajewicz J., 'Serbowie nadłabscy', Kraków 1948.

2. The Slavic name of the river Elbe is 'Łaba'. Hence the Slavs who settled at that river called themselves 'Polabians' or 'Polabs'. With time the name was applied to all Slavic nations who lived west of the river Odra.

3. Archaeologists found remnants of the Slav stronghold of the 7th-9th centuries in Feldberg near Neustrelitz in Mecklenburg on the high bank of the Luzin Lake. Strongholds similarly situated were numerous in the Vyeletian territory from the 8th to 9th centuries, hence they are classified as the strongholds of the type Feldberg.

4. Lech Leciejewicz, 'Slownik kultury dawnych Słowian', Warszawa 1972, p. 258-274.

5. It is difficult to reconstruct the Polabian language since written sources almost do not exist and nobody uses it today. Some traces are left in onomastics. Unfortunately, the genuine names were usually corrupted by the Latin writers first and the German later. Since Polabian was close to Polish, geographic and personal names are given here in Polish, because they probably had similar sound in the past. Moreover, many names have counterparts in Poland today.

6. By the 17th century Slavonic survived only in a tiny patch in the east of Hanover about Luchow, where a few words were still understood at the beginning of the 19th century. The population of the district still goes by the name of 'Wends'. The chief remains of the language are a 'paternoster', a few phrases and a short vocabulary written down by Pastor Chr. Henning about 1700 and the diary of J. Pauns Schultze in 1734.

7. The Burgwards were the administrative-military units formed by the Germans in Slavic subdued territories. The Burgward had a centrally situated 'Burg'-stronghold usually of Slavic origin and with a Slavic name with several villages around it.

8. Strongholds Radogoszcz was 'Rome' for the Polabs at first. There stood 'Swarożyc', the well known Slavic deity and 'Radegast' his successor. When the German destroyed Radogoszcz in 1068 the Polabs established there another 'Rome' at Arcona on the Isle of Rugen with 'Świętowit' their new deity.

224

CHAPTER XXXII

THE BALTIC SLAVS

The West Slavs territories were seriously shaken in the second half of the last millennium before our era, when the Lusatian culture came to its end. This was caused by pressure from German nations from the island of Bornholm (Rügians and Burgunds) and from middle Sweden (Goths and Gepids) on the southern Baltic shores between the mouth of the Elbe, Odra and Vistula. At the turn of the era these nations moved south to the Roman Empire borders.

As time went by (1), the empty spaces between the Elbe and Odra were occupied by Slavs moving west and crossing the Elbe and the Saal at many points. The records show the Slavic presence at the Baltic Sea in the second century A.D. in the times of Ptolemy (2). In the first millennium of our era, the Slavs became the only settlers of the southwest Baltic coast, from the mouth of the Vistula to the city of Lübeck in Germany (3)

The final settlement west of the Odra ran in two phases: the period from the 5th to 10th centuries, with the archaic system of military democracy and the period from the 11th to 12th centuries with an early feudal system. It is necessary to mention that in these periods, Poland, Russia (Rus) and Bohemia were progressing well in social, economic and political development. They already laid grounds for their early feudal system in the 9th and 10th centuries. Because of that, the Polabian and Baltic Slavs became the object of attacks for the better organized states, especially Germany and Poland (4).

Scandinavian countries established their power in the early period, also. They managed to replace the archaic clannish community by the early feudal system in the 7th and 8th centuries. All three Scandinavian countries — Denmark, Sweden and Norway — introduced the feudal monarchies at the end of the 10th century.

The early feudal Slavic states established their strength on agriculture. The big landowners formed the ruling party. Unlike them, the Scandinavian countries, having feeble agriculture, based their feudal strength on trade, seafaring, craftsmanship and piracy.

Trade contacts between the Baltic Slavs and Scandinavia started in the period between the 1st and 5th centuries A.D., but developed in two periods: between the 6th and 8th centuries and between the 9th and 10th centuries (5).

Following the trade and piracy expansion on the Slavic shores, political pressure took place. The Danes started to attack the commercial center, Rerik of the Obodrits. They destroyed it in 808 and forced the Slavic merchants to resettle into the Danish haven Hedeby (6).

The relationship between the Danes and Obodrits was not stable. Both nations managed to unite and cooperate when they were endangered by the Saxons. When Slavic coastal navigation developed, their ships anchored at the Rugen Isle and the port Wolin. The Slavs settled also on the near Danish islands like Lolland, Falster and others (7), and the Danes tried to settle in Wolin. There are many records about the Danish invasions on the Slavic territories, but the Slavs must have undertaken counteraction because the reprisal was a common procedure in those times.

Traces of trade and other cultural relationships between the Slavs and Scandinavians are numerous especially on the Rügen Isle. This island was a good stop in commercial navigation from the port Hedeby to Baltic countries and Russia.

Vikings were busy on the Baltic. Their homeland was Scandinavia, but they penetrated all West Europe as far as Spain and Sicily and East Europe to Byzantium and Greece. The Baltic became the bridge of Viking invasions.

Viking invasions all over Europe were numerous during early feudal times. Their task was to enrich the home country at the expense of others, because their own agriculture was on such a low level that it could not support their states.

There is nothing unusual in the Vikings' activity. Many other European countries converted from military democracy to feudal states by the way of piracy.

The Viking's action took the form of piracy in the 7th and 8th centuries. Next to trade, the Vikings also organized units to live on spoils. In the middle of the 10th century, the kings united those units and employed them to invade the neighboring countries, especially

England, as the Danish king Sven (986-1014) and his son Canut (1014-1035) did.

Since the 7th century the expansion of Scandinavian merchants and pirates passed by the Baltic Slavs, directing itself toward the Prussian and Latvian shores.

What was a reason of this turn of events?

It appears that the main cause was the weak economic production of Scandinavia and Slavic countries which were just beginning to organize cities and craftsmanship. Being much more developed, the Mediterranean countries lured the Scandinavians. They used the western route as well as the eastern to Russia and Byzantium. Slavic lands were not attractive to them, as few and rather poor findings of Scandinavian origin indicate. The Slavic resistance to Scandinavian penetration was the last cause for lacking a relationship (8).

But the Baltic Slavs as well as other Baltic nations learned piracy from the Vikings. They took part in booty expeditions against England. Having had good relations with the Danes (9), the Slavs battled the Norwegians. The Slavic-Danish armada defeated the Norwegian navy at the "Hjorning Bay in 985.

As mentioned before Scandinavians started to compose themselves by cementing their early feudal states, but piracy did not die out. The Baltic Slavs and other nations took over the Vikings' tradition.

The Baltic Slavs took active part in politics in northwest Europe. According to Scandinavian sagas, they helped the Danish king Sven to fight the Norwegian king Olaf Harald in the battle at Canterbury in England in 1012.

The good relationship between the Slavs and Danes lasted over a century. It was warm especially during the reign of Canut, the king of Denmark.

When in 1018 the Slavic Lutitsi defeated the Obodrits and chased their prince Mścisław out of the country, Canut invaded Sclavinia (10), expelled the Lutitsi and restored the throne to Uto, the son of Mścisław, in 1019.

After the death of Canut the Slavs started to attack Denmark. Racibor, the prince of Obodrits, suffered defeat from Danes in 1043. To avenge his death the Obodrits invaded Denmark destroyed the country as far as the city Ribe in middle Jutland. King Magnus met them at Hedeby and crushed them. Many Slavic warriors among them eight of Racibor's sons fell in the battle.

In 1135 the huge Slavic sea expedition with over 300 war ships led by the prince Racibor passed Sund and attacked the Norwegian port

Konungahela. After a short battle the invader completely destroyed the city.

A year later the Danes organized the reprisal expedition. Their armada of 1100 war ships attacked the Slavic Island of Rügen. They crushed the resistance and imposed Christianity upon the pagan inhabitants who promised to be baptized. But when the Danish navy left the Rugen ports, the natives chased out the bishop and returned to their gods.

After 1140 the Baltic Slavs found themselves under the strong pressure of Germany from the south and Poland from the east. The struggle lasted 30 years in which the political base of the Baltic Slavs had been destroyed for good.

Fig. 55. The Isle of Rugen

In 1170 Denmark joined the sea offensive and with help of Saxons conquered the island of Rugen, but the Baltic Slavs did not lose their identity in that time (12).

When the Baltic Slavs became politically active, two of their cities played important roles — Wolin and Lubeka.

Since the city of Wolin had ceased to exist, for a long time the question troubled scholars if it were a real or a legendary city.

In Scandinavian sagas and written sources there are many mentions about the city 'Jumne', 'Jumme', 'Julin', 'Jóm', 'Jómsborg', 'Yumneta', 'Vineta' etc. For a long time scholars were not sure if it was one city with different names or many cities. Now, they agree it was one city with the Slavic name 'Wolin' on the island at the mouth of the Odra River (13). There is no doubt it was Slavic (14).

It existed many centuries and was known to the Romans. Since they called the Slavs "Veneti', they named the port 'Urbs Veneti' —

Venetic City, or Vineta. For chronicler Helmold it was Jumneta which looks like a corruption of the word 'Vineta'.

The archaeological findings prove that on the island Wolin there existed down through centuries a mighty harbor. Its area was over 65,500 square yards. Among the items discovered were many articles made of amber, glass pearls made of rock crystal, articles of silver and bones and ceramics made on a potter's wheel.

The Wolin stronghold was not only a big harbor but a center of the craftsmen's production for export. Traces of houses running miles along the river Dziwna and remnants of enourmous ramparts built of wood and earth might have made a big empression upon visitors. Thus, the statement of Helmold that it was the biggest city in Europe seems to be not much exaggerated.

Based on trade and piracy, Wolin became a power of the Baltic. How important it was is indicated by the fact that Harald, king of Denmark ousted by his son, Harald Jr., found refuge here.

The Jómsvikings of Slavic origin were so active that Magnus, king of Norway, attacked and destroyed it in 1043. The Slavs rebuilt the city and continued their activities.

Prince Warcisław of Pomerania conquered Wolin and imposed Christianity upon the inhabitants. Bishop Otto of Bamberg converted the city in 1124-1128, which shortly after declined and fell completely.

Every Slavic port formed an independent republic. Endangered by Scandinavians these republics organized an alliance of the Baltic cities with the seat perhaps in Wolin first and then in 'Lubice', 'Lubeka (Lübeck, today). Its name is unknown (15). It lasted until the Baltic Slavs were subdued by crusadors.

Germans took over the Slavic ports and it looks like they did not bother to change the name of the alliance. It appears that their name 'Hansa' for 'Hanseatic League' might be of Slavic origin.

Germans ran the Hanseatic League by the rules established by the Slavic 'Law of Lübeck'. Moreover, they did not write off the word ''Wenden' which is the German expression for the Slavs who lived west of the river Odra, but pronounced it with great respect. The capital of the Hanseatic League was always Lubeck, till the end of this organization. Its district was called 'Wendische Provinz' — Province of Wends. The best fishermen were named 'Wenden'. The richest and oldest families in Hanseatic cities proudly proclaimed their 'Wendisch' origin.

NOTES TO CHAPTER XXXII

1. **Bibliography:** Adam Bremensis, 'Gesta Ham burgensis ecclesiae pontificum', ed. B. Schneider, Hannover-Leipzig 1917; Bronsted J., 'The Vikings', London 1960; Filipowiak 'Wolin — największe miasto Słowiańszczyzny', Warszawa 1958; Giesenbrecht L., Wendische Geschichten', Berlin 1843; Hollander L.M., 'The Skalds. A Selection of their Poems with Introduction and Notes', New York 1947; Helmoldi 'Chronica Slavorum', Hannoverae 1937; Jedlicki Z., 'Kronika Thietmara', Poznań 1953; Kiersnowski R., 'Legenda Winety', Kraków 1950; Kock E. A., 'Den norsk-islandska Skaldediktningen', Lund 1946; Krijn S., 'De Jómsvikingasaga' Leiden 1914; Larson L.M., 'Canut the Great and the Rise of Danish Imperialism during the Viking Age', New York 1912; Leciejewicz L., 'Początki nadmorskich miast na Pomorzu Zachodnim', Warszawa 1962; Noack U., 'Nordische Fruhgeschichte und Wikingerzeit', Munchen-Berlin 1941; Ohnesorge W., 'Einleitung in die lübische Geschichte', Lübeck 1906; Pieradzka K., 'Walki Słowian na Bałtyku w X-XII wieku', Warszawa 1953; Schuldt E., 'Die slawische Keramik in Mecklenburg', Berlin 1965; Steenstrup J.G., 'Venderne og de Danske for Valdemar den Stores tid', Kobenhaven 1900; Wachowski K., 'Jomsborg-Normanowie wobec Polski w X wieku', Warszawa 1914; Wehrmann M., 'Geschichte von Pommern' Gotha 1919; Weibuhl L., 'Sverige och dess nordiska granmakter under den tidigare medeltiden', Lund 1921; Wigger F., 'Mecklenburgische Annalen bis zum Jahre 1966', Schwerin 1860; Wilde K.A., 'Die Bedeutung der Grabung Wollin', Stettin 1939.

2. H. Łowmiański, 'Początki Polski', Warszawa 1963.

3. W. Lammers, 'Germanen und Slaven in Nordalbingen', 1957, p. 17; J. Kostrzewski, 'Zagadnienie ciągłości osadnictwa' p. 12.

4. W. Wachowski, 'Słowiańszczyzna zachodnia', Poznań 1950.

J. Żak, Studia nad konkluzjami handlowymi', p. 196; L. Leciejewicz, 'Początki nadmorskich miast', p. 36.

6. M. Vasmer, 'Spuren von Westslawen auf die dännischen Inseln', 1942, p. 313-315.

7. J. Żak, 'Importy skandynawskie na ziemiach zachodniosłowiańskich od IX do XI wieku', Poznań 1963.

8. E.A. Kock, 'Den norsk-islandska Skaldadiktningen', Lund 1946, p. 34.

9. Harald, king of Denmark (964-986) married Tove, daughter of Mściwój, prince of the Slavic Obodrits and had good relation with the Slavic city republic of Wolin, where he found refuge.

10. Adam of Bremen describing the Polabs and Baltic Slavs calls their territories 'Sclavinia' (Adam Bremensis, Gesta' lib. II. c.22, p. 87).

11. Laskaris Kananos a Byzantinian explorer travelled on the Baltic states in 1438-1439 and left report what he saw and heard. He noticed that the city of Lubeck was in Slavonia, and its inhabitants spoke the same language as the Zygiots in Peloponesus. Commenting on this statement G. Labuda in 'Fragmenty dziejów Słowiańszczyzny zachodniej', p. 260-269, mentions, that the Slavs on Peloponesus kept their identity until the 15th century. Especially active were two nations, the

Milengoi and Ezeritai, settling in the mountain region west of ancient Sparta. The name of Slavonia was applied to Mecklenburg in Germany, down the centuries as the records indicate, and the hanseatic cities from Lubeck to Kołobrzeg at the Baltic had been called as the "Wendischer Quarter' as long as the Hansa existed.

12. The presence of the Slavs at the Elbe confirmed Polish historian Jan Długosz (1415-1480) (Joannis Dlugossii, 'Historiae Polonicae', Kraków 1873, Vol. I., p. 83) and two Polish ambassadors to the city of Rostock, Jan Kosta and Marcin Kromer in 1564 (Acta Tomiciana, Poznań 1906, Vol. XII, p. 196).

13. Why did Wolin have so many different names, like Jóm, Jómsborg, Jumne Jumme, Yumneta, Vineta, Julin? G. Labuda (op. cit. p. 127-131) maintains that the name 'Julin' is closest to the name 'Wolin', but chronicler Adam of Bremen introduced 'Jumne' in his writings because his informers about Wolin were the Scandinavian travellers and to them 'Wolin' was 'Jóm' or 'Jómsborg'. Since then the name of Wolin took so many different names.

14. G. Labuda, op. cit. p. 129-131.

15. There are some speculations about the Slavic ports alliance. In Old Slavonic the word 'ązać' or 'ązati' meant to bind, which in the Polish language of today is 'wiązać'. It is possible that the name of the alliance was 'Anza'. But it is possible too, that it derives from another Old Slavonic word 'chąsać' — to steal or to rob. After all, the Baltic Slavs for some time did what the Vikings had done all the time — the piracy. From these two Slavonic words — 'ązać and 'chąsać' — is easy to create the German word 'Hansa' for the Hanseatic League, which is in use even today, for the German Air Lines is called German 'Lufthansa'.

231

CHAPTER XXXIII

POLAND

The year 626 A.D. ends the history of the Ancient Slavs. Two events closed Slavic antiquity: the defeat of the Avars at Constantinople and the emergence of the first Slavic tribal state created by Samo. Although Great Moravia after the death of her creator plays no role for some 200 years, the other Slavic nations were so far advanced that they made their own states more or less stable (1).

How did this process evolve in the Polish territories? What happened in the lands which were once the cradle of Slavdom after many Slavic tribes migrated? Some historians refer to this epoch as the Proto-Poland history which lasted from 626 to 1000 A.D. (2).

There were at least four tribal states before Poland emerged: 'Ślężanie' — the state of the Silesians; 'Wiślanie' — the state of the Vistulans; 'Lędzianie' — the state of the Lenthans; and 'Polanie' — the state of the Polans.

When the strong tribe of the Obodrits left Silesia to migrate west and south, the small Slavic tribes who remained absorbed the remnants of Obodrits so even their name vanished from the map of Poland.

According to the 'Description of Regions and Countries on the North Side of the Danube' written by the so called 'Bavarian Geographer' of the 9th century A.D. (3), there was a tribe of the 'Golęszyce' — Golenshits in Upper Silesia near the Moravian borders (4). They had 5 fortified towns (5).

On both banks of the river Odra lived the 'Opolanie' — Opolans. They had 20 strongholds. No doubt, the city of Opole which plays an important role in Silesia today, was their capital.

To the north-west of the Opolans the Silesians had their habitat.

Their 15 strongholds were centered at the middle Odra near the Sobótka Mountain.

In the region of the city of Legnica resided the 'Trzebowianie' — Tshebovians; near the city of Bolesławiec the 'Bieżuńczanie' — Byeshuntchans and the territory of the middle Bober River was occupied by the 'Bobrzanie' — Bobshans.

To the north and east of them in the region of the city Bytom on the Ćuıa, Głogów and Krosno the 'Dziadoszanie' — Diadoshans, sometimes called the 'Dziadoszyce' — Diadoshits had 20 strongholds.

It is worth mentioning that the tribes with the ending 'anie' — ans like Silesians or Opolans took their names from the names of regions (Opole) or rivers (Silesians — the 'Ślęża' River). The tribes with the ending 'ice' — its, took their names from the founders of their tribes who mostly were mythical persons. Thus, the ancestor of the 'Golęszyce' was 'Golęsz' and the 'Dziadoszyce' — Dziadosz. The two names of this tribe means that with the course of time people forgot the origin of their name, from a founder or a river, so they used both names.

Those tribes were independent at the beginning but being endangered from the outside the four of them organized the tribal alliances. In this way the tribal alliance of the Silesians came into existence, as the so called 'Silesian Ramparts' indicates.

To the south west of the city of Zielona Góra on the both banks of the river Bober in the direction toward the city of Krosno run the remnants of the ramparts. Here and there they are vanishing, destroyed by time and agriculture. In some places they are marked by the convexity of the terrain only. But there are places where three ramparts running parallel with fosses between them are remarkably well preserved. These ramparts were over 70 miles long and were armed with palisades.

Like the Maginot Line in France, the Silesian Ramparts were not built against the strong enemy who could break through at any point they liked and invade the country. But they were effective against the small booty expeditions. To force three guarded ramparts was not an easy task for a little group ad even if they had managed to break through, they were sacked inside and destroyed.

Everything indicates that the Silesians Ramparts might have been built against the Slavic Serbs of Lusatia, who in small units, made the booty expeditions.

Could the tribe of Diadoshits alone raise those ramparts? As the record says, they had 20 fortified towns which means they were not able to build three parallel running ramparts over 70 miles. Somebody had to help them. Since not only Diadoshits but other Silesian tribes were menaced, too, it is possible that the Bobshans, Tshebovians and Silesians joined them.

The Silesian state was the base of the united tribes. It must have been a political body who directed the building of such long ramparts and kept them in fighting readiness for over one hundred years. The four tribes could meet together during one of the religious festivities on the Sobótka Mountain (6). Those rites were so famous that people travelled long distances to take part in them long after accepting Christianity. The stronghold at the foot of the 'Holy Mountain' could have been the capital of the Silesian tribal state. In this way might be explained the curious fact that after the Obodrits left Silesia a small tribe with only 15 fortified towns took over the whole country and gave it its name.

The Silesian Ramparts were raised either at the end of the 8th century before the establishment of the second Great Moravian state or after its fall in 906.

Why did the Silesians not create a modern state? Instead of Poland it could have been Silesia, today.

The Silesians had little chance to do it. North of their territory a powerful state of Polans developed; and south, first the Great Moravia and then the Bohemian state came into existence. Both neighbors fought down through the centuries among themselves to keep Silesia inside their own borders.

Neither did the second tribal alliance in the Polish territory east of Silesia have a chance. Its name is derived from the river Vistula which is 'Wisła' in Polish. There were the Vislans (Vistulans) living along the upper Vistula.

Contrary to the tribal alliance of the Silesians whose existence is based on supposition, there are records acknowledging that the tribal alliance of the Vislans was not only a reality but that it played quite an important role in this region. An unknown writer of the life of St. Methodius writes in the 10th century A.D.: "A mighty Pagan Prince residing in Wisla (region of the Vistula) scoffed at Christians and mocked them in every way. Hence, sending unto him said (Methodius): It would be well, my son, if thou wouldst accept baptism freely in thy own land, for otherwise thou willst be taken into bondage and forced to receive baptism on alien soil, recalling the word I had spoken. And so it came to pass".

This unhapy event took place around 885 A.D. Unfortunately the writer did not mention the name of this Pagan Prince.

The existence of the Vislan state was acknowledged also by the Bavarian Geographer in the 9th century A.D. who called it 'Uislane" and Alfred the Great, King of England (871-901) in his book 'The Description of Germany' noted that to the east of Great Moravia is the 'Visleland'.

How did the tribal state come into existence?

After the Croats left the territory, now called 'Little Poland', the small tribes who remained took over. It is possible that Samo incorporated the region into his Great Moravia state. At that time there were built the powerful strongholds in Chodlik, Stradów and Szczaworyż at the northern borders of the state of Vislans.

The death of Samo caused the end of his mighty state. His numerous sons could not run it, fighting each other for the father's heritage. Thus, the tribes north of the Carpathian Mountains decided to take their own road.

The same situation could have happened as in Silesia. Three tribes: Golenshits, Opolans and Vislans made an alliance to defend themselves under the leadership of the Vislans.

Why the Vislans?

Similar to the Silesians they had special circumstances in their favor. They lived on fertile soil and had saltworks at Bochnia and Wieliczka and it seems that the industrial center at Igołomia was still working.

The Vislans had a center of Pagan cult, too. It appears like it was situated in the city of Cracow upon the hill called 'Zwierzyniec'. The name might be a corruption of the word "Swarożyniec' used until the 16th century A.D. (7). Similar to the Sobótka event in Silesia three tribes made a union at Zwierzyniec during the festivities. The town at the foot of the hill became their capital.

The tribal state of the Vislans was a dynamic one. It expanded and its borders were the Carpathians in the south, the Sudets in the west, the rivers Styr and Bug in the east. Further expansion was halted by the invasion of Svetopluk, the Prince of Great Moravia.

The message sent by Methodius to the prince of Cracow was not a prophecy but a normal warning. Svetopluk tried to imitate Samo. Probably he asked the prince of Cracow to join his state as a vassal, but he met refusal. Thus, he decided to invade the state of the Vislans under pretext to baptize the prince and his subjects by force because the prince "scoffed at Christians and mocked them in every way". As archbishop Methodius knew about the preparation for invasion he tried in vain to help the Vislans (8).

Map XIX. Poland in the year 1000, after R. Portal, 'The Slavs'

The invasion tok place about 880 A.D. Svetopluk probably destroyed Chodlik, Stradów, Szczaworyż, Wiślica and other fortified towns.

Then, the rapid Christianization of the Vislans followed in Slavonic rite of the Western Church, called Methodianism.

At least two bishoprics were established, one in Wiślica and another in Cracow. Digging in Wiślica the archaeologists found a baptismal font used for the mass-baptism of Pagans. Such bapisteria usualy were made at bishoprics in those days. Scietific research revealed the baptismal font at Wiślica was erected about 890, which indicates in this time the city was a seat of a bishop (9).

236

In the same time the wooden church of St. Spass (Savior) was built at Zwierzyniec in Cracow in the place where the stone church of St. Salvator is standing today. The missionaries of the St. Methodius rite normaly raised churches of St. Spass in places of Pagan cult (10).

There is another proof that the tribal state of the Vislans was converted to Christianity in 890-ies. It is a letter from the German bishops to Pope John IX in 900 A.D. stating that the missionaries of St. Methodius baptised all the Vislans.

The Byzantinian Emperor Constantine Porphyrogenitus in his treatise about the administration of the country, writes: ''It is necessary to know that the family of the Proconsul and patrician Michael, son of Wyszewic, came from Pagans living at the Vistula River and settled at the Zachluma River (11).

Who was Michael, son of Wyszewic? How could he make such a career at the Byzantine court?

According to the Life of St. Mehodius, the prince of the Vislans was captured and baptized by force in an alien country. Emperor Constintine indicates that there was another prince, too, by the name of Wyszewic. If we accept the possibility, that the unknown prince ruled in Wiślica and was taken prisoner and Wyszewic was the prince of Cracow, the situation becomes clear. When Wyszewic heard about the fate of the prince of Wiślica and not seeing any possibility of confronting Svetopluk, he took his family, all his treasures and with troops left Cracow. Since he had valuables and warriors it was not difficult for his son Michael to obtain the title of Proconsul and patrician which in those times had honorary meaning only in the Byzantinian court.

The fall of the second Great Moravian state in 907 brought independence to the Vistulans for a short time before they were subjected by the Bohemians which was recorded by Ibrahim ibn Jacob in 965.

The tribal state of Vislans was absorbed by the Polans at the end of the reign of Mieszko I. It is obscure as to how it happened. There are no traces of the Vislans being subjected by war. It is possible that their land came into possession of the Piast dynasty by succession. The third wife of King Boleslas the Great was Emnilda, the daughter of the Slavic prince Dobromir, who according to the chronicles ruled in Western Slavdom. She might have been the daughter of the prince of Cracow.

Vislans as well as Silesians had no chance to develop their tribal state to modern states being subjected by two bigger Slavic states, once by the Bohemians and another time by the Polans (Polcs).

East of the Vislans was the third tribal state of Lenthans. The name is derived from the word 'lęd' which in Old Slavonic meant the fallow (12) which applied to agriculture across the Polish territories. Thus, in Great Poland are the cities called "Ląd', 'Lądek', 'Lędnica', etc.

Did the Lenthans create a tribal state?

The Emperor Constintine Porphyrogentius, the same who left the notice about Wyszewic and his son Michael, mentions that among the princes who in 944 arrived to Constantinople to negotiate the peace treaty between the Byzantine Empire and Russian Kiev was a prince of the Lenthans. He must have made a good impression at the court since the Emperor gave him special mention in his book and added that the state of Lenthans was depended from Kiev (13).

What areas belonged to the tribal state of Lenthans?

The answer to this question could only be given by linguistics. The Pole is 'Lakh' in Ukranian, 'Lengyel' in Hungarian, 'Lankas' in Lithuanian. All those words indicate relationship. They are derived from the name 'Lenthans'.

The name indicates that the tribal state of Lenthans had borders with Hungaria in the south, Russian Kiev in the east, Lithuania in the north and with the state of Vislans in the west. Its capital could be the city of Przemyśl. This city is first mentioned in the chronicle of Nestor. According to the Polish historian Jan Długosz, the prince founded the city and gave it his name. Out of gratitude the inhabitants of Przemyśl raised him a mound. Since a similar legend about Krak or Krakus the founder of the city of Cracow and his mound was recorded by Długosz, too, it could be that the legend of Cracow was applied to the city of Przemyśl, also.

After 944 A.D. the state of Lenthans was either independent or belonged to Mieszko I, prince of Polans. Nestor indicates that in 981 Vladimir the Great, the prince of Kiev, attacked the Lenthans (Lakhs) and captured theit fortified cities, Przemyśl, Czerwień and others.

As a heritage from the Lenthans comes the name of Poland which was accepted by the nations north, east and south of Poland. The Pole is 'Lankas', 'Lakh' and 'Lengyel'. Tartars and Turks took the name from Kiev. Poland· is 'Lechistan' to them.

The tribal state which played a dominant role in emerging Poland was the state of Polans.

After the Serbs left nortnern Poland to migrate west and south, the small Slavic tribes took their places. The Bavarian Geographer mentions that the 'Glopeani' had 400 or more strongholds and they occupied the territory known today as 'Kujawy'. It might be that the

German writer twisted the name. The Gopło Lake is in this area. Probably, the tribe who lived in its vicinity was called the 'Goplans' (Goplanie) and the writer overheard it and recorded 'Glopeani'. He is right about the strongholds. Although the number might be exaggerated but around the Gopło Lake archaeologists found the remnants of many small strongholds.

The capital of the Goplans would be the city of Kruszwica. It is situated at the shores of the lake and it was fortified in ancient times. According to chroniclers Kruszwica could be a cradle of Poland.

Legends say that the rulers of the Goplans were Popiel I and Popiel II. The second one lost his life in unusual circumstances. Mice ate him.

After Popiel II the ruler was Piast, his son Ziemowit, grandson Leszek and great-grandson Ziemomysł, the father of Mieszko I. They were princes of the Polans.

One fact puzzles the historians. Why did not the Bavarian Geographer in listing the tribes in the Polish territories mention the Polans who were the founders of Poland? It appears that this tribe was so small and insignificant in those times that the chronicler did not notice them.

It is possible that the Goplans under the leadership of Popiels were the masters of tribal alliance in the eastern part of northern Poland. According to the legends, Popiel II was a cruel ruler hated by his subjects. It is possible that the man named Piast made a "coup d'etat" and took over the Goplans. Not trusting the inhabitants of Kruszwica he established the capital in his tribal city of Gniezno which in that time had the name 'Gniazdo' (Nest).

The base of the emerging state was the area situated in a triangle consisting of three large strongholds: Kruszwica, Gniezno and Poznań. The distance between them is about 30 miles. There was no other stronger concentration of fortifications in the Polish territories as in this area.

The triangle of Polans was densely populated. Its inhabitants had an intensive agricultural system and had also developed industry. In Kruszwica was a famous center of glass production.

Gniezno was surrounded by small strongholds, such as Kłecko, Ostrów, Lednicki, Giecz, Ląd, Trzemeszno, Mogilno and Biskupin. Having such a strongly fortified base, the Piasts could direct expansion to unite all tribes in the Polish territories.

Gniezno was not a political center only. It was a place of religious cult, too. According to legends, in this city stood a temple of the goddess 'Nya', widely worshipped by the Pagan Slavs.

The same thing could happen here as in the states of the Silesians and the Vislans. Political power developed supported by a religious cult. The temple of the goddess Nya could have played the same role here as the Sobótka Mountain in Silesia and Zwierzyniec in Cracow.

There is a view generally taken that Mieszko I was converted to Christianity in 966 and with him all the Polish nation. Facts tell something different. According to the letter of the German bishops sent to Pope John IX the entire state of Vislans (Little Poland) was baptized about 900 A.D.

The legend says, that before Piast took over the power in northern Poland two angles visited him and because he was good to them, they promised him and his dynasty a great future. The St. Metodius missionaries always worked in pairs. It could be that one pair visited Kruszwica and being chased by Popiel II they went to Gniezno and helped Piast to overthrow Popiel II.

If this is right, then Piast had to be converted to Christianity of the St. Methodius rite because the missionaries would not help a Pagan prince if he were not baptized. Piast and his followers could be Christians but Mieszko I did not receive baptism, he only changed the St. Methodius rite into the Latin rite (14). The same situation took place in Great Moravia a little earlier. The prince Svetopluk changed the rites. Thus, it could be accepted that Poland was converted to Christianity of the St. Methodius rite in 900 and then, in 966 changed the rite into the Latin one.

The tribal state of Poland found itself in an exceptionaly good situation. The other states faced confrontation with powerful neighbors. It was quite different with the Polans. Having had weaker neighbors they could enjoy peace and had time to fortify their towns. When they felt strong enough they started their expansion. Miszko I attacked the tribal state of Vyelets which occupied West Pomierania. His success brought him fame. Ibrahim ibn Jacob considered Mieszko I the most powerul prince in all Slavdom.

The West got to know the Polans first from the tribal states which existed in those times in the Polish territories. The name of Polans which described the settlers on the cleared fields 'polany' covered the whole country. In this way we have 'Polska' — Poland and 'Polacy' — Poles. These names are only a small transformation of the name of Polans.

As mentioned before, the Lenthans and Polans gave two different names to Poland. The craddle of Slavdom is for some eastern nations 'Lechistan' and for the others — 'Poland'.

When did the epoch of tribal states end in the Polish

territories? Many people believe that the history of Poland began in 966, when Mieszko I was supposedly baptized. Poles are religious people so they like the idea of connecting the origin of their modern state with some religious event. But in view of archaeological findings this date is difficult to defend. Poland was baptized a half century before 966. It would be better to accept the year 1000 A.D. as the beginning of modern Poland, when the Emperor Otto III visited Boleslas the Great in Poznań, Poland, and declared his host as a king equal to the emperors. This fact is clearly recorded.

NOTES TO CHAPTER XXXIII

1. **Bibliography:** Buczek K., 'Ziemie polskie przed tysiącem lat', Wrocław 1960; 'Cambridge History of Poland' Cambridge 1950; Dowiat J., 'Polska krajem średniowiecznej Europy', Warszawa 1968; and 'Chrzest Polski', Warszawa 1966; Dvornik F., 'The Slavs', Boston 1956; 'Encyclopedie polonaise', Lousanne-Paris 1920; Gall, 'Kronika Polski', Wrocław 1968; Gradecki R., 'Polska Piastowska', Warszawa 1969; Hensel W., 'Polska przed tysiącem lat', Wrocław 1967; 'Historia państwa i prawa Polski', Warszawa 1964; 'Historia sztuki polskiej', Kraków 1965; Jobert A., 'Histoire de la Pologne', Paris 1953; Kostrzewski J., Chmielewski W., Jażdżewski K., 'Pradzieje Polski', Wrocław 1965; 'La Pologne', Warsaw 1964; Łowmiański H., 'Początki Polski', Warszawa 1963; 'Początki państwa polskiego', Poznań 1962; 'Polen', Cologne 1959; 'Polska i jej kultura', Warszawa 1927; Potkański, K., 'Lechici, Polanie, Polska', Warszawa 1965; Trawkowski S., 'Jak powstawała Polska', Warszawa 1963; Tymieniecki K., 'Polska w średniowieczu', Warszawa 1961; Wojciechowski Z., 'Polska nad Wisłą i Odrą', Katowice 1939.
2. The word 'Prapolska' — Proto-Poland, was probably introduced by Józef Kostrzewski, who published 'Kultura prapolska', Poznań 1949. Paweł Jasienica in his book, 'Świt słowiańskiego jutra', Poznań 1953, uses the words 'Prapolska' and 'Prapolak' very often — so do some other writers.
3. H. Łowmiański, 'O identyfikacji nazw Geografa Bawarskiego', SZr. 1958, Vol. 3.
4. S. Trawkowski, 'Jak powstawała Polska', p. 118-122.
5. Since in those times every 'opole' had a stronghold we could accept that the territory of Golenshits constituted five 'opoles'.
6. About the religious significance of Sobótka Mountain since the time of Celtic penetration of the Polish territories down through the centuries H. Cehak-Hołubowiczowa dedicated three historical delibrations: 'Śląski Olimp', 'Kamienne kręgi kultowe na Raduni i Ślęży', and 'Monumentalne zabytki kultowe na górach Ślęży, Raduni, Kościuszki'.
7. One of the oldest descriptions of Cracow from the 13th century A.D. gives the Latin name of 'Zwierzyniec' as 'Sverinzia'. According to 'Larousse Encyclopedia of Mythology', London 1966, p. 304, 'Svarog' was the Slavic god of the sun and fire. Between the words 'Sverinzia' and 'Svarog' is a striking resemblance. It could be assumed that in the place where 'Zwierzyniec' is today a thousand years ago was the sacred grove 'Sverinzia', 'Sveriniec' or 'Svarożyniec', in which the statue of the Slavic

241

god of the sun and fire stood. This supposition is supported by the description on the church built in 1622 in Zwierzyniec by the abbess Kątska that the church had been raised in the same spot where once a Pagan temple stood.

8. K. Lackorońska, 'Studies on the Roman-Slavonic Rite in Poland', Rome 1963. p. 10-11.
9. K. Lanckorońska, op.cit., p. 167-170.
10. St. Salvator is a strict Latin translation of the Slavic St. Spass.
11. S. Trawkowski, op.cit., p. 130.
12. A. Bruckner, 'Słownik etymologiczny języka polskiego', p. 289.
13. According to Prof. Stefan Kuczyński, 'Problemy' 1969; in 944 Igor, the prince of Kiev sent his representatives to Constantinople to sign the peace treaty with the Byzantine Empire. Among them was the prince 'Wołodzisław' as the Russian 'letopis' — chronicler mentions. The name 'Wołodzisław' is not a Russian one but Polish. In the course of time it was transformed to 'Włodisław' and then to 'Władysław'. The last form is very common among the Poles. The Emperor Constantine Porphyrogenitus talked to Wołodzisław inquiring about the situation in the north and that is why in his treatise Constantine writes that 'Lendzaninoi' — Lenthans, paid tributes to Kiev. The Slavic linguist Tadeusz Lehr-Spławiński thinks since the Emperor wrote the word 'Lendzaninoi' he must have heard it from someone who came from Polish territories, because the Russian envoys would have given him the name 'Lakhy', as the Kiev Russians called the Lenthans. The Emperor did not mention the name of the prince of 'Lendzaninoi', perhaps he forgot it when he wrote his treatise; but following the Russian chronicler we can assume it was Włodzisław, the prince of Lenthans. Prof. Kuczyński thinks the state of Lenthans belonged first to the Great Moravian state and after Moravia collapsed in 905 Lenthans asked Kiev for protection because they were endangered by the Pechinges invasion. This could be the reason why they paid tributes. Since Włodzisław was associated with Kiev, prince Igor sent him with the Kiev delegation to sign the treaty in Constantinople.
14. K. Lanckorońska, op.cit., p. 9, 22.

GENERAL CONCLUSIONS

Is there much difference in the behavior between the Ancient Slavs and the Slavs of today — Bulgarians, Byelorussians, Croats, Czechs, Macedonians, Poles, Russians, Serbs, Serbo-Lusatians, Slovaks, Slovenes, Ukrainians? Rather not. One who chances to have a closer look on these nationalities, can easily find it for himself.

Ancient Slavs displayed amazingly strong features of their character in fighting misfortunes. The anonymous author of "Strategikon" recorded it, observing the Balkan Slavs in the 6th century. Widukind arrived at the same conclusion five centuries later when watching the western Slavs at the Elbe. "They inured to hardship and bear easily heat, cold and foul weather, lack of cloth and food" — says Strategikon. "They are accustomed to hardship, poorest meals, and what to our people looks like a heavy burden, the Slavs consider a pleasure" — repeats Widukind.

The strength of perseverence in the Slavs is astounding, also. They had been crushed and harassed by Huns, Avars, Pechyngs, Tartars, Turks, Byzantinians, Franks, Hungarians, Northmen and Germans and sold as slaves to Rome, Constantinople, Cordoba and Mahgreb, but they managed to survive. What is more, being at the bottom of the foreign society, many of them rose from slavery to the top.

Ancient Slavs displayed another strength — the strength to endure humilation. As slaves and subjugated people they had been exposed to all kinds of cruelty as far back as they appeared on the political arena to Hitler's era. No matter how ferocious and disastrous the torture it did not break their spirits.

"They are so fond of freedom that they in no way let themselves be subjugated and ruled, especially on their own land" — records the Strategikon. "They fought — Saxons for fame spoils, and big country, the Slavs for freedom from foul dependence" — states Widukind. Many other writers observed the unusual love of freedom among the Slavs. Perhaps this feature of character had given them the strength to survive. One after another all the Slavic nations lost their freedom, but not their hope of some day regaining it again. Some, like the Poles, waited 130 years for that hapy moment, others like the Slovaks almost 1000 years. From all the Slavic nations, only the Polabs at the river Elbe in Germany and the Slavs in Peloponesus, Greece, lost their national identity. The rest are on their feet again, as they were a thousand years ago.

Someone who wants to overcome all hardships of life must have enormous strength of body and mind. This feature among the Slavs had been recorded by the chronicler. "All of them are tall, extremely strong" — says Procopius. His observation was repeated by many doctors during the Second World War, while nursing Slavs as allied soldiers or prisoners of war.

"Slavs in general are very skillful and courageous warriers" — notes Ibrahim ibn Jacob. "The Antes are very courageous" — states Jordanes. But Theophile Simokata underlines: "They live a quiet, peaceful life". "They are not villians nor eager to wrong doings" — admits Procopius, and Helmold adds: "There is no other nation more honest and god-natured". Slavs warred with many nations but not for spoils only, like the others did, but mostly to fight back the invader.

Their good-natured character allowed them to develop another feature — hospitality. "They are friendly to visitors, giving them all they want" — states the Strategikon. "What concerns morality and hospitality there was no other nation" — observes Helmold. This feature, deeply rooted in Slavic character, is a relic of times when the sharing of food and clothes was a common practice. Many nations changed it into an egoistic attitude but the conservative minded Slavs stood by their tradition.

"They farm and seek for food with great ardor, in which they surpass all northern nations" — records Ibrahim ibn Jacob, and the Strategikon mentions: "They have a great number of cattle and crops". Love of soil is proverbial among the Slavs. The Mother-Earth became the great goddess to them, honored and venerated with great respect, because the farm land was all the Slavs wanted.

Love of freedom found full expression in the institution called the wiece — gathering. All chroniclers underline the democratic way of Slavic life. "Slavs and Antes are not ruled by one man but by themselves, and all good and bad matters are done in general meetings" — writes Procopius. Ibrahim ibn Jacob relates: "The żupan or kniaz was elected by the tribe from the oldest amd most

244

respected people. He was the supreme judge, leader and high priest, but in all important matters his authority was limited by the council of elders. If a prince attempted to abuse his power or to undertake a despotic action, he was rapidly removed from his office. The Slav spirit of independence did not tolerate any infringement on the rights of the tribe or any injustice". This is why the very powerful Polish king Boleslas the Great "distinguished himself with great justice and admittance" — as Thietmar records. It means, being tightly controlled by the gatherings, he could not afford to follow his whims.

This democratic system deeply rooted in their minds, barred them from developing a sense of sacrificing their privilages in time of emergency to save the country. The results were disastrous. "The tribes lived independently and there was no possibility for them to become united" — writes Ibrahim ibn Jacob. Then he adds: "Slavs in general are quick to quarrel and aggressive, and if their discord had not caused the division of many tribes, no nation could equal them in power". The Strategikon expresses the same opinion and gives advise on how to exploit: "As there are among them so many chiefs who fight with each other it is not difficult to win over some of them by promises and gifts, inciting particularly those at the borders to fight the rest. That is why the Slavs are unable to organize themselves as a nation or to build a modern army".

The advise of the Strategikon was followed by all Slavic enemies. One by one the Slav nations lost their freedom. The lack of a sense of reality in it was shown by the Poles. Their love of "golden freedom" led them to introduce the insitiution of "liberum veto" in 1652, which provided that one deputy to the Sejm — diet could destroy every legislative action by saying the simple word "veto" — I protest. This unrealistic approach to political matters destroyed one of the most powerful kingdoms in Europe and brought bondage to the Poles for 130 years.

Many nations tried to destroy the Slavs. Hitler had a plan to exterminate 100 million Slavs and to banish the rest behind the Ural Mountains into Asia. Slavs, like the mythical Phoenix, are reborn from ashes. Nations should understand that instead of loosing money and armies to battle the Slavs it is better to cooperate with them. The Slavs possess attributes needed by the society of tomorrow.

Some people could not understand why communism was born in one Slavic country and met little resistance in other Slavic countries. To find out the proper answer it is necessary to glance into the past.

When the backbone of society was the clan no class system existed. All people were equal. The feudal system destroyed equality. Society was split into classes, closed one to another. The industrial revolution broke up this system, giving room for the philosophy that every man is boss for himself. If he is poor it is his own fault. To ease its conscience this society developed the charity organizations and projects to help the needy people.

Slavic nations knew no industrial revolution. Those at the bottom, the peasants, perpetuated the clannish morality, sharing each others joys and sorrows and even wealth. It was a traditional Slavic hospitality admired by many visitors.

When the feudal system in Russia met its tragic end the victorious communists based their system on clannish morality cherished down the centuries by the Russian people. In this way they met little resistence.

Another attribute deeply roted in the Slavic minds and accepted by communism is the system of councils. Fighting for freedom of speech and gatherings, Slavic nations, one after another, lost their independence. Communism was aware of that, and introducing a totalitarian regime, instituted councils on every level of government. People have the right to speak their minds and the government is sometimes harshly criticized in the meetings. This makes the communistic system unique among totalarian states, where a small clicque makes decisions and the whole nation, as the soldiers in the army, have to listen and obey without a word of resentment.

The philosophy "every man is boss for himself", on which our society is based, does not work anymore. Old and sick people have lost the power of caring for themselves because of spiralling costs and the changing mood in society. Social Security, Medicare and other projects remove the charitable organizations. With National Health Service and Welfare properly managed we are returning to long forgotten clannish morality — sharing joys and sorrows, costs and wealth as it was a common practice some thousand years ago. Technical progress and overpopulation force us to do it.

Lenin, the prophet of communism, stated that the communist system is not everlasting but a transitory one leading people from the bad to the better society. Being afraid to loose power, communist leaders do all they can to perpetuate their system, saying that the time has not come yet for these changes.

It loks like the West, as it was in the past, will establish a better society about which Lenin dreamt: the democratic system with freedom for anyone to speak his mind and sharing costs and wealth in society. We are on the road to acheive those goals, and as history shows we have here natural friends and supporters — the Slavs.

The End

246